SCHIZOPHRENIA:
BEHAVIORAL ASPECTS

APPROACHES TO BEHAVIOR PATHOLOGY SERIES
Brendan Maher—Series Editor

Robert D. Hare : PSYCHOPATHY : THEORY AND RESEARCH

Sheldon J. Lachman : PSYCHOSOMATIC DISORDERS : A BEHAVIORISTIC INTERPRETATION

Barclay Martin : ANXIETY AND NEUROTIC DISORDER

Joseph Mendels : CONCEPTS OF DEPRESSION

Theodore Millon and Herman I. Diesenhaus : RESEARCH METHODS IN PSYCHOPATHOLOGY

Kurt Salzinger : SCHIZOPHRENIA : BEHAVIORAL ASPECTS

SCHIZOPHRENIA: BEHAVIORAL ASPECTS

KURT SALZINGER

Biometrics Research, New York State Department of Mental Hygiene and Polytechnic Institute of Brooklyn

John Wiley & Sons, Inc.

New York · London · Sydney · Toronto

To Joseph Zubin

Library of Congress Cataloging in Publication Data :

Salzinger, Kurt.
        Schizophrenia : behavioral aspects.

        (Approaches to behavior pathology series)
        Bibliography : p.
        1. Schizophrenia. I. Title
[DNLM :   1. Schizophrenia. WM 203 S186s 1973]
RC514.S312   616.8'982   73-1276
ISBN 0-471-75091-3
ISBN 0-471-75090-5 (pbk)

Photoset at Thomson Press (India) Limited
Printed in the United States of America

10 9 8 7 6

PREFACE

The purpose of this book is to present, in brief form, the behavioral theories and findings related to schizophrenia. The literature on this subject is an ever growing one—the malady seems undiminished in prevalence. I hope that, by presenting to the student the victories and the defeats of research in this area, I can help him learn something of greater significance than if I presented the vaguer generalities about the disorder. No book of this size can even pretend to be complete but, by following up the references for statements made here, the alert student should be able to satisfy his curiosity further.

I will let the book speak for itself. For me, the most important measure of success of the book will be the number of students who, having read it, will decide to enter the field of abnormal psychology to bring order to it.

The behavior that goes into the writing of a book is, of course, acquired over a period of many years through the mediation of many people. Most important among these people has been Joseph Zubin, who convinced me early in my graduate career that it is worthwhile to apply experimental techniques to problems in abnormal psychology, and who has consistently supported me in my research ever since. In gratitude, I dedicate this book to him. I have also been most fortunate in my research career to work at Biometrics Research (created by Joseph Zubin), and to have had at my side two such remarkable people as Richard S. Feldman and Stephanie Portnoy. I thank them for working with me. Finally, I am grateful to my wife, Suzanne Salzinger, who also has done research with me, and who once again took the time and effort to convert a book of mine into a more readable one. Thanks, Suzy.

My research in schizophrenia has been supported by various grants from the National Institute of Mental Health and the Division of Psychopharmacology. Most of the actual research took place at Brooklyn State Hospital, first under the directorship of the late N. Beckenstein and, more recently, under the directorship of M. B. Wallach, and some at the New York State Psychiatric Institute under the directorship of L. C. Kolb. With their support I was able to learn about schizophrenia firsthand. My thanks go to them.

I would also like to thank Helmut Gruber, who as Chairman of the

Department of Social Sciences at the Polytechnic Institute of Brooklyn, made it possible to try out some of my explanations of schizophrenia to students, and who facilitated the typing of the manuscript. I owe a debt of gratitude to Jean Patenaude, who took such care in checking the references in the book. Finally, I would like to thank Brendan Maher for reading the text and making useful criticisms.

New York City, 1972   Kurt Salzinger

CONTENTS

INTRODUCTION

Imagine that you are given the following task: you are to describe the unicorn, explain where it comes from, and specify how to capture it. If you know anything about unicorns you will immediately go to the library and start looking under Mythology. There you will find descriptions of a fabulous animal with one horn and, in the more expensive books, you will discover colored illustrations. The pictures and verbal descriptions will show that the unicorn comes in assorted colors and sizes, and that it has a single horn in the middle of its forehead. If you stop at that point you will arrive at a satisfactory description, but if you delve further you will find that the unicorn cannot be captured except by a virgin, and even then only rarely. What's more, the essential conditions are not very well specified. You will soon realize that the descriptions differ depending on the particular mythology book you are reading. Thus, although the heraldic unicorn most often consists of a horse's body, a lion's tail, and a spirally twisted long horn, not all representations of the unicorn are the same. The Old Testament, to take but one example of peculiar practice, uses the word, unicorn, to refer to a *two-horned* animal.

How does this relate to schizophrenia? Let me state the relation in as simple and as straightforward a way as I can: schizophrenia is a unicorn. In neither case do we have definitive information about the cause for its appearance. In both cases a voluminous literature is available, and in both cases various authors have written about the phenomenon lacking the

1

knowledge of what others proposed. Schizophrenia, like the unicorn, is described in various ways by various people. And its elimination, like the capture of the unicorn, appears to require some special conditions, not all of which have yet been specified. Finally, whether or not these conditions exist, belief in their existence has had significant consequences.

The implication of all this is that the subject of schizophrenia requires special treatment. The many uncertainties about it demand that we devote a good deal of space to the methods that produced the descriptions in conflict, that we not pretend to be able to describe this disorder simply, and that, at least in the areas of greatest dispute, we avoid drawing definitive conclusions. Furthermore, it implies that no formal and complete definition of schizophrenia is yet available. Rather, the book will present approximations to a definition by setting forth the behavioral findings on patients labeled schizophrenic (with the labeling procedure itself also undergoing our scrutiny).

Instead of presenting an oversimplified, and therefore incorrect, view of schizophrenia—in the hope that another book, more courageous than this one will provide the more complete although less finished picture—we will seek to make clear what we know, what we don't know, and what, because of our inadequate knowledge, we continue to quarrel about in schizophrenia.

CHAPTER ONE

ON THE NATURE AND CONCEPT OF SCHIZOPHRENIA

In discussing the abnormal behaviors that are often summarized by the term schizophrenia, I will argue in favor of describing them in an objective, abstract, and nonanecdotal manner. In order, however, to orient the reader in a general way to the kind of people who are diagnosed as schizophrenics, I will begin by presenting some case histories. For a full explanation of the official meaning of schizophrenia and its subtypes, the reader is referred to the Appendix, which is excerpted from the Diagnostic and Statistical Manual of Mental Disorders and prepared by the American Psychiatric Association.

A patient, diagnosed as a schizophrenic, simple type (Kolb, 1968), was hospitalized at the age of 21 after being caught peeping into someone's window. His childhood was described as quiet, but people around him had some difficulty in understanding his behavior even then. At age 19, after working for two years, he suddenly decided to stop, pointing out that since his father and sister were working there was no need for him to work too. At about this time he was first caught peeping into a woman's bedroom. He became careless of his appearance and did only occasional work. A year later he was again arrested for peeping. He spoke less and less and became antagonistic to his father and sister. After his third arrest he was committed to a mental hospital. He showed no concern over his predicament, laughing about it in a silly manner. While in the hospital he was apathetic, inactive, and preoccupied, but he never expressed delusions or hallucinations.

A schizophrenic patient of the hebephrenic type was described by Strecker and Ebaugh (1940). The patient was hospitalized at age 25. She was characterized as having been very seclusive and reserved from childhood. The onset of her illness came after a visit to a dentist's office where she said the dentist had exerted some influence over her and loved her. She became careless of her appearance after the visit to the dentist, talked irrelevantly, began hearing voices, had long periods of laughing and smiling to herself, and was depressed at other times. At the examination, her speech was extremely irrelevant and she said that people had been talking about her for years. Her voices accused her of self-abuse and told her that she must die. She said that she was under the control of electricity and influenced by telepathy and thought waves. In the hospital she showed progressive deterioration, becoming more and more sloppy in her habits and appearance. She became more delusional and claimed that the doctors caused her to masturbate day and night. She continued to laugh and smile to herself.

Landis and Bolles (1950) described a schizophrenic patient of catatonic type. The patient was a 27-year-old laborer who had led a relatively normal life. Three weeks before he was admitted to the mental hospital he started to show peculiar behavior; he became seclusive, had difficulty sleeping, and became sloppy about his person. At a bar he accused a person he had known for many years of "talking behind my back." He became very excited, so much so that even after he had been brought home he still stood at the window shouting and spitting at people who ostensibly were trying to "get" him. In the hospital, at first he was monosyllabic and slow. In the next few days he became completely mute and refused to eat. After five weeks of severe symptoms, including incontinence and standing in peculiar positions, he became somewhat more cooperative, but even after one year of hospitalization he rarely answered questions, still showing himself to be disoriented. Through his limited conversation, it became clear that he had auditory hallucinations, occasionally becoming assaultive.

O'Kelly and Muckler (1955) supplied a case history of a paranoid schizophrenic patient. This patient entered a psychiatric hospital after having failed to obtain a body for his "experiments in restoring life." He had been in the army for 16½ months without being hospitalized, despite the fact that he had been psychotic during that entire period. The patient had a number of delusions, including one that people had been trying to kill him for about eight years. According to him, he had been changing into a woman for the last five years and would soon be able to bear children. Of interest is the fact that this patient existed in society for quite awhile before his paranoid ideas came to be known, resulting in his hospitalization.

Despite the existence of such cases as those cited above, doubt and disagreement linger among honest men about whether an abnormality called schizophrenia exists, and if so, whether it is a single disease or many, whether it is socially or physically caused, whether it changes over time, when it starts, and how it responds to various therapeutic (or purportedly therapeutic) agents. Psychiatrists differ about whom to designate as schizophrenic, and at least one psychiatrist thinks it wrong (morally) to designate anyone by this appellation. In fact, the greatest agreement about schizophrenia is on our ignorance of the phenomenon.

In marked contrast to this uncertainty, there is the certain knowledge that large numbers of patients in psychiatric hospitals do not respond to the treatments used. No one treatment appears to be effective in curing people who are classified as schizophrenic, but there is evidence that about one-third of the patients in hospitals recover—independently of the treatment administered and even independently of *any* treatment. There is the additional peculiar fact that almost any *new* treatment is effective with large numbers of patients, but this effect lasts only until the enthusiasm of the psychiatrists, nurses, attendants, and patients has worn off.

Schizophrenia has attracted scientists in disciplines ranging from molecular biology and mathematics to anthropology, sociology, and the science of ecology. New techniques and developments in related and unrelated sciences have been applied to schizophrenic patients and to this area of research. Almost every conceivable model for explaining the various inexplicable aspects of schizophrenia has been investigated, not only for the patient but even for the observer, in an attempt to explain the phenomena in question. Nonetheless, the information collected has turned out to be more useful to the sciences mentioned than to the unraveling of the mystery that is schizophrenia.

Despite the many problems inherent in the study of schizophrenia, some behavioral aspects are known and agreed upon; both the problems and the behaviors form the subject matter of this book. Much of the research reported here has attempted to describe the very phenomenon we cannot quite define or, for that matter, eliminate. The justification for attempting a description of a phenomenon whose definition, not to say existence, is questioned, is the faith in the ultimate victory of science, the fact that as many as one percent of the population are afflicted with this poorly defined condition, and the fact that those who are called schizophrenic in our society (whether correctly or not) are dealt with in a way different from those who are not so labeled.

According to a National Institute of Mental Health report (Segal and Kety, 1964), about 25 percent of the patients admitted each year to state mental hospitals are diagnosed as schizophrenic, and 50 percent of the resident population in these hospitals also bear that diagnosis. Schizophrenia derives its importance not only from the numbers it strikes but the productive years of each life that it eliminates. Of all first admissions to state hospitals in this diagnostic category, 75 percent are between the ages of 15 and 44 years old, with a median age of 33 years, as compared to a median age of 51 years for all other admissions. In a book dealing with various aspects of schizophrenia, Hoch and Zubin (1966) estimated that the cost of maintenance and loss of income attributable to this behavior disorder comes to 660 million dollars per year! In the National Institute of Mental Health report (Segal and Kety, 1964) the amount of money reported given away in grants for research in schizophrenia from 1948 to the end of the fiscal year 1963 was $ 54,019,379—making up 1849 different grants and constituting 21 percent of the total number of grants and 27 percent of the total amount of money awarded.

Segal and Kety (1964) describe this research as follows (p. 2): "Clues to prevention, etiology and treatment are being sought in the chemistry of the body as well as in the quality of the mother-child relationship, in the mechanism of the brain along with the social structure of the community, in the effects of psycho-active drugs and the dynamics of the patient-therapist relationship." And they describe our chief concern in this book (p. 2): "One of the most difficult problems posed in research involving the mentally ill is that of making accurate measurements of the patient's overt behavior— his degree of psychopathology, his change as a result of treatment, his symptom patterns."

Before moving on to a short history of schizophrenia, let us look at one more assertion about it. Romano (1967) states (p. 1): "The magnitude of the prevalence of schizophrenia, the lack of agreement about its diagnosis and course, the multiple conjectures about its origins, all attest to the fact that it constitutes modern psychiatry's greatest challenge." To which I must add that it is a challenge to all science and to scientific method in general.

SOME HISTORY ON SCHIZOPHRENIA

In a recent paper on the history of schizophrenia, Lewis (1966) says that the condition of schizophrenia has probably always existed among civilized people. It is interesting to note that, like all other statements concerning schizophrenia, even this broad statement is qualified by a reference to social condition; "civilized" suggests that the disorder is a function of some environmental variables, even if it is caused by something physical. Lewis refers first to Indian "Works of Wisdom," which, in approximately 1400 B.C., described behavior similar to the kinds of clinical description often given for schizophrenia. It is also interesting to note that apparently even then an attempt was made to differentiate functional diseases (a category of disorder, including schizophrenia, for which no physical cause has been discovered or clearly specified) and physically caused disorders. This dichotomy, as we shall see (especially Chapter 5) has contributed to a continuing dispute among investigators, but is a false dichotomy, leading to inadequate research. It implies that only one set of factors (environmental or physiological) needs to be considered for each type of disorder, when taking account of both will allow complete study. Lewis also cites a description by Hippocrates (460–377 B.C.), who differentiated schizophrenia from physically caused disorders such as alcoholic disturbances, epilepsy, and acute febrile (high temperature) reactions.

In the history of schizophrenia, the last two centuries are no doubt the most important, or at least the best documented. Kraepelin's (1856–1926) conception of schizophrenia, which he called dementia praecox (and which, at least in part is still used), apparently originated in 1674 with Willis, a famous British anatomist. The term dementia praecox, to Kraepelin, meant a disease process that began in adolescence or early adulthood and had a deteriorating effect culminating in a dementia (impairment of mental powers). Wender (1963) points out that the first use of the term dementia praecox, ironically enough, may well have been applied to a case of neurosyphylis (infection of brain tissues by a syphylitic organism).

Bleuler (1857–1939), who is responsible for the term schizophrenia, in contrast to Kraepelin, rejected the idea of deterioration as an inevitable aspect of schizophrenia. No doubt the idea of the inevitability of deterioration, with poor outcome as part of the definition of schizophrenia, was responsible, in part, for the inadequate care given such patients. While Kraepelin stresses such symptoms as hallucinations (perceptions in the absence of a stimulus), delusions (false beliefs supported by emotional factors), disorders of attention (a narrowing of attention), stereotypes of motion (persistent repetitions of movement serving no apparent purpose), reduced capacity for work, judgment disorders (inability to compare facts and ideas, and to organize them to draw conclusions), and considering them as effects of underlying somatic disturbances, Bleuler (1950) viewed many of symptoms as secondary elaborations of primary disturbances in affect (emotional blunting and expression at inappropriate times or inappropriate places) and association (ideas connected in a fragmented, illogical, tangential manner).

Gerard's description of the causes hypothesized for schizophrenia and a listing of some of the remedies employed may be a fitting conclusion to this very brief history: "The cause of schizophrenia is not known. The Egyptians thought it was gas in the ventricles of the brain; during much of the Medieval period it was believed to be a demon possessing the individual; later it was attributed to a bad colon or to bad teeth, or a bad nervous system, or a bad environment, or bad heredity—not all mutually exclusive. And the treatment depended pretty much on the mood of the day. For possession, the evil spirit was exorcised by whatever way seemed appropriate; teeth were extracted; colons were excised; brains were exposed by trephining or lobotomy; shock was given; psycho-and sociotherapy were directed to environmental factors; drugs are being used; nobody has yet done a great deal about a hereditary cause" (1964, p. 311).

DIAGNOSIS

The recognition of schizophrenia depends on a system of classification of the so-called mental disorders. For some years, systems of classification were based simply on schemes preferred by different psychiatrists in various hospitals. In more recent years, and particularly as more types of treatment are being promulgated, the need for a universal method of classifying behavior disorders has increased. Thus, a second edition of *The Diagnostic and Statistical Manual of Mental Disorders,* published by the American Psychiatric Association (1968), attempts to provide a uniform system of classification (see Appendix). In addition, many countries are considering adoption of a World Health Organization International Classification of Diseases. An international system would, of course, make possible badly needed cross-cultural comparisons, which would reveal more clearly the contribution of cultural environments to various behavior disorders.

Once a qualified psychiatrist or psychologist has obtained sufficient information, usually by way of an interview with a patient, with relatives, with the police, or with some other agent who brings the patient to the hospital, he makes an attempt to classify the patient's behavior. The label he finally assigns is his *diagnosis.* The purpose of the diagnosis is, as Zubin (1967) explains, "threefold: aetiology [study of causes or background], prognosis [prospects for recovery], and selection of therapy." The logic of this approach (the *medical model*) is good; it has been successful for many physical diseases. It does, however, assume that behavior is symptomatic of some other, more basic, cause—the disease to be treated. As we shall see, there is another way of viewing behavior: as the phenomenon that itself is to be treated. It is of some interest to note that a shift from the classical medical model is evidenced even in such a respected book on psychiatry as Kolb's (1968), which suggests that "a classificatory diagnosis is less important than a psychodynamic study of the personality." He states that such labeling is only one aspect of what the psychiatrist must do before he can help his patient; the psychodynamic explanation of the patient's behavior that consists of a detailed study of the "meaning" of his behavior in terms of underlying motivations, the therapeutic program that is outlined for him, and the prognosis do not seem to derive automatically from the diagnosis. This is so because the same pattern of behavior resulting in one descriptive diagnosis may in fact be caused by different factors in the patient's life.

Thus, although much is made of diagnosis for legal purposes and record keeping, such serious decisions as what treatment to assign a given patient are made more often on the basis of evaluation of the behavior itself, rather than on the basis of diagnosis.

Although I reject Laing's operational definition (1967, p. 139) that (schizophrenia is the name for a condition that most psychiatrists ascribe to patients they call schizophrenic," I do agree with Stengel (1967, p. 2) that "schizophrenia, as an operational concept, would not be an illness, i.e., a biological reality...but an agreed operational definition for certain types of abnormal behaviour." From this point of view it seems that what the field needs is a better, more workable definition. One major attempt to arrive at a workable classificatory system for schizophrenia is that of the American Psychiatric Association (see Appendix).

The American Psychiatric Association Classification

In the APA manual, schizophrenia is defined as follows: "This large category includes a group of disorders manifested by characteristic disturbances of thinking, mood and behavior. Disturbances in thinking are marked by alterations of concept formation which may lead to misinterpretation of reality and sometimes to delusions and hallucinations, which frequently appear psychologically self-protective. Corollary mood changes include ambivalent, constricted and inappropriate emotional responsiveness and loss of empathy with others. Behavior may be withdrawn, regressive and bizarre" (p. 33).

The Manual describes 11 types of schizophrenia (see Appendix). Case histories related to some of these categories have been presented above. As to the definitions of the various terms used, I must point out that the process of diagnosis is more art than science. The definitions are usually made concrete through the process of watching accomplished diagnosticians make their diagnoses, although more detailed descriptions than those given in the APA Manual are to be found in books such as Kolb's (1968). Nevertheless, the general lack of precision in definition, as will be seen in the section on the classification system, contributes substantially to the failings of diagnosis.

Reliability and Validity of Diagnosis

Most patients do not display symptoms as clearcut as the case examples above; the result is poor reliability. The concept of reliability is basic to any science. It means that measuring instruments must yield the same results over a number of specified conditions of measurement, or else they must be improved until they do. Nobody would use a yardstick that expanded and contracted from time to time so that the same table measured 5 feet one time, 3 feet another time, and 7 feet a third time. The diagnostic measurement procedure must be challenged on similar grounds. If the same patient is sometimes placed in one diagnostic category and sometimes in another, then here too we have a problem of low reliability. Jackson (1967) has summed up the situation: "For many years there has been a general discontent with psychiatric nosology [classification of diseases]. The hope we once had that individuals could be classified with rigorous diagnoses has slowly dissipated. Not only is there dissatisfaction with specific diagnostic labels, but the concepts on which these labels are based are continually being questioned" (p. 111). He points out that such labels as schizophrenia result in too hetero-geneous a group of individuals; he also suggests that the use of the label schizophrenia becomes more probable the longer a patient remains in a psychiatric hospital. As a substitute for a diagnosis based on the concept of disease, he suggests classifying the context in which an individual lives, rather than his attributes. What may, on first consideration, be thought to be an intrinsic part of the disorder may turn out, on second look, to be a natural response to a particular, albeit abnormal, environment.

Some Data on Reliability. On what is the dissatisfaction with diag-nosis actually based? Essentially, it is based on the fact that agreement on any given diagnosis by any two psychiatrists is not very high. Zubin (1967) summarizes some relevant data. Based on five studies of schizophrenia, agreement between any two psychiatrists varied from 53 to 80 percent; a sixth study, admittedly based on too small a sample (six patients) obtained no agreement. Zubin concludes (p. 383) "that the degree of overall agreement between different observers with regard to specific diagnoses is too low for individual diagnosis." Note that specific diagnosis means such broad cate-gories as schizophrenia, not subtypes such as catatonic schizophrenia. In his review of the consistency of diagnosis (the percentage of times that the same diagnosis is made when a patient is reexamined within four weeks), Zubin finds that agreement varies widely—from 37 to 70 percent. The subtype schizoaffective disorder shows an agreement score of 28 percent; the subtype nuclear schizophrenia (a category corresponding most closely to process schizophrenia in this country, see pp. 18–20 for a discussion) shows 87 percent agreement. We must conclude that diagnosis is not consistent.

In still another approach to the problem of reliability in diagnosis we can compare the frequency of occurrence of certain diagnostic categories in comparable samples of the same population. When comparable samples show different distributions of a given diagnosis, we may conclude that there is a disagreement about the kind of patient who should be assigned that diagnosis. Thus, the study by Pasamanick, Dinitz, and Lefton (1959) indicated that the percentage of occurrence of the diagnosis of schizophrenia varied from 22 to 67. In general, we are forced to conclude that all the bases for examination of the reliability of the diagnosis of schizophrenia yield figures that should make us believe this classification system could be improved.

Some Data on Validity. In reviewing the validity of diagnosis, by which we mean the extent to which it accomplishes what it sets out to do (for example, to predict the kind of treatment a patient should receive), Zubin reports that statistically significant degrees of agreement can sometimes be obtained for the kind of therapy appropriate for a *group* of patients; this agreement is unfortunately not high enough for correct assignment of treatment to individual patients. As to the relation of diagnosis to prognosis, (a second attribute of validity of diagnosis), Zubin, et al (1961) reviewed 364 studies. Among these they found 119 studies showing that catatonic schizophrenia is associated with good outcome, but only two studies showing an association with poor outcome. On the other hand, in 55 studies the diagnosis of paranoid schizophrenia was found to be associated with unfavorable outcome, and in 39 studies with favorable outcome. Thus, since some diagnoses (but by no means all) seemed to have prognostic significance, we might assert that the diagnosis of catatonia is associated with a good prognosis, but we would not hazard an assertion about the relationship between the diagnosis and outcome of paranoid schizophrenia. We can only conclude that, in general, the relationship between diagnosis and prognosis is too variable to be useful. The medical model of disease also requires that we infer etiology from diagnosis but the dearth of knowledge about the etiology of schizophrenia makes satisfaction of this requirement quite out of the question.

The problem of validity can be viewed from another vantage point. Let us take each construct said to underlie a given diagnostic category and test for its existence as follows: compare patients having one diagnosis with those having another, and with normals. If the measure of the construct does not relate to the appropriate diagnostic category or relates to the same degree to all patients and even normals, then assume no validity for that construct. If the measure is found to occur in the predicted diagnostic category but not elsewhere, then assume validity for that construct. This approach is common in current behavioral investigations of schizophrenia and will contribute substantially to the chapters to follow.

One word of caution is in order. Inglis (1966) points out that even when the diagnosis relates to both the abnormality that it is labeling and the behavioral measure, it does not follow that the behavioral measure relates to the abnormality. The relationship may simply reflect agreement on nonabnormal behavior that both the diagnosis and the behavioral measure are picking up. As a preventative to such dangers, Inglis suggests the study of behavior independent of diagnostic systems now extant. Such new measures have, as we shall see in our discussion of the process-reactive categorization, already led to new or additional systems of classification.

The Nosological System. Before looking at remedies to the problem of classification, it might be well to list some of the other difficulties with diagnosis. Zubin (1967) mentions that the nosological (classification of diseases) system constructed by the American Psychiatric Association (1952) was decided upon by a majority voting procedure because of the large amount of disagreement. In accounting for the disagreement in diagnosis, some investigators have estimated the contribution of the inadequacy of the nosological system (as opposed to inconstancy of the diagnostician or patient) to be greater than half (Ward, et al, 1962). In a now-classic article on psychiatric diagnosis, Zigler and Phillips (1961a) pointed to the fact that the current nosological system still focuses its efforts, albeit only theoretically, upon etiology (thus requiring an inferential), instead of an empirical approach to diagnosis. Despite the fact that symptoms are supposed to form the basis of diagnosis, Zigler and Phillips (1961b) found, on empirical examination, such a slight relationship between the two that few symptoms could be predicted based upon knowledge of diagnosis. In another study Phillips, Broverman, and Zigler (1966) obtained a more significant relationship between diagnosis and symptomatology by ordering the symptoms on scales of social competence or maturity. The critical aspect of a symptom is not how it relates to an hypothesized underlying disease process but, instead, the extent to which it reflects the social competence of the patient.

The Influence of the Interviewer. I have already implicated the nosological system in the low reliability and validity of diagnosis. Now let us examine the interview—the method used to arrive at diagnosis—for its contribution. Taking one of the symptoms considered to be critical in the diagnosis (and prognosis) of schizophrenia, that is, the lowered expression of emotion or affect, Salzinger and his colleagues evaluated the effect of the behavior of the interviewer on the behavior of the patient and, therefore, on diagnosis. In the first study, Salzinger and Pisoni (1958) defined a response class of self-referred affect in a reliable manner and standardized the behavior of the interviewer in such a way as to carry out what is basically a learning experiment. Using what to the patients was simply another intake interview, they examined schizophrenics diagnosed that way at the state hospital where the research was being conducted and at the intake hospital. The interview lasted 30 minutes and was divided into three consecutive 10-minute periods. For one group, the first 10 minutes consisted of operant or initial performance level, a period of time during which the interviewer asked questions of a general nature only, for example, "Why are you here at the hospital?" and "How do you spend your free time?" The second 10 minutes consisted of conditioning, during which the interviewer continued to ask general questions but, in addition, reinforced positively (rewarded) every self-referred affect statement (that is, a statement beginning with the pronouns "I" or "we" followed by one of an explicit list of affect verbs and adjectives, such as, "I hated that," "We couldn't stand him," "I loved him," and "I am quite happy now") by saying "yeah," "yes," "uhhuh," "I see," or "I can understand that," after each emission of a self-referred affect statement. The third 10 minutes consisted of extinction (the period following conditioning and during which no further reinforcement is given), for which the same procedure was followed the operant level condition. Another group of patients was given the same interview except that the entire 30 minutes consisted of operant level, that is, no reinforcements were given at all. The patients emitted the largest number of self-referred affect statements during the conditioning period. Furthermore, despite the fact that the conditioning and operant level groups emitted the same number of self-referred affect statements in the first 10 minutes, the conditioning group emitted a larger number of affect statements in the second 10 minutes (when reinforcement was given to one group but not to the other). Figure 1-1

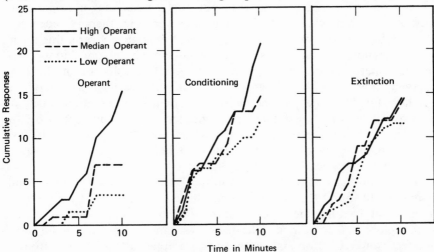

FIGURE 1–1. Individual cumulative response curves for three patients who showed the conditioning effect. (Courtesy of K. Salzinger and S. Pisoni, "Reinforcement of affect responses of schizophrenics during the clinical interview," *Journal of Abnormal and Social Psychology, 57,* **1958, pp. 84–90.** Copyright 1958 by the American Psychological Association and reproduced by permission.)

shows the cumulative curves of emission of affect statements for three of the subjects of the experimental group. The three patients were selected so that a high, a median, and a low operant level subject were presented.

A subsequent study, using the same general procedure, shows that the reinforcement is equally effective whether it comes during the first or second 10-minute period of the interview (Salzinger and Pisoni, 1961). In other words, the effect could not be ascribed to the establishment of rapport by the second half of the interview, which might allow the patient to confide more easily in the interviewer. This study also demonstrated that patients who manifested the highest rate of acquisition emitted the largest number of responses during extinction. The interviewer influences the very behavior he is trying to assay, but the degree of this effect is influenced by how fast the patient conditions.

The rate of conditioning is important with respect to prognosis. Salzinger and Portnoy (1964) found that patients who increased in the number of affect statements from operant level to conditioning were likely to leave the hospital six months after hospitalization, while those who did not show the conditioning effect were likely to remain in the hospital. There are two ways in which one can interpret these results. Remembering that the conditioning occurred one week after the patient was hospitalized and not just prior to his release from the hospital, the relationship between conditioning and outcome may reflect the patient's potential for changing in response to therapy given him while in the hospital; however, since therapy depending upon verbal reinforcement in a state hospital is relatively rare, this interpretation is not as convincing as it may at first seem. The relationship suggests another interpretation. The patient may manifest behavior in the first interview that stands him in good stead when the psychiatrist interviews him later for discharge. In other words, a patient who conditions easily in the experimental interview may also condition well, be influenced by, or "cooperate"[1] when facing a psychiatrist at an evaluation interview; the fast rate of conditioning may (albeit indirectly) influence the psychiatrist to believe that the patient is ready for discharge.

Let us look at two other studies in this series. The first (Salzinger and Pisoni, 1960) found that schizophrenics have the same operant level and condition at the same rate as normals; they differ only in that they extinguish more rapidly than do normals. The diagnostic importance of the shallowness of affect (lowered emotional responsiveness) appears to stem, not from a

---

[1] In none of these interviews was the patient or normal subject aware of being influenced or of cooperating to please the interviewer. The subjects did not even know that they were participating in an experiment. The point is that a person's behavior can be modified whether or not he or his modifier knows what either is doing.

general emotional deficit, but instead from the way its expression is influenced by the withdrawal of positive reinforcement. Still another possibility is that it reflects the generally greater diminution in response produced by withdrawal of reinforcement in schizophrenics. The final study (Salzinger, Portnoy, and Feldman, 1964a) was a methodological control for the possibility that the questions themselves (even though care was taken to keep them general and to prevent them from leading toward or away from the expression of affect) might have led to an increase in self-referred affect statements independent of the reinforcement. The study also examined the effect of reinforcement on speech in general. It corroborated the previous findings on affect and showed, in addition, that it is possible to condition speech in general.

What are the implications of these studies? They make it clear that the interviewer, while trying to obtain information on which to base a diagnosis or other evaluation, influences the behavior he is trying to evaluate. The fact that the typical interviewer does not reinforce in a *planned* way, does not mean that the typical interviewer reinforces in random fashion so that every response class is equally affected. It is more likely that the interviewer's reinforcing behavior is itself influenced by the behavior in the patient that interests him most, whether this interest stems from theory, conviction, or just plain prejudice; as a consequence, he is more likely to reinforce the behavior of the patient that agrees with his prejudgment than the behavior that disagrees with it. The very conduct of the interview, which is usually unplanned, almost promotes disagreement in the final diagnosis because it is susceptible to the idiosyncracies of the individual interviewers. The interested reader may consult Salzinger (1960) for a more detailed discussion of the problems of the interview in the assessment of behavior.

Errors of Observation and Interpretation. Another important and related source of error in the diagnosis of schizophrenia, as in diagnosis in general, is the fact that uncontrolled observation is susceptible to a number of errors produced by response biases. An experiment by Chapman (1967) demonstrates the phenomenon quite clearly. He presented pairs of words to subjects in such a way that each of the left-hand words occurred equally often in combination with each of the right-hand words. However, some of the left-right word combinations were meaningfully associated with each other, as in bacon-eggs, and some were not. Furthermore, one left and one right word were considerably longer than any of the other words on both lists. Having seen the various word pairs equally often, subjects were asked how often each pair occurred. They tended to report pairs of words meaningfully associated with each other in preference to the other combinations. They also reported the longer words to have occurred together more frequently than they actually did. Thus, those events that people tend to associate (whether they are associated in the verbal behavior of the subject or whether they simply share a distinguishing property such as length) are reported by them to have occurred together independent of their actual co-occurrence. For a diagnosis that feeds on the co-occurrence of events, this implies that different diagnosticians, having experienced different co-occurrences, will tend to be differentially influenced by them to report different co-occurrences and will, therefore, arrive at different diagnoses.

Another source of error responsible for the situation in diagnosis is that the diagnostician is encouraged, if not forced, to make interpretations of whatever facts he confronts, instead of being encouraged first to record the behavior and only then (if at all) trying to interpret it. Ayllon, Haughton, and Hughes (1965) did a pertinent study. A patient, 54 years of age, classified as schizophrenic, chronic undifferentiated type, who had been hospitalized for 23 years, was generally inactive, either lying in bed or on a couch most of the time. She had been idle for 13 years, during which time she did nothing but smoke cigarettes. She was restricted to only one cigarette per meal for a period of 25 days. Then conditioning began; the patient was handed a broom; at the same time she received a cigarette. This produced self-initiated broom-carrying behavior, which was eventually maintained by an intermittent schedule of reinforcement. After maintaining this behavior for 294 days, the experimenters extinguished it by withholding further reinforcement. This bizarre behavior was started by means of positive reinforcement and was eliminated by the subsequent withholding of that reinforcement. (The use of reinforcement as a therapeutic tool will be described later.) Of particular interest is the interpretation that a psychiatrist gave when he was asked to view this behavior without having been told about its origin. He said (Ayllon Haughton, and Hughes, 1965, p. 3): "Her constant and compulsive pacing, holding a broom in the manner she does, could be seen as a ritualistic procedure, a magical action... Her broom would be then: (1) a child that gives her love and she gives him in return her devotion, (2) a phallic symbol, (3) the sceptre of an omnipotent queen... this is a magical procedure in which the patient carries out her wishes, expressed in a way that is far beyond our solid, rational and conventional way of thinking and acting." Need more be said about the pitfalls of interpretation?

Improvements in Diagnostic Procedure. A number of solutions have been suggested to improve the state of diagnostic evaluation. Most prominent among these has been the utilization of rating scales, which consist, essentially, of some systematic way of viewing behavior. The structured clinical interview (Burdock and Hardesty, 1966)—one such technique—consists of a series of questions such as: "Tell me, what's troubling you now?" "What kind of an imagination do you have?" "What has your social life been like?" "How has your family been getting along?" and "Tell me something that interests you in the news." The questions are always asked in the same way, with the interviewer following up a question by repeating it or by asking "Can you tell me more about it?" if the answer given is not clear. The questions are, on the whole, relatively neutral, thus being serviceable for hospital populations as well as for community surveys. The interviewee's responses are scored with respect to an inventory of maladaptive behaviors that form the basis of the evaluation of psychopathology. This structured interview has already yielded interesting results whose findings can be evaluated by means of quantitative techniques. In a more recent development, a computer program was applied to a structured interview (Spitzer and Endicott, 1968) in order to eliminate the problem of variability of combining observations.

Lorr and his colleagues have constructed the In-patient Multidimensional Psychiatric Rating Scale (Lorr, Klett, and McNair, 1963). The interviewer obtains quantitative scores based on consideration of such factors as hostility, disorientation, guilt, auditory hallucinations, slowed speech and movements, and delusions of grandeur. In the application of rating scales to the evaluation of the behavior of the patient on the ward, Burdock, et al (1960) have devised an instrument that allows the nurses and/or attendants to rate the behavior of patients for a predetermined time sample, such as 48 hours, as either true or false with respect to a given series of items. Examples of such items are "joins in social games" (cards, for example), "is able to make own bed", "talks insistently about getting out", and "has to be reminded what to do." Goldberg, Klerman, and Cole (1965) used both the Lorr and the Burdock instruments in the evaluation of drug treatment. Having included in their design of the experiment one group that received a placebo (an inert substance having no known chemical effect on behavior) and one that received an active drug, these investigators were able to show the following: both the placebo and the active drug produced improvement in the behavior of the patients; however, the particular behaviors that improved were not the same; thus one group of behaviors—irritability, slowed speech and movements, so-called hebephrenic symptoms, self-care, and indifference to the environment—changed in response to the active drug but not in response to the placebo. This finding is significant in that it demonstrates the advantage of using a detailed description of the behavior of the patient. Undoubtedly, rating scales are an improvement over the global, unsystematic, subjective evaluation that forms the basis of the typical interview and gives rise to its unreliability. Some of these scales do, however, still suffer from a number of defects. Some of them simply consist of the arbitrary application of a number for the evaluation of a concept (for example, anxiety) that is, to begin with, inadequately defined. Other problems relate to the manner in which the numbers are combined, for example, when an investigator arbitrarily assumes that the difference between the numbers 1 and 2 is the same as the difference between the numbers 3 and 4 on a 7-point rating scale of anxiety. Finally, as we shall see below, there is the question of the appropriateness of the behavior that is rated to the particular model under consideration. Most of the rating scales are based on psychiatric concepts and on the medical model. We shall see that there are different ways of conceptualizing abnormal behavior; these would, of course, lead to the rating of behavior in different units and in relation to different variables.

Process-Reactive Schizophrenia

Before leaving the topic of diagnosis, it is important to describe a relatively new approach to the evaluation of schizophrenia. It stems from some of the dissatisfactions with the currently used diagnoses. Because of its relative novelty, it has been subjected to more empirical validation than the older psychiatric diagnoses. Although proponents of this system of classification are still debating whether one should view the process-reactive distinction as a continuum, that is, a dimension with two extreme poles, or whether one should view it as consisting of two different types, it is useful for purposes of exposition to describe the two extreme types of schizophrenic patients. In general, the process schizophrenic has been sick for a long period of time, having had a history of insidious onset (slow and inconspicuous process of becoming abnormal) and social inadequacy and who has little chance of recovery, while the reactive schizophrenic has experienced a sudden onset of the disorder, has a history of social adequacy, and has a favorable prognosis. As pointed out by Herron (1962), the process-reactive distinction had its implicit origin in Bleuler's work, in the sense that he rejected the Kraepelinian approach to schizophrenia as an incurable deteriorative disorder and allowed for the fact that some patients do recover. In addition to Herron's (1962) review, additional attempts to survey, the burgeoning literature have been made (Higgins, 1964; Garmezy, 1965; Kantor and Herron, 1966; Higgins and Peterson, 1966; Phillips, 1966). One of the points on which these reviews concur is that the diagnosis of schizophrenia yields too heterogeneous an assortment of patients to allow us to discover anything about the etiology or treatment of the disorder. All of the writers point out that the process-reactive distinction provides, at least potentially, the means for reducing this variance, citing studies where the distinction injects some lawfulness into the results. These studies will be described in the chapters appropriate to each particular type of behavior.

In addition to the Rorschach (Kantor and Herron, 1966), two other methods of arriving at the process-reactive diagnosis are the Elgin Prognostic Scale (Wittman, 1941) and the Phillips Scale (1953). Only a few reliability reports have been made on the Elgin Scale, but these (Garmezy, 1965) ranged from + .87 to +.97. Nevertheless, many investigators have not been able to use the Elgin Scale because of vagueness in wording (for example, "poor bite on life"), the requirement of an either-or judgment, the rating of items composed of several dimensions as if they constituted a single dimension, and the inclusion of many items that depend on life history data usually unavailable to a rater. The Phillips Scale has the advantage of demanding less case history data than the Elgin Scale; it has also retained only those items that relate to prognosis, and has had more substantial work done on its reliability. In a recent study, Zigler and Phillips (1962) used a social competence score based on age at onset, intelligence, education, occupation, stability of employment, and marital status; this is perhaps the easiest type of score to use. The investigators concluded that the process-reactive distinction is reducible to a social maturity dimension that applies to all of psychopathology, not merely to schizophrenia. This view of psychopathology as a response to the environment is one that is very much in accord with the view of behavior theory, as the reader will see below (especially Chapter 5).

Turner and Zabo (1968) found parts of the social competence score to correlate – .40 with the percentage of time the patients spent in the hospital (the lower the social competence, the longer the stay in the hospital). They pointed out, however, that the social competence score, which is considered to be an index of ability or maturity by Zigler and Phillips (1962), should more properly be viewed as an index of achievement rather than one of potential. Although a chronic process schizophrenic patient is very low on the social competence index, not everyone who is low on this index is a process schizophrenic; Turner and Zabo remind us that the factors that determine a person's score on individual items (such as whether he is married, steadily employed, or well educated) do not depend on the characteristics of the person alone. Differences in social competence also depend upon differences in cultural background.

Chapman and Baxter (1963) took the influence of culture in the process-reactive evaluation into account in a more explicit manner; they related the social class of the fathers of patients to the social competence index assigned to the patients. Their findings suggested that the characteristics of the specific population being rated on social competence might well prove to be an important factor in the relation of the process-reactive distinction to outcome of illness.

Because the process-reactive distinction has been somewhat more explicitly related to outcome of illness, it has encouraged a larger number of direct tests than the older, more tradition-bound type of diagnosis. The means for arriving at the process-reactive categories, however, are not totally objective and often require data that are most difficult to obtain (life history data are not usually available in case records or even potentially available in some cases because of the passage of time and lack of informants). In addition, the more objective indices tend to suffer because they are too much affected by unrelated factors. Another problem is posed by the application of the process-reactive classification on top of the unreliable diagnosis of schizophrenia. On the other hand, this new form of diagnostic evaluation has propelled investigators to examine the adjustment the individual makes to his environment. Since it is that adjustment that brings him into the hospital and, after discharge, keeps him in the community (whether or not there is a physical or psychological cause underlying his problem), patients will at last be evaluated on a relevant dimension.

PROGNOSIS

As already indicated, Kraepelin included poor outcome as a criterion in his definition of dementia praecox. For many years, a diagnosis of dementia praecox and, later, even the diagnosis of schizophrenia, was considered incorrect if the patient recovered instead of deteriorating. This view of schizophrenia was modified, under Bleuler's influence, to allow for the possibility of recovery. The estimate of improvement or recovery for patients diagnosed as schizophrenic is approximately 40 percent; the other 60 percent remain the same or deteriorate (Kolb, 1968). Description of the outcome of schizophrenia is still generally pessimistic. Thus, Kolb says that occasionally a patient with only a mild schizophrenic episode has no subsequent recurrence of illness; in many cases, however, the favorable outcome must be characterized as a social recovery, rather than as a cure or full recovery, suggesting that even though the patient can function in his previous social environment, he is left with a number of minor signs of schizophrenia. With respect to paranoid schizophrenia, for example, there are "surly and bitter attitudes."

The reader should also be reminded of the importance of the criterion of outcome in the process-reactive classification. A diagnosis that leads to a prediction about the outcome of a disorder is obviously superior to one that does not. In addition, the current availability of drug therapies, whose effect may be great with some patients and small or even adverse with others, makes the inclusion of a prognostic factor still more important. Only by knowing how soon and how much a patient would improve without any special treatment will we be able to gauge the effects of different kinds of treatment. Furthermore, by isolating factors related to good outcome, we might be able to modify the behavior of other patients to resemble those with favorable outcome.

The area of prognosis, like the rest of the literature on schizophrenia, abounds with studies that suffer from the failings already listed for the category of diagnosis, as well as from some of their own. First of all, the followup of schizophrenic patients must depend on who is to be included in the sample. In addition, there is the problem of deciding when the outcome is good and when it is poor; sometimes this is done on the basis of a followup of symptoms only, sometimes it is based upon an extensive psychiatric examination, sometimes on the simple, relatively objective criterion of being either "in" or "out" of a hospital (it should be noted, however, that the evaluation of whether the patient is ready for leaving a hospital is currently left up to the subjective judgment of the psychiatrist), and sometimes on information about the ex-patient's adjustment in terms of his job history and family life. All the criteria of outcome have failings; the use of different criteria causes still further confusion. Other aspects of this problem are discussed by Astrup and his colleagues (Astrup, Fossum, and Holmboe, 1962; Astrup, 1966; Stephens, Astrup and Mangrum, 1966), who, unlike many others in this field, call attention to the presence of schizophrenic psychosis in close relatives as a sign for poor outcome of illness.

In 1954, Zubin and Windle pointed out the need for taking into account the kind of treatment given to different patients, since the prognosis may well change in accordance with it. A collaborative group of research workers (NIMH-PRB Collaborative Study Group, 1968) examined this question. They related social and psychiatric history factors to an outcome variable of symptom reduction for four groups of patients: one was given a placebo only, one fluphenazine, one thioridazine, and one chlorpromazine (all three active drugs employed were phenothiazines). The study uncovered three clusters of predicting variables: one cluster predicted equally well for all treatments, one predicted outcome for the placebo and not for the active drug groups or vice versa, and one predicted differently for different active drugs. Without going into all the factors in this study, let us look at the variable of marital status. Many studies have found that married individuals have a better prognosis than single individuals. In this study, where prognosis was examined separately with respect to each kind of treatment, this relationship held only for patients treated by chlorpromazine (the correlation was +.34) and fluphenazine (the correlation was +.53), but not at all when the patients were given a placebo or thioridazine. Although the writers supplied no theoretical explanation for the result, they did demonstrate that marital status made it more likely for patients to improve only when treated by particular drugs.

I have already mentioned that patients who conditioned relatively quickly were more likely to be out of the state mental hospital six months after hospitalization (Salzinger and Portnoy, 1964). Another study (Salzinger,

Portnoy, and Feldman, 1966) shows that patients whose speech is more comprehensible also have a better outcome; although the correlations between speech comprehensibility and outcome were obtained on relatively small samples of patients, they did reach significance, and in one case showed a correlation as high as +.88. The exact procedure used will be explained in the chapter on verbal behavior; at this point, I merely wish to indicate that some hope exists for measures of performance at the time of hospitalization for predicting outcome of illness.

Zubin and his colleagues (Zubin, 1962; Zubin et al, 1959; Zubin et al, 1961) reviewed the literature consisting of approximately 800 articles on prognostic indicators. Many methodological difficulties inhere in these studies. We shall discuss here those variables least open to criticism. Seven hundred and eight studies noted that sudden onset of illness implied good outcome, 21 studies poor outcome, and 11 studies no prediction. Despite the overwhelming uniformity of opinion on this variable, the subjectivity with which it is usually determined leaves us with quite a few problems. The reader will recognize, in this variable, the kind of premorbid judgments of social competence that are currently used in the process-reactive dimension. The subcategories of schizophrenia as predictors of outcome have been discussed in the section on validity of diagnosis. Other variables examined with respect to prognosis include bizarre mannerisms, emotional expression, and abstract ability. It is enough to say that a number of behaviors in schizophrenics have at least the potential for use as prognostic indices. Only a very few, however, have been studied experimentally to check on their validity. To take the example of lack of emotional response, referred to above, it is not the emission of affect per se that relates to outcome; instead, it is the conditionability of the emotional responsiveness that relates (Salzinger and Portnoy, 1964). Thus, although the clinical literature may be helpful in uncovering relevant variables as a focus for more controlled study, for the most part they call attention to variables only tangentially, if at all, related to prognosis.

THERAPY

I will not attempt to review even large parts of research in therapy in schizophrenia; instead, I shall again rely on reviews in the literature. To begin with, it is interesting to see what a book on clinical psychiatry has to say on the subject. Kolb (1968) notes that the use of a phenothiazine (that is, chlorpromazine) is a preferred method of treatment today; but he warns that the longer a patient has been ill, the less chance there is that the treatment will be effective. In psychotherapy, it is important to consider not only the therapeutic hour but also the patient's day-to-day activity, since it is in the latter that the effects of the therapeutic hour must ultimately be gauged. In regard to this, Kolb states that although some patients become permanently isolated from their environment, for most the degree of improvement varies as a direct function of the amount of attention they receive. Kolb indicates that psychoanalytic treatment has never been successful with schizophrenia. He goes on to warn (p. 397) that "complete resolution of the schizophrenic process... is rarely obtained, even by therapists of the greatest experience and patience." He describes insulin coma therapy (the injection of insulin deprives the brain of oxygen and thus causes a brief period of unconsciousness) as having failed to prove to be sufficiently effective, and mentions that electroconvulsive therapy (the application of brief electric shock to the forehead, inducing a period of unconsciousness), another shock treatment given to schizophrenic patients, is often preferred to insulin shock therapy because it involves fewer hazards to life and limb and is simpler to apply. Electric shock therapy itself has been displaced, at least as maintenance treatment, by drugs. Psychosurgery, the last type of treatment Kolb discusses, has lost popularity in recent years and is employed only if all else has failed; yet Kolb maintains that even when everything else has been tried, there are conditions under which psychosurgery should still not be used, for example, when the patient is chronically deteriorated with no emotional response.

Physical Methods

In a recent review of the physical (all but psychotherapy) methods of treatment of schizophrenia, Cawley (1967) points out that, while clinical benefits undoubtedly accrue from the current physical treatments (p. 109), "there is no evidence that they have in themselves any curative action or permanent effect." One side effect of tranquilizers, Cawley tells us, is a new optimism about the success of treatment (sometimes referred to as a placebo effect); another is the possibility it provides of giving the patients other treatments (since it calms patients down) to which they were previously not amenable; a third is the return of Pinel's moral treatment (in which the staff handles the patient in such a way that his dignity as a human being is not forgotten, and thus his interaction with his environment is positively reinforced). It is, perhaps, ironic that the placebo effect is one of the most important deterrents to obtaining information about the action of the so-called active drugs.

In a review of the effectiveness of the pharmacotherapy, Lehmann (1966) maintains that drugs are the treatment of choice because they are superior to any other single therapeutic procedure "in terms of rapid effectiveness, sustained action, general availability, and ease of application." At the same time, he freely admits that they are not a cure, despite the "definitive evidence of the superior performance of the major tranquilizers in the treatment of acute and chronic schizophrenic patients" (p. 393). One of the benefits of the advent of drugs has been the introduction of a new era of research concerned with the problem of evaluating treatment. One such new procedure is the so-called double-blind procedure. In accordance with this method, neither the investigator who is evaluating the effect of the drug (even if he does so by objective means) nor the patient knows what drug, or how much, if any, the patient is getting. Furthermore, drugs have also stimulated the interest of government agencies, such as the Veterans Administration and the National Institutes of Mental Health, to engage in large collaborative studies on the basis of which proper evaluation is possible. Nevertheless the problems of diagnosis and objective evaluation of improvement still require further research in order to achieve a valid evaluation of the various treatments.

Another review, although completed before evaluation of drugs was widespread (because they had not yet been in use long enough), is instructive and should be briefly mentioned. Staudt and Zubin (1957) surveyed studies evaluating the effectiveness of a variety of somatotherapies (physical therapies), including insulin convulsive therapy, metrazol, electroconvulsive therapy, lobotomy (psychosurgery), and prolonged narcosis (state of drowsiness induced by barbiturates), and found an advantage of treated groups over untreated groups in the short range, but no such advantage on long-term followup. Interestingly enough, the rate of improvement of patients during the era in which no physical treatment was given was higher than that of the later control patients compared to the somatotherapy-treated groups. This suggests that the control patients were not randomly chosen but included, most probably, those patients with the relatively poorer prognoses. Another possible interpretation is that patients during the preshock era were recipients of more attention because no other kind of treatment was available except for the social interaction resulting from occupational therapy and the like. The control-group patients during the shock era might have been largely ignored because of the belief at that time that only a form of somatotherapy would be helpful. Still other interpretations are, of course, possible; they refer to differences in diagnoses, differences in evaluation of improvement, differences in criteria of hospitalization and, finally, differences in the public's hesitation to confine a relative or friend in a mental hospital.

The use of the various somatotherapies has been pragmatic, encouraged in large measure by clinical speculation. Nevertheless, some interesting experimentation has been done. Zubin (1948) and Zubin and Barrerra (1941) found that while the electroshock treatments interfered with *recall* of recently experimentally learned material, the interference with the *recognition* of the same material was nowhere as great. Furthermore, they found that shock affected only recently acquired material, not old memories.

Hunt and Brady (1951) showed that a so-called conditioned emotional response (CER) in animals could be eliminated by means of electroconvulsive treatments. The animal was first conditioned to press a bar on an intermittent positive reinforcement schedule (only some responses were reinforced). After the animal had learned to emit the bar-pressing response at a stable rate, a stimulus (a clicking noise) was introduced. It lasted for a period of three minutes and was terminated by the delivery of an electric shock. The general effect of this CER procedure was to cause the eventual cessation of responding by the animal while the clicking noise was occurring, even though the positive reinforcement contingency had not changed. After the establishment of the CER, electroconvulsive treatments were administered and the animals were tested in the regular bar-pressing situation again. The animals given the electro-convulsive treatments showed restoration of the operant response rate and virtually no emotional responses at all to the clicker, except for some initial exploratory behavior. In other words, this experiment showed that the shock treatment eliminated a nonadaptive response (emotional behavior and cessation of the adaptive response for food) that was engendered in the laboratory. It is of interest to note in this context that the review by Lewis and Maher (1965) shows the effect of electroshock treatment to be better interpreted as a conditioned inhibition of responses than as an interfering agent in memory consolidation.

A study by Lindsley and Conran (1962) demonstrates an ingenious method for measuring the depth of coma induced in electroshock treatment. The subject was trained to squeeze a palm switch in order to reduce the intensity of a loud tone coming to him via ear phones. As long as he responded at a rate higher than 50 per minute, the intensity of the tone was reduced below his threshold. By presenting the patient with the tone during the course of his shock treatments, the investigators were able to trace, in an objective way, the depth of the coma by monitoring the response rate on a continuous basis, rather than by the more usual rough-and-ready methods of calling the patient's name, pinching him, and raising his eyelids, for example. The availability of this objective measure of the depth of coma should allow future investigators to relate this variable to rate of recovery from schizophrenia.

A recent article by Dies (1968) provides a learning theory explanation for the effect of electroconvulsive therapy. Essentially, Dies views the shock treatments as negative reinforcements to which the patient responds by making escape and avoidance responses, since he "expects that his pathological behavior is what leads to the punishment of the shock treatments." Dies goes on to explain the lack of any long-range effects of this treatment by pointing out that while the pathological behavior of such patients is suppressed, no one teaches them alternative responses to use once they are discharged from the hospital. Only by using psychotherapy as an adjunct to shock therapy, says Dies, can we expect to have a better long-term outcome. Let us, therefore, look at psychotherapy more closely.

Social Methods

In a review of social treatment of schizophrenic patients, Wing (1967) shows that most therapies are either symptomatic (that is, not directed at the "underlying disease process") or simply arbitrary. These therapies have caused change, however. He attributes much of the decrease in abnormal behavior in mental hospitals not just to the advent of drugs but to improvement in the social conditions that prevail there. He makes the further provocative point, despite the usual pessimistic view of psychotherapy with schizophrenic patients, that they are quick to respond to social changes. Other bits of evidence also show that schizophrenic patients respond to their environment. The placebo effect, which is such a large problem with respect to evaluation of drugs, is another source of evidence for the schizophrenic's susceptibility to social stimuli, or at least to environmental stimuli. Rosenthal and Frank (1956) believe in taking the placebo effect into account when evaluating the effectiveness of psychotherapy as well as of drug treatments. The placebo can be powerful indeed, since "it can significantly modify the patient's physiological functioning, even to the extent of reversing the normal pharmacological action of drugs; and . . . it may be enduring" (Rosenthal and Frank, p. 296). Other articles on the placebo effect (Honigfeld, 1964a and b) have implicated the social environment and have suggested that the conditioning model explains how the placebo works.

The questionable effect of psychodynamic psychotherapy (Eysenck, 1960), even with neurotics, has begun to stimulate behavior theorists to use their modification techniques to produce a change in the behavior of schizophrenic patients (for example, Grossberg, 1964; Kanfer and Phillips, 1969). We will have more to say about this in Chapter 5. It is enough to say here that behavior therapy, because both its modification techniques and its target behaviors are explicit, is easier to evaluate than the psychodynamic therapies.

The fact that various kinds of psychotherapy have been reinforcing behavior was recently demonstrated, even for the proverbially "noninterfering" nondirective therapy (Truax, 1966; also discussed at length by Inglis, 1966). It is in fact fair to say that the operant conditioning of verbal behavior is a significant aspect of all types of psychotherapies (Salzinger, 1969b). One really cannot decide to use reinforcement, only how to distribute it, if one makes any attempt at long interactions with another human being. Behavior theory studies show that the well-known learning paradigms can be put to good advantage as far as the patient is concerned.

METHODOLOGICAL PROBLEMS IN THE STUDY OF SCHIZOPHRENIC PATIENTS

Much of what has been discussed so far has involved consideration of methodological problems such as diagnosis, evaluation of therapy, and prognosis. There are still others. A rather angry paper by Bannister (1968) asserts that what we need is not more data but rather a more logical delineation of research in the field of schizophrenia. Bannister's first logical requirement is the redefinition of schizophrenia. The second logical requirement is the linking of conceptual and operational definitions. He criticizes research of a completely empirical nature that simply asks, "Do schizophrenics differ from normals on this?" without making any attempt to relate such a difference to a network of theory that has been supported by other data. Zubin (1965b) presents a classification of the research done in psychopathology in general and schizophrenia in particular, in terms of levels of observed behavior (physiological, sensory, perceptual, psychomotor, and conceptual) on one hand, and types of stimuli on the other (configuration, signs, and symbols). While this does provide a scheme for looking at the disparate techniques and results obtained with them, it cannot function as a substitute for conceptualization when the original experiment is done. Bannister's methodological point is really one of methodology of conception rather than of execution.

Cooperativeness

Shakow (1963) has, for many years, taken the variable of cooperativeness into account. He rates the behavior of the patient being tested, contending that, when he takes the level of cooperativeness into account, differences between normals and schizophrenics are often reduced and sometimes even eliminated. Winder (1960) points out that the relationship between performance and cooperativeness is found only for schizophrenics and not for patients given such diagnoses as organic disorder. The problem with procedures like Shakow's, in which one rates the extent of cooperativeness while aware of the patient's performance on the task with which the rating is later to be correlated, is that response bias may inadvertently enter the rating. Thus the experimenter may unwittingly assign low ratings of cooperativeness just because performance on the task was poor. The problem, however, cannot just be ignored.

It may be useful to analyze cooperativeness in terms of behavior theory.

Let us take a task where the subject is given instructions to memorize a series of nonsense syllables as fast as he can. Obviously, one of the discriminative stimuli (a stimulus, in the presence of which a response is rewarded, for example, by approval of the tester) in the situation consists of the instructions; there may, however, be others, such as the discriminative stimulus that a subject provides for himself. Examples might be: "I can't learn this stuff," or "If I learn this well, he'll say I can go home. I'd better pay attention," or "I'll be damned if I'll do this—it's too stupid for words!" (and then look away from the memory drum). The point is that the patient may present himself with discriminative stimuli either at variance or in agreement with the performance required by the task. For some patients, however, cooperativeness may reflect directly the psychotic control exerted over the patient's behavior by his hallucinatory voices. In other words, cooperativeness may be an artifact of the experiment or a clear expression of the disorder. To avoid experiment-induced lack of cooperativeness, the following measures must be taken. The patient should not know what the experimenter is after, and behavior that is consonant with the instructions should be followed up by positive reinforcement. Conditioning experiments, such as Salzinger and Pisoni's (1958), demonstrate how the patient can be tested in a familiar situation (talking in an interview), where the patient's performance is evaluated by a measure (rate of conditioning) of which he is unaware, and where reinforcement is deliberately dispensed or withheld. This, at least, partially obviates the subject-produced discriminative stimuli that might conflict with those presented by the experimenter. The use of speech samples is still another example of how an experimenter can circumvent the problem of cooperativeness, since the subject's participation in the experiment is minimal, that is, all he has to do is talk. Such experiments allow the investigator to study the coherence of what the patient is saying, or the topic he discusses, or the relevance of his speech to the question asked, and in this way the problem of cooperativeness is either avoided or emphasized, depending on what is measured.

Hospitalization

The effect of hospitalization may well account for the many disagreements in the literature concerning the "typical" schizophrenic since, more often than not, the critical information of length of hospitalization is not even specified in the description of the population being tested. I have already mentioned that schizophrenic patients are responsive to social changes; it is, therefore, axiomatic that the particular institutional environment should affect the patient. It follows that the particular ward and the particular hospital (and the length of stay) in which the patient is confined will have a significant effect on his behavior. In addition to the factors over which the patient has no control at all, there are concommitant, or secondary effects of the schizophrenic disorder. Mednick (1967, p. 179) describes the problem as follows: "Schizophrenia is a complex life condition which has consequents. These consequents include longterm hospitalization, bachelorhood, economic and social failure, as well as educational and even dietary deprivation." He cites studies that show a similarity in the differences between nonpsychiatric prisoners of long duration and those of short duration, and differences between chronic and acute schizophrenic patients. Part of the problem, as we shall note again when we review social factors in schizophrenia, is to discover what is cause and what is effect, that is, is social failure a cause or an effect of schizophrenia? Many of the artifacts in biochemical research have been shown to be due to the diet offered by the hospital or produced by the strange eating habits of the patient.

Murray and Cohen (1959) related degree of abnormality to social organization in three different wards. One was a nonpsychiatric experimental ward for the long term study of metabolic diseases; the patients were restricted to the ward but they were ambulatory. A second was a closed ward for disturbed psychiatric patients; these patients were treated by somatotherapy. The third was a closed ward in which the disturbed patients were treated by milieu (the social environment is used to produce social rehabilitation) and group therapy. The milieu therapy ward showed a greater degree of social organization than the somatic therapy ward and about the same degree of organization as the nonpsychiatric ward. It is also interesting to note that in sociometric choices, paranoid schizophrenic patients showed a greater tendency to choose other such patients rather than different types of patients. Paranoid patients seem to wish to be with patients who are equally deluded rather than with patients who have other symptoms. There is the definite possibility that paranoid patients reinforce each other positively for their respective delusions; it is also possible, however, that other common characteristics (for example, higher intelligence) may bring them together. In any case, the environments of patients of different diagnoses may well differ from each other, even on the same ward. Although one can view this study as showing either the effect of the disorder or of the type of therapy on behavior, it does make clear that, in presenting results on patients, the type of ward atmosphere should be specified, for it may well be responsible for some of the different results found by various investigators. One would certainly expect that at least some of the differences in patient behavior picked up by tests are related to the patient's placement in different kinds of wards.

Testability

The various inferences made about schizophrenic patients are limited by the extent to which all patients are tested. Wilensky and Solomon (1960) studied a group of 101 male, chronic schizophrenic patients who constituted the entire population of two wards. Three tests were given to these patients: the Rorschach (a projective personality test), part of the Wechsler Adult Intelligence Scale, and six months after administration of the first two tests, a tapping test (subject is required to tap two targets as rapidly as possible), which, unlike the first two, was administered on the ward. Performance on the first two tests used as a criterion of testability yielded two groups of untestable patients: a refusal group and a confused group. The untestable group differed from the testable group in some important respects. Thus, out of 36 patients diagnosed paranoid schizophrenic, 25 were testable on at least one test, one was not testable because he was confused, and 10 were untestable because they refused. The testable patients were younger than the untestable patients. Those who were untestable because of confusion had been hospitalized for the longest period of time, while those who were untestable because of refusal had been in the hospital only a little longer than the testable ones. The authors concluded that the test results of any sample of patients represent a biased sample of the population of hospitalized patients. Use of the tapping test incurred a loss (untestable) of only 9 percent of the patient population. In addition, ways of observing behavior can be used with even greater success in obtaining a complete, or almost complete population. Social interaction on the ward, analysis of speech samples, and tests whose purpose is so disguised that the patient cannot "refuse", since it is not clear to him what he has to refuse in order to be uncooperative, are examples.

Committal

The question here relates to the selective factors that bring patients to the attention of the authorities and, subsequently, into the hospital. Apparently, the lower socioeconomic groups sustain the greater risk of being in a mental hospital. Langner (1961) describes these patients as being "older, poorer and less educated performing manual labor in low status occupations." Smith, Pumphrey, and Hall (1963) describe the critical incidents resulting in the request for hospitalization of 100 schizophrenic patients. For 53 of these patients, hospitalization was requested because they either had actually committed, or threatened to commit, a dangerous act, For 38, it was requested because they exhibited behavior that was socially unacceptable, such as shouting, nudity, irrational talk, and inexplicable behavior. Only nine patients were hospitalized because someone claimed that their illness required treatment (including four requests from the patient himself, one family request, and four medical recommendations). When prior incidents (those incidents that occurred before the critical incident) were reviewed, it became obvious that socially unacceptable behavior was tolerated to a much greater degree than behavior that resulted in, or could have resulted in, danger to the patient or others. These results are not precisely the same for all hospitals. Nevertheless, actual hospitalization does not occur until the patient's behavior is quite extreme, thus giving rise to a biased sampling of schizophrenic behavior in the hospital.

In a study relating hospitalization to the social network of the nuclear family, Hammer (1963-1964) also found that only extreme behavior, such as violent and grossly bizarre behavior, consistently resulted in the patient being brought to a hospital. Nonperformance of tasks in the community elicited hospitalization by persons close to the patient. In addition, she found that patients in critical positions in the family were hospitalized more rapidly than those in noncritical positions (critical referring to the making of a regular financial contribution to the household or caring for the children). Patients with symmetrical ties (close to people who were equally close to them) were more likely to receive personal care, therapy, and hospitalization from such a person, illustrating still another factor that influences hospitalization. Furthermore, we have no way of knowing, at present, how these differences in reasons for hospitalization influence the choice of patients who are selected for testing for various behaviors or biochemical faults, but this results in still another way in which populations of patients being tested by different investigators may differ from one another as well as being unrepresentative of patients having that abnormality.

Having been exposed to the methodological pitfalls in research, the reader may well wonder what the implications are for the behavioral descriptions to be presented in this book. The first implication is to look to these methodological factors to explain some of the discrepancies found in various studies. The second is to view such a listing of methodological complications as a challenge to future research. The challenge has, in fact, been accepted by some investigators already. Mednick (1967) has begun a long-range research program on the children of known schizophrenic mothers. Such children constitute a population of high risk for schizophrenia, since genetic studies have indicated a much higher incidence of schizophrenia for them than for the population at large (see Kallmann, 1946). These children will provide subjects who have not yet been affected by hospitalization or, for that matter, by any of the other secondary effects of schizophrenia; it will also make it possible to study the onset of schizophrenia. Finally, such a population should eventually profit from preventative therapy, made possible by the identification of indicators of the onset of schizophrenia. Mednick's pioneering study will undoubtedly make important contributions to our knowledge of schizophrenia.

VARIABLES RELATED TO THE ONSET AND MAINTENANCE OF SCHIZOPHRENIA

This category is generally called etiology, but the very use of this term pre-judices the entire discussion, since it stems from the medical disease model, the appropriateness of which has been questioned by a number of researchers. I therefore chose the more neutral term, "variable". The reader will also note that I have separated those variables that started the disorder from those that maintain it. In practice, it is very difficult to separate them com-pletely; however, it is critical to realize that the factors we are discussing and, which the various warring theorists maintain cause the disorder, may all be involved—some primarily with respect to onset and others primarily with respect to maintenance. First thought suggests that to prevent a disorder we must prevent its onset, but this is not always the most effective method; vaccinations produce onset but prevent maintenance of the disorder. From the point of view of therapy, the variables that maintain the aberrant be-havior may loom larger, but even here no clearcut preference for one set of variables over another is possible. It may turn out that some behavior once initiated by a biochemical flaw will tend to return, even if the maintain-ing conditions are changed.

The Medical Model

Schizophrenia has not always been viewed as a medical problem. The concept as we know it today, however, was named by a medical man, and patients so labeled are almost exclusively under the care of physicians. It is, therefore, not surprising that most people view schizophrenia as a disease and try to treat it as one. What is the medical disease model? It consists of two basic concepts: one is the underlying cause of a disease that must be treated if the patient is to improve; the other is the symptom, a mere mani-festation of the disease, which, even if treated, will not help the patient because other symptoms will arise to take the place of those eliminated. In physical medicine this model has been very powerful, functioning in such a way that description and classification were followed by discovery of a foreign organism or lesion that was responsible for the symptoms. Taken over into psychiatry, this approach has not always led to the search for a physical cause. Since Freud, it has often implied that the behavior is the unimportant symptom and that the underlying factors must be searched for deep in the unconscious part of the mind. When such factors are uncover-ed (the goal of psychoanalysis), then it is suggested, the behavioral symptoms will disappear. Many have criticized this model of abnormal behavior. In many cases, only the direct treatment of the abnormal behavior is necessary to eliminate some disorders (Ullmann and Krasner, 1965), and the predicted symptom substitution does not in fact occur. Let us, nevertheless, examine the results of the medical model approach.

Perhaps the most important development of this approach is the nosological system already discussed. The problems of diagnosis that have resulted from it have also been cited in detail. It is enough to say that the classification system has not been notably successful.

The Genetic Variable. Another development of the medical model is the search for a biochemical cause of the disease. Kallmann's (1946) work on the genetic aspects of schizophrenia gave it much impetus. Meehl (1962) has described the discovery of the genetic variable in the etiology of schizophrenia as probably the single most important fact known about schizophrenia. We have already mentioned that Mednick used the genetic information to locate a high-risk-for-schizophrenia population. Yet even this apparently unassailable finding has been questioned. Kety (1959) points out that even if one accepts Kallmann's figures of greater concordance (agreement in both members of a pair having or not having schizophrenia) of schizophrenia in identical than in fraternal twins, one cannot conclude that only genetic factors are responsible for the disorder, since some 14 to 30 percent of the monozygotic twins had schizophrenia in only one twin. Furthermore, monozygotic twins separated some years before the study showed less concordance than those not separated.

In 1967, Shields, Gottesman, and Slater reviewed Kallmann's 1946 schizophrenic twin study. They note that Kallmann's concordance rates for identical twins are higher than a number of other studies that followed his, the other concordance rates being (identical twins versus fraternal twins) 65 versus 9 percent, 60 versus 12 percent, 0 versus 10 percent, 38 versus 14 percent, 42 versus 9 percent, and 30 versus 0 percent. Kallmann's higher concordance rates for identical twins are explained by the fact that his starting sample came from the chronic cases of state hospitals, resulting in a greater proportion of severely disturbed cases of schizophrenics. They nevertheless conclude that "genetic factors...remain largely responsible for the specific nature of most schizophrenic disorders."

In another review of genetic studies of schizophrenia, Kreitman and Smythies (1968) also specified a number of methodological problems. Like Shields, et al, they emphasized the importance of the selection of the beginning sample. By beginning with a hospital population, one is more likely to find concordance, since a family is more likely to have at least one concordant twin hospitalized than the single schizophrenic of a discordant pair. This results from the fact that one schizophrenic individual is easier to deal with than two. They further pointed out that Kallmann had to estimate zygosity (whether identical or fraternal twins) by clinical means that were not entirely independent of the clinical judgment of presence of schizophrenia. Despite their criticisms, these writers also conclude that the genetic factor cannot be ruled out from consideration in the etiology of schizophrenia.

Lest the reader believe that there is unanimity of opinion on the etiological importance of the genetic factor, we must refer him to some studies by Kringlen (1964, 1966, 1967). He finds relatively low rates of concordance with somewhat higher rates for the monozygotic than for the dizygotic twins. Although the rates are significantly different statistically, the magnitude of the difference is so small that Kringlen concludes the genetic factor to be less important than some investigators have claimed. It is difficult to reconcile the fact that even the most severe cases of schizophrenia are often paired with a twin who is normal. However, this result is also difficult to deal with by an environmental theory of the causation of schizophrenia. He concludes that a biochemical breakthrough (whose significance is based largely upon the genetic determination of schizophrenia) may well not be enough to produce an understanding of schizophrenia.

Biochemical Faults. The fact that some genetic influence over schizophrenia is undeniable has, of course, encouraged the search for a biochemical fault as the mechanism responsible for the schizophrenic behavior. The discovery that certain drugs (called psychotomimetic) can generate schizophrenic-like behavior has further promoted the interest in the biochemistry of schizophrenia. The progress of this type of research has had its ups and downs, however, as is well documented in Kety's review of biochemical theories of schizophrenia (Kety, 1959). He listed a series of errors made in such studies, many of which I have discussed under methodological problems. Additional methodological factors in biochemical research have produced more artifacts in research than information about schizophrenia. In some studies, Kety showed the diet, rather than a biochemical fault, to be the critical factor that differentiated the schizophrenics from the normals. No attempt will be made here to review the research concerning the biology of schizophrenia. Let us merely quote some remarks made by proponents of this approach. Friedhoff (1967) said (p. 27): "While the etiology and pathogenesis of schizophrenia remain largely uncertain, it seems reasonable to assume that the marked psychological and behavioral changes in the schizophrenic are mediated through altered biochemical mechanisms or disturbed patterns of physiological organization. Whether these biochemical aberrations are inborn and primary or secondary to emotional trauma, they must play an important role in producing the symptoms of this illness." Kety (1967) recently discussed the relevance of biochemical studies to the etiology of schizophrenia (p. 39): "The nurture-versus-nature controversy is becoming as obsolete in the study of schizophrenia as it is in the rest of medicine. It is no longer a question of which is involved but how much, and the most important task appears to be the precise definition of the specific biological and psychosocial factors involved and the mechanisms by which they interact in the production and development of various forms of schizophrenic illness."

Another reason for the biological approach to the study of schizophrenia given by Zubin and Kietzman (1966) and later by Al-Issa (1968) is for purposes of cross-cultural study of schizophrenia. They propose that culture-free indicators of psychopathology are more universal than other indices for classifying behavior disorders. Recent studies in conditioning, particularly those carried out in Russia, have demonstrated the modification of so many internal organs of the body by well established conditioning paradigms as to question the existence of truly culture-free measures. A more reasonable description of these measures would be to place them in a culture-fair category, that is, where comparable social factors, rather than no social factors, are involved in their measurement.

In summary, we can say that although the medical disease model begins by positing a biological cause and deprecates attempts to modify "mere" symptoms, current investigators have become less convinced of the possibility of finding a biological cause independent of social causes; they have even suggested that the biological involvement need not be primary. I maintain that it is critical to examine the *behavior* of the patient and that it is, therefore, critical to view it in terms of a behavioral model, the only model that is capable of containing within one scheme both biological and behavioral variables.

The Behavioral Model

Dissatisfaction with the medical model of abnormal behavior has run rampant for some years. Szasz (1960) refers to the myth of mental illness. In a similar vein, Adams (1964) describes the concept of functional illness as a verbal analogy; since it involves interpersonal behavior, mental illness is neither a health nor a medical problem. Shakow (1965), not usually in opposition to the medical model, questioned its utility in solving the classification problem. The process-reactive classification (mentioned in detail above) attempts to make the schizophrenia category more useful by examining the patient's premorbid social behavior in a way not called for by the medical model. A paper on the anatomy of abnormality (Herron and Kantor, 1966) maintains that abnormality needs to be viewed in terms of interactional analyses and, even more important, that analysis of abnormality must concentrate, not only on the description of the behavior in question, but also on the context in which it occurs. In a paper on culture and abnormal behavior, Hammer and Zubin (1968) suggest that psychopathology be defined in terms of reduced cultural predictability; they admit that this definition also includes the reduced cultural predictability of genius but they differentiate the genius from the abnormal individual in terms of the latter's greater "internal" redundancy (that is, more repetitions in his idiosyncratic remarks) than the genius.

Clearly, students of abnormal psychology have had to take into account a variety of social-cultural factors in the effort to attain a better understanding of psychopathology. In psychiatry, this has come under the heading of epidemiology (Hoch and Zubin, 1961; Zubin, 1961). Epidemiological studies have found a larger number of psychotic individuals among lower socioeconomic groups than among higher ones (Brody, 1967). The implication of such a finding is not entirely clear, but current researchers are inclined to conclude that psychopathology causes the lower socioeconomic group membership, rather than that the group membership is responsible for schizophrenia (Hare, 1967). Other interesting findings in this area are the apparent invariance in the rate of schizophrenia over the last 150 years (when reasonably accurate records were kept), the higher frequency of schizophrenia among migrant groups, but not in all cultures, and finally, a higher rate in those members of minority groups who live among the majority than in those who live in the midst of their own group.

These findings emphasize the importance of social factors in considering abnormal behavior. What we need is a model for a mechanism demonstrating how such social factors express themselves in the abnormality. I propose that the behavior theory model accomplishes essentially this. At a conference called to consider objective indicators of psychopathology, Salzinger (1968) listed a number of ways in which behavior theory could be applied to the study of psychopathology. In the past, behavior theory was used to translate another theory (notably psychoanalytic theory) and in the creation of behavior modification techniques. With respect to this discussion, however, behavior theory is useful in supplying vocabulary for the lawful description and analysis of behavior.

Concepts of Behavior Theory. In order to consider behavior theory, we must first explain some of the important concepts. The explanation offered will be brief, and the interested reader is advised to read more extensively (Keller and Schoenfeld, 1950; Skinner, 1953; Millenson, 1967; Salzinger, 1969a). There are two paradigms for learning. One is called respondent or classical conditioning; unconditioned responses are elicited by unconditioned stimuli (by stimuli that evoke these responses without any special training). The placement of food in the mouth is an example of an unconditioned stimulus; the unconditioned response to it is salivation. The pairing of such unconditioned stimuli with conditioned stimuli (stimuli that have no eliciting effect without special training) produces the conditioned responses. In other words, respondent conditioning is a procedure by means of which stimuli initially neutral elicit responses that formerly could be elicited only by unconditioned stimuli. The sound of a bell is an example of a conditioned stimulus that after some pairing with the unconditioned stimulus of food, comes to elicit the conditioned response of salivation. This type of conditioning deals with "involuntary" responses, such as heart rate and sweating, and has found application in the explanation of aspects of psychosomatic medicine. The concept of anxiety is related to respondent conditioning by defining it as the period intervening between the onset of a conditioned stimulus and an aversive unconditioned stimulus, (for example, the sound of a metronome followed by an electric shock). The intervening period is called anxiety because during that time the animal produces a number of emotional responses and ceases to make responses that interact with the environment. The equivalent for a student might be the waiting period between being told a test is forthcoming and the actual test administration.

In operant conditioning, the response acts upon the environment and the critical stimulus, the reinforcement follows it; the stimulus which marks the occasion for the availability of the reinforcement, provided the animal responds, is the discriminative stimulus. There are two types of stimuli (reinforcements) that can follow a response to cause conditioning: a positive reinforcement, which is one whose occurrence after the response increases the frequency of that response, and a negative reinforcement, which is one whose elimination or avoidance by the response increases the frequency of occurrence of that response. The discriminative stimuli take on some of the properties of the reinforcements with which they become associated by this paradigm. The S^D is the discriminative stimulus for a response whose occurrence is followed by positive reinforcement; the S^Δ is the stimulus in the presence of which a response is *not* positively reinforced, that is, the S^Δ is the stimulus indicating extinction. The S^D becomes, through this procedure, a conditioned positive reinforcement, that is, it takes on the properties of the primary positive reinforcement and becomes capable of conditioning other responses. The S^Δ acts like a conditioned negative reinforcement. In the same way, a stimulus associated in this manner with a negative reinforcement becomes itself a conditioned negative reinforcement and the stimulus associated with the cessation of a negative reinforcement becomes itself a conditioned positive reinforcement.

Two other points need to be made. An animal responds to a reinforcing stimulus after having been deprived of it. To take an example, an animal that has been deprived of food for 24 hours can be conditioned by food acting as a reinforcement. Such deprivation is said to produce a drive. Drive is more important at the beginning of learning than for its maintenance. After the behavior has been acquired, it is very effectively controlled by the discriminative stimuli. These discriminative stimuli demonstrate their control by setting the occasions for the reinforcement of different patterns of responding, particularly the intermittent schedules of reinforcement.

One of Skinner's most important discoveries was that every response need not be reinforced for an animal to continue to work. Intermittent reinforcement is in fact the rule in nature. Furthermore, different kinds of intermittent reinforcement produce typical kinds of performance; thus, reinforcement that is essentially contingent on a piece-work basis (ratio reinforcement schedule) produces high rates of response in comparison to reinforcement contingent on a time basis (interval reinforcement schedule). In the ratio reinforcement schedule, the larger the number of responses emitted, the larger the number of reinforcements the animal receives; in the interval reinforcement schedule, only a minimal number of responses must be emitted for the animal to receive reinforcement. In the ratio schedule, the animal may be reinforced for approximately every 60th response (fixed ratio) or for every 60th response *on the average* (variable ratio), that is, sometimes the reinforcement may come after one response, sometimes after 120 responses, but on the average it comes after every 60th response. In the interval reinforcement schedule, the animal may be reinforced for the first response made after 15 minutes are up (fixed interval) or for the first response after 15 minutes are up *on the average* (variable interval), with some responses being reinforced after one minute and some after 30 minutes but, on the average, after 15 minutes are up. The combinations and permutations of these schedules and many others appear to be unlimited. Such schedules can engender combinations of responses in particular orders, at particular rates, and in response to all sorts of stimuli. The exquisite complexity that the behavior theory approach makes possible is perhaps best illustrated in Honig's *Operant Behavior* (1966), and it is this complexity that gives us the confidence that behavior theory can cope with the tangled skein of abnormal behavior as well.

Acquisition of Abnormal Behavior. In a paper already referred to, Salzinger (1968) describes a number of models for the generation of abnormal behavior. Such models tell us how the usual paradigms for the acquisition of behavior can be posited as the mechanism for the acquisition of many forms of abnormal behavior as well. And yet, if abnormal behavior is acquired in the same manner as normal behavior, how do we account for the fact that some individuals become abnormal and some do not? The explanation might well lie in a biological fault of the organism. It is also conceivable, however, that the fault lies not in the individual but in his environment (present and/or past). It might take the form of a particular defect, sensitizing the individual to the input of certain kinds of stimuli whose more frequent occurrence in juxtaposition with certain kinds of behavior brings about the abnormal behavior. Or, it might be entirely environmentally determined, that is, in certain impoverished circumstances, the patient's parents may become discriminative stimuli for negative reinforcement ("No, you can't have any more food") rather than the more usual discriminative stimuli for positive reinforcement.

But let us look more closely at a specific behavior that is often ascribed to schizophrenic patients. They are often said to be suffering from a lack of contact with reality. One of the paradigms for the acquisition of behavior that can be characterized as showing a lack of reality, is superstitious conditioning. It consists of the following: a food-deprived organism is placed in an experimental compartment and food is made available on the basis of a purely temporal contingency, that is, every nth minute food is made available. Although the animal can make any number of responses in the time intervening between reinforcements, no response made by the animal controls the reinforcement at all. Under these circumstances the animal acquires a special response (often a complicated chain of responses) that did not exist before the noncontingent (independent of responses) reinforcement procedure was introduced. In the complex society in which we live, such noncontingent reinforcements are present very often, giving man the opportunity to acquire many superstitious chains of responses. Herrnstein (1966) views such chains as style; he includes in this category the way in which an individual writes, the way he twists his hair when trying to think of ways to answer a question, and the way he rings a doorbell, for example. Individuals acquire such behavior through the purely chance co-occurrence of responses and positive reinforcements.

There are, however, less benign forms of superstitious conditioning, such as delusions. Herrnstein (1966) has shown that the stimuli that happen to be present while an animal is emitting a particular response, and that exert no control over the response at that time may, at a later time, exert such control. The individual who attributes certain powers to himself or other people may well have come under the control of an accidentally present, but unrelated, stimulus. A man who finds himself unable to work in the presence of his wife (for reasons, let us assume, completely unrelated to his wife) may therefore be a good candidate for acquiring the delusion that his wife has some sort of supernatural power over him that prevents him from working. The paradigm describes the sequence as follows: a stimulus that is accidentally present while the individual is working badly eventually acquires the power to make him work badly, and evokes delusional thoughts (which normal individuals might presumably have also). These delusional thoughts themselves may then become conditioned and thus increase because they remove the individual from the more aversive thought (the negative reinforcement) that he cannot work well. Such a model should also tell us why particular individuals have a greater tendency to become conditioned in this manner than others. Is it merely chance that some people are reinforced for such responses, or is there something else about the reinforcement history of their neurophysiological functioning that accounts for it? It may be difficult to imagine the acquisition of the bizarre schizo-phrenic behavior through conditioning, but we must remember that addi-tional reinforcement might well act to further maintain such behavior, independent of how it is first acquired.

The weakest acceptable statement about the role of behavior theory in the acquisition of abnormal behavior is that conditioning must be involved. A schizophrenic patient may differ from normals in terms of the types of stimuli to which he is likely to respond; he may differ from normals in having a unique set of conditioned stimuli (for examples, any object having a red color may elicit the same conditioned anxiety response from him that, in normals, is elicited by the appearance of a snake), in having a higher drive level which controls the emission of his responses, in responding more to so-called concrete stimuli than to so-called abstract stimuli, or more to immediately present stimuli than to remoter stimuli, or more to social than to nonsocial stimuli, or more to unconditioned than to conditioned stimuli. The overriding point is that the principles of behavior theory still hold—even though only within the limitations set by the patient's peculiarity or defect.

All sorts of animals are controllable by the same general principles of learning, and even mentally retarded individuals with known brain damage and whose major difficulty is one of learning, can learn provided the proper conditions are present. No drug or other type of somatotherapy can influence an individual very much independently of environmental control through learning. The somatotherapy may act to make aversive stimuli less aversive, or, as is suggested by some, may serve to suppress, through forgetting, some of the aversive stimuli that control the patient's abnormal behavior, or it may serve to suppress certain responses of an aberrant nature more directly, making the patient, in all cases, more amena-ble to the administration of positive reinforcement for healthy responses.

Another dramatic form of abnormal behavior in schizophrenics consists of hallucinations, where a patient "senses" a stimulus that is in fact not there. Two learning theory mechanisms may explain such behavior. One is the respondent conditioning paradigm, where a conditioned stimulus comes to elicit the same, or at least a similar, response to that of an unconditioned stimulus. Such a conditioned stimulus might well serve as a discriminative stimulus for an operant response of "seeing" something that is not there. The simple positive reinforcement of certain kinds of responses (recognition responses) might serve as another way of conditioning hallucinations. Goldiamond and Hawkins (1958) demonstrated such a process. They first reinforced the emission of recognition responses by presenting different nonsense syllables a different number of times each. Then they presented discriminative stimuli for the presence of these nonsense syllables, without presenting the nonsense syllables themselves. Under these conditions normal subjects reported the occurrence of stimuli that were not in fact there. In an even more dramatic demonstration of this phenomenon, Hefferline and Perera (1963) conditioned normal subjects to respond to a slight thumb twitch whose occurrence they were not able to report verbally, but to which they had previously been trained to attribute the quality of a tone. The procedure was as follows: first, the experimenter turned on a tone whenever he detected a thumb twitch electromyographically; the subject was required to report the occurrence of the tone; second, the experimenter gradually reduced the intensity of the contingent tone until it ceased occurring completely and, finally, under the conditions of no tone, the subject continued to report the tone, even though there was none, when he made his thumb twitch responses.

Diagnosis. The examples given above are only some of the paradigms that could account for the abnormal behavior characteristic of schizophrenia. It is enough, however, to show that this approach warrants further exploration. Here, I wish to examine the usefulness of behavior theory in diagnosis. I have already given some examples of the actual use of operant conditioning during the course of interviews (Salzinger and Pisoni, 1958, 1960, 1961; Salzinger and Portnoy, 1964; Salzinger, Portnoy, and Feldman, 1964a). In a study of the unplanned interview, Nathan, Schneller, and Lindsley (1964) monitored the listening and looking behavior of the patient through a closed-circuit television setup. The patients' rate of looking, listening (the patient had to respond continuously to keep the TV on) and talking correlated negatively with the severity of their illness, that is, the more severe the illness, the less the patient responded to talking, seeing, and hearing the interviewer. By making the attention-giving response into a measurable operant response, the investigators were able to assess the consequences that control the patient's attention-giving behavior; they also provided an index of the degree of illness.

Lindsley (1962) constructed a very simple operant device housed in a bare experimental cubicle for diagnosing patients. When the patient pulls the plunger a series of programmed consequences follow, including such reinforcers as candy, pictures of nudes, cigarettes, money, and a social reinforcer that gives the patient the opportunity of feeding a hungry kitten. He also showed how the expansion of this device to two responses and two stimuli allows the experimenter to test the subject's ability to discriminate between stimuli and to differentiate between responses.

In a study of the functional aspects of hallucinations, Lindsley (1963) concluded that vocal hallucinations compete with strongly reinforced nonpathological behavior (that is, they decrease when the competitive behavior is increased through reinforcement), yet at the same time they are not influenced by direct application of reinforcement. Such considerations might help in formulating a more precise definition of abnormal behavior and more measurable data.

Some years ago, Crandall and Bellugi (1956) devised a social reinforcement index based on Rotter's (1954) social learning theory. Individuals' experiences are rated as either rewarding or frustrating. The ratings proved to be reliable and were used to assess degree of adjustment. Somewhat more sophisticated uses of behavior theory for assessment were recently suggested by Greenspoon and Gersten (1967), and Weiss (1968). Both papers describe the response-reinforcement contingency, and both speak of the need for devising instruments to measure a person's susceptibility to different kinds of reinforcement.

Most important of the recent developments in the area of assessment is the work of Kanfer and Saslow (1965, 1969). They constructed a method of behavioral analysis, as an alternative to diagnosis that is particularly useful for behavior therapy. The assessment procedure consists of the following: a description of the behavioral excesses and deficits and the behavioral assets (behaviors likely to be followed by positive reinforcement in our culture), a listing of the sources of reinforcement (positive or negative) that maintain the various behaviors, a survey of developmental aspects of the patient's behavior (including biological considerations, to see if any of them are relevant to his complaint and treatment), an analysis of the patient's ability to present himself with stimuli that the therapist might want to recommend (self-control) and, finally, an analysis of the patient's social-cultural-physical environment to determine the extent to which a change in his behavior is congruent with the environment in which he must live.

Information collected for a behavioral analysis should not be restricted to a typical interview but should include a number of samplings of real life situations, such as a discussion between the patient and one of the people with whom he has a particular difficulty, or a tape recording of his speech on the telephone, if he has special difficulties in this area. Kanfer and Saslow also suggest using special devices for presenting stimuli, such as projectors to show pictures of nudes, to provide the therapist with information about the patient's homo- or hetero-erotic feelings. The authors stress that it is essential to discover, by any means possible, the stimuli that are contingent on the patient's behavior.

Although behavioral analysis has been used for a relatively short time, the reader should realize that its insistence on the description of behavior rather than on inference, its utilization of the information about the patient for the specific purpose of therapy, rather than for purposes of classification only, and its stress on direct methods of observation, rather than on indirect ones (such as free association in the therapist's office) make this form of patient examination a very hopeful development for an increased understanding of many types of abnormality, including that of schizophrenia.

SUMMARY

The purpose of this chapter was to describe both the characteristics of schizophrenia and the attributes of the concept of schizophrenia. It includes some of the clinical descriptions of the disorder and the ways in which these clinical descriptions are arrived at. It covers, therefore, some studies of the reliability and validity of diagnosis. It shows that the currently used diagnostic system is not very reliable and that its validity is so low that, in practice, diagnosis is useful only for the purpose of counting noses and for technical legal matters. To decide what kind of treatment to employ with a given patient, the clinician must regularly appeal to other sources of information and, in fact, is advised to do so by current textbooks in psychiatry.

The chapter describes a relatively new system for the classification of schizophrenic patients. It is based on a distinction that derived from the premorbid social history of the patient and is anchored in the outcome of the disorder. In other words, the distinction is explicitly based on outcome of illness; furthermore, it measures the premorbid history in terms of at least some semiobjective measures. One category derived from this classification system is called process schizophrenia (insidious onset of disorder and poor outcome); the other is called reactive schizophrenia (sudden onset and good outcome of disorder).

A discussion of prognosis in general follows, and shows how being in or out of the hospital can be used as a criterion for the validity of various behavioral measures.

An examination of therapy applied to schizophrenia shows that treatments have, in the past, been primarily empirical in nature because of a lack of knowledge about the variables responsible for the onset and maintenance of the disorder. No treatment is known to effect a cure, while many, at least when they are first initiated, appear to produce changes in the patients.

Next, the chapter deals with some of the vexing methodological problems that any investigator of this disorder must face. In addition to the problems of diagnosis and criteria for the evaluation of outcome, the investigator of schizophrenia must deal with the problem of cooperativeness (how much is an expression of the disorder and how much is peripheral to it), the effect of hospitalization either on the biochemistry or the behavior of the patient, the selective factor of who is hospitalized and after exhibiting what kind of behavior and finally, the biasing variable of who is tested in a hospital.

The final section of this chapter deals with the variables related to the onset and maintenance of schizophrenic behavior. The traditional medical model is discussed first. It is supported by some of the research done on the genetic aspect of schizophrenia that in turn, inspired the research in biochemistry. Nevertheless, despite the large amount of research that has been done in this area, little concrete evidence for a biological cause of schizophrenia has been found. Furthermore, the notion of symptom substitution, which comes directly from the concept of disease is in doubt, because of the success in eliminating many kinds of abnormal behavior without incurring the formation of new symptoms. In general, proponents of the medical disease model have, more recently, taken the stand that a biological factor need not be the only, or even the primary cause of schizophrenia.

Discussion of the behavioral model follows; it stresses the fact that an abnormality in behavior requires at some point an explanation in terms of behavioral principles, even if only a biological cause is involved at the onset of schizophrenia. For it is only in the relation between behavior and the stimuli that precede or follow it that we can see how the biological fault expresses itself. After describing some of the basic principles of behavior theory, the chapter presents a number of possible paradigms for the generation of abnormal behavior often found in schizophrenic patients. The last part of the chapter suggests an alternative to the current diagnostic classification in the application of a behavioral analysis to abnormal patients. The advantage of such an approach lies not only in the objectivity of a behavioral description, but also in the fact that a behavioral analysis determines directly the kind of therapeutic program that the therapist can subsequently utilize. Its reliability is insured because the therapist uses a mode of description that does not require interpretation, but simply observation; its validity is insured because the behavioral analysis determines the therapeutic strategy directly.

CHAPTER TWO

LANGUAGE: ITS REGULATORY AND COMMUNICATIVE FUNCTIONS

Many conceive of thought as the purveyor of language, as a kind of distributor of the goods. First you "think" and then you express the thought in language. Yet, consider your speech or if you can be objective only with the speech of others, reflect on that for a moment or two. Surely it must be self-evident that not all speech is preceded by thought, for much of what is said is foolish and much serves to disguise rather than express thought.

In the psychological analysis of the functions of language, it is altogether better to avoid speculating about thought, which is not amenable to direct measurement, and to deal with language in the two forms in which it expresses itself and can be measured: *regulatory* and *communicative*. I will describe each of these functions in detail. For now it is enough to say that by regulatory I mean that man can plan and direct his own behavior by his verbal behavior; by communicative I refer to his capacity to affect the behavior of others. Probably no behavior emitted by human beings serves one of these functions exclusively. Nevertheless, it is useful for purposes of exposition to deal first with the regulatory and then with the communicative functions of language.

THE REGULATORY FUNCTION

Luria's work (1967) is relevant to regulatory function in schizophrenia even though it concentrates on children with and without pathology, rather than on adult schizophrenics. Using a simple experiment as his basic paradigm, he demonstrated the growing effectiveness of experimenter-control and self-instruction control over a bulb-pressing response as a function of age. In this way, he made the definition of regulatory function explicit by saying it is the way in which a person tells himself to do something.

For instance, in a sorting task where a subject has to place a number of objects into categories, the subject instructs himself to put objects of one kind in one pile and objects of another kind in another pile. The sorting test reveals the principle, if any, by which the subject directs himself to place objects into categories and the consistency with which he follows such a principle. Nevertheless, even a superficial analysis of the sorting task reveals its complexity. The purpose of the earlier experiments (Kasanin, 1944a) was to bring objectivity and measurement to the various sorting tests. Based on such a task, Goldstein (1944) presents arguments for using the abstract-concrete dimension for the characterization of schizophrenics' conceptual behavior, or as he puts it, for the characterization of their total behavior. He offers, as one example, the case of a patient given a task of sorting colors; when presented with different shades of green, the patient tended to assign each of them a different name, such as, "peacock green," "emerald green," "taupe green," and "baby green," for example, instead of grouping them all under the rubric "green". He explains this behavior by asserting that words for the schizophrenic are tied to specific situations or objects (behavior is concrete) and do not function as categories, as they do for normals. He also shows that the interesting similarities between organic patients and schizophrenics fail to make their forms of malfunctioning equivalent. Unlike the organic patient, the schizophrenic patient does not simply show a concrete resolution of a problem of categorization; his sorting relates to many more stimuli in the environment than does the organic patient's.

Kasanin (1944b) describes the application of a test originally developed by N. Ach and used by Vigotsky and Luria on three different samples: schizophrenic patients, patients suffering from organic brain disease, and normals. The test consists of a number of blocks of different size, shape, and color. The subject's task is to classify the blocks into four groups according to a principle. Kasanin explains the task in terms of theory testing: the subject sorts according to a principle and, if it fails to work, tries another until he finds the correct one. Schizophrenics do not perform this task well; they combine blocks into a single group on the basis of such statements as, "they are all policemen" or "all little people," despite the fact that the blocks bear no relationship to the referents, and are quite dissimilar as a group.

Unlike the preceding investigators, Cameron (1944) views the behavior of schizophrenics on sorting tests as showing not so much a form of concrete thinking as an isolation from the social environment. He views the schizophrenic problem as one in communication in which patient and investigator misinterpret one another's remarks. He believes it is impossible to separate thinking from communication since thinking is influenced by the language that the child acquires in the process of communicating with his social environment. He argues that patients are unable "to maintain the boundaries of the problem and to restrict their operations within its limits." (Cameron, 1944, p. 56). Given the task of sorting blocks, the patients include other objects in the testing office, such as desk blotters, the telephone, the experimenter's pencil, his wristwatch, and his shirt. In other words, the schizophrenics suffer from overinclusiveness. Furthermore, although patients say they are sorting according to one principle they are, in fact, often sorting according to quite another.

Another early contributor to this area of research, Benjamin (1944), used proverb interpretation as a way of evaluating schizophrenic thinking. He asked patients to explain the meaning of such proverbs as "when the cat's away, the mice will play." Some of the schizophrenic responses to this particular proverb were: "When there's nobody watching, they do things they wouldn't if the cat were there" and "If there isn't any cat around, the mice will monkey around, and maybe get into things." Schizophrenics of high intelligence do not perform this task any better than others. On the basis of testing some 169 subjects, Benjamin concluded that literal interpretations are typical of schizophrenics.

A paper by von Domarus (1944) is considered a classic for its description of the so-called laws of logic in schizophrenia. He claims that the schizophrenic indulges in paralogical thinking, that is, he concludes identity on the basis of the identity of predicates, as in the following example: certain Indians are swift; stags are swift; therefore certain Indians are stags. Von Domarus provides a dramatic example from a patient who apparently believed that "Jesus, cigar boxes, and sex were identical." The reason for this strange belief was based on the fact that all three are encircled: the head of Jesus was encircled by a halo, the package of cigars by the tax band, and the women by the sex glance of the man.

It might be well, before we go any further, to inject a note of caution about the concept of paralogical thinking, and about many other interesting characterizations of the schizophrenic patient. Many investigators used, and some still do, the dramatic example as grist for the theory production mill. Von Domarus, like many others of that period and genre, apparently felt little need for such corroborating evidence as some basic data on incidence of such thinking in patients and normals, a clear operational description (the conditions under which such behavior may be observed) of the techniques used to elicit such thinking, or a quantitative measure of the extent to which different patients show this behavior. Such empirical evaluation of the concepts will be taken up later.

A more contemporary investigator, Arieti (1955, 1966), speaks of schizophrenic thinking as undergoing "teleologic regression," which results in various forms of concretization. Translated, this means that the schizophrenic converts various forms of abstract concepts into concrete, palpable experiences, as in the following case: a patient who thought of himself as having a "rotten" personality before becoming psychotic developed an olfactory hallucination of a bad odor emanating from his body. Arieti views such behavior as regression (going back to an earlier stage of life). According to him, it removes the patient from his feelings of anxiety. Arieti's concept of concretization is somewhat different from Goldstein's notion. Arieti accords the schizophrenic the ability to conceive of abstract things but claims that he is not able to sustain such abstractions because of the anxiety engendered by them. Arieti mentions three types of concretization: adualism (inability to separate the possible from the actual), paleologic thought (primitive ancient kind of thought), and awholism (inability to see whole systems, paying attention instead to parts only). Arieti's concepts of schizophrenic thought, like most of the others mentioned above, have never been validated directly by experiment. Nevertheless, these intuitions have given rise to experiments by investigators who set themselves the formidable task of deriving operational definitions for the vague concepts. Before we take up the experiments, let us review the concepts: schizophrenic thought is described to be concrete, relatively uninfluenced by social consensus factors, overinclusive (taking into consideration many stimuli not relevant to the task at hand), awholistic and, finally, logical in a very special way.

Intellectual Deficit

In the Schizophrenic. Since Kraepelin had originally stated that schizophrenia (dementia praecox) is characterized by intellectual deterioration, psychologists used the intelligence test to quantify the concept. Reviews by Payne (1960, 1968) have led that author to conclude that there is some intellectual deterioration in some patients—apparently little in paranoid schizophrenics but more in other types of schizophrenia. Progressive deterioration occurs over the course of the disorder, but at least part of it must be attributed to the effects of hospitalization rather than the illness.

Using different items from several intelligence tests, Senf, Huston, and Cohen (1955) find the greatest intellectual deficit when the patient must attend closely, when the situation presents little structure for the response (incomplete sentence versus multiple choice item), and when the items involve personal reference. Another series of studies (Foulds and Dixon, 1962a, 1962b; Foulds, et al, 1962), using a vocabulary and performance test, find a considerable intellectual deficit in schizophrenics as compared to neurotics, particularly on the performance test. Furthermore, the intellectual deficit is not progressive and it is greatest among catatonic schizophrenics. These studies are particularly important because of the relatively large N (270 schizophrenics).

Vocabulary tests are often less sensitive for differentiating schizophrenics from normals than abstraction tests (Hall, 1951). The fact that the vocabulary test differentiates schizophrenics from others less effectively than some other tests, most notably the abstraction tests, stimulated Willner (1965) to examine vocabulary tests more closely. He constructed a special test on the basis of unusual meanings instead of the most frequent meanings that typically characterize most vocabulary tests. Willner concluded that the deficit in abstraction in schizophrenics is because of their experience of alteration in individual word meanings, while the impairment in abstraction in brain damaged individuals is a function of a diminished ability to form relationships between words. His conclusions rest upon the fact that brain damaged individuals show impairment in an analogy test (requiring ability to *relate* words) but not in the unusual meanings vocabulary test, while schizophrenics show impairment on both tests.

Broadhurst (1958) reports that repeated administration of a *speed* test produces more improvement in schizophrenics than normals, to the extent that the speed of the schizophrenics on the fifth day reaches the speed of the normals on the first day. A comparison of performance on the *level* test shows that both groups improve significantly, although the normals tend to improve more than the schizophrenics.

In the Preschizophrenic. An important question concerning intellectual functioning in schizophrenia is whether a decline in that function precedes the disorder, possibly bringing it on, or whether the decline is part of the disorder itself. This question can be answered only by examining preschizophrenic intellectual functioning. Furthermore, testing the schizophrenic before he exhibits the behavior that brings him to the hospital circumvents the artifacts of low motivation, effects of hospitalization, and others already mentioned in Chapter One. For these reasons, it makes sense to examine the performance records of children who have become adult schizophrenics (Lane and Albee, 1967). In the first study, Albee, et al (1963), compare the premorbid (before illness) IQ's of 112 adult schizophrenics to their IQ's at the time of hospitalization. They find no significant difference. The low IQ found in schizophrenics on hospitalization is apparently already present when the preschizophrenic child is in second grade. In another study of hospitalized schizophrenics, however, Lane and Albee (1963) find a statistically significant drop in IQ between early (5 to 8 years of age) and late childhood (11 to 14 years of age) IQ's, as compared to a comparable group of children sampled from the same school system but not in the state hospital system as adult schizophrenics. A reexamination of these conflicting results by Lane and Albee (1968) showed that the conclusion of a lowering of the IQ in preschizophrenics was unwarranted because the comparison was based upon two different intelligence tests, which thus introduced statistical artifacts. The evidence militates against a difference in the change of IQ of preschizophrenic and normal children from early to late childhood.

Albee, Lane, and Reuter (1964) compare the intelligence of preschizophrenic children to a control group that takes into account the lower socioeconomic class from which schizophrenics in state hospitals typically come. The control group consisted of children in the same school and class as that attended by the preschizophrenic children. The preschizophrenic children scored significantly lower than children in the school system as a whole and, what is more important, they scored significantly lower than their peers in the same class and school in the second grade, the sixth, and in eighth grade. In followup studies (Lane and Albee, 1964, 1965), they instituted an additional control taking into account the family in which they were raised. Children raised in the same family as the preschizophrenic child ought, in general, to be exposed to the same degree of intellectual enrichment or impoverishment. The preschizophrenic children had significantly lower IQ's than their siblings, while a control group chosen to match the preschizophrenic child in school, class, and IQ showed no significant difference from their own siblings.

In another study of the same problem, Schaffner, Lane, and Albee (1967) examined the intelligence test scores of suburban children to generalize their findings to a higher socioeconomic class level (the above studies were based primarily on lower socioeconomic classes). They found that here too the preschizophrenic children had lower intelligence test scores than their siblings (statistically significant results in two of three comparisons). Although the IQ's of all the children (preschizophrenics included) are above average, only the preschizophrenic children scored below their siblings. It is, of course, not clear whether the lower IQ portends the beginning of the schizophrenic process or simply a higher likelihood of (greater susceptibility to) development of schizophrenia. Another interesting result cited by Lane and Albee (1967) is that neurotic children do not differ significantly from their siblings in intelligence, thus suggesting that their findings are specific to schizophrenia. Lane and Albee (1967) conclude that schizophrenia does not lower intelligence, since lower intelligence is found long before schizophrenic behavior occurs. A final study by these investigators relates the preschizophrenia intelligence score to the process-reactive classification.

Heath, Albee, and Lane (1965) find that process patients have significantly lower IQ's than their siblings in childhood, but reactives only tend to have lower scores than their siblings, thus offering some data in favor of the classification system.

In a critique of these studies, Mednick and McNeil (1968) point out that the lack of a national psychiatric register produced a sample of schizophrenics who did not move from their place of residence, while the control groups contained both mobile and nonmobile individuals, thus yielding comparison groups differing on schizophrenia *and* on mobility. Nevertheless, since the Albee-Lane group showed the same effect of IQ difference within the family as between matched preschizophrenics and nonpreschizophrenics, the objection is less serious. The results might conceivably hold only for nonmobile schizophrenics. The reader is directed to Roff and Ricks (1970) for a discussion of these points between Mednick, and Lane and Albee.

What can we say about intellectual deficit? First, there is no reliable evidence for deterioration in intellectual ability. Second, there is at least some evidence that aspects of the deficit (speed) can be eliminated by giving patients a little practice. Is an intellectual deficit a basic aspect of schizophrenia or is it part of a more general deficit, perhaps in the effect on behavior of social stimuli, as suggested by Cameron (1944)? Even the lower intelligence test performance in the preschizophrenic child is no certain evidence that an intellectual deficit is an important aspect of schizophrenia. It may simply be an early manifestation of an inability to get along in society. The reader must be reminded here that the intellectual deficit shown in the preschizophrenic child is a deficit only in comparison to his siblings or peers; it is not a deficit in absolute terms. Two interpretations seem possible: one suggests that the family pressures on a child who does less well than his siblings constitute an important etiological factor; the other suggests that the preschizophrenic is functioning below his own optimum level as a result of the presence of one form of the disorder.

Cognitive Deficit

In this section, I will review some of the interpretations and data-collecting devices used to describe cognitive deficit.

Overinclusiveness. Dissatisfaction with the abstract-concrete dimension arose rather early with Cameron's (1944) emphasis on social factors. He also proposed the concept of overinclusiveness, by which he meant a tendency to include in the stimulus field many things that normal individuals typically exclude. This concept has in recent years been embraced by Payne (1961, 1966, 1968; and Inglis, 1966). In one of the studies, Payne, Mattussek, and George (1959) compare schizophrenics to neurotics, to determine the extent to which the concept of concreteness (as opposed to the concept of overinclusiveness) succeeds in differentiating them. Unlike the overinclusiveness concept, the abstract-concrete dimension largely failed to differentiate the populations.

A very interesting theoretical inference that Payne made is that an overinclusive individual is more likely to be paranoid since his inclusion of unrelated facts in his reasoning is likely to produce unwarranted conclusions. Payne, Caird, and Laverty (1964) confirmed this inference, taking the number of words to interpret a particular proverb as the measure of overinclusiveness. A paper by Goldstein and Salzman (1965) did not confirm the results, although it must be noted that they failed to tape record the responses, thus leaving their word counts more open to error. Another study (Lloyd, 1967) confirmed Payne et al's findings, but found theoretical fault with the use of a word count as an index of overinclusiveness: the larger number of words might reflect either a relatively well-integrated explanation based upon a single wrong premise, or a great deal of general confusion on the part of the patient. Nevertheless, the relationship between over-inclusiveness and delusions receives some support. Most recently, Foulds, and others (1968) used the proverb elicited word count and an object sorting test as measures of overinclusiveness. They found a significant positive correlation between overinclusiveness and the presence of delusions in three of four groups, with the object classification test showing a clearer relationship. Craig (1965) factor analyzed a battery of tests and found that over-inclusion was more prominent in the delusional and thought-disordered groups than in the others.

Overinclusiveness has also found its critics. Chapman (1961) contends that schizophrenics make errors of overinclusion and overexclusion on conceptual sorting tasks and that they result from the schizophrenic's use of categories of a specific breadth, regardless of their appropriateness. To test his contention, he had his subjects sort picture cards into categories of various breadths. The results showed that the errors of overexclusiveness increase with the breadth of the category required. Nevertheless, the schizophrenic patients did, on the whole, make more overinclusion than overexclusion errors, while a sample of organic patients showed the opposite trend.

Although Payne and his colleagues have maintained that the excessive concreteness often found in schizophrenic patients is actually an expression of their overinclusiveness, Sturm (1965) performed an experiment that resulted in seemingly opposite conclusions. Sturm revised Epstein's (1951) inclusion test so that he was able to extract from it both an overinclusion score and a concreteness score. In this way, Sturm was able to compare the validity of the two concepts on the basis of using the same instrument on the same subjects. In addition to his schizophrenic group, which he divided into process and reactive types, he included a brain-damaged group and a normal group hospitalized for approximately the same duration as the schizophrenic patients. His results showed a significant difference between the groups on the concreteness score, but not on the overinclusion score. The concreteness score was highest for the process schizophrenics (15.07), next highest for the brain damaged group (13.88), next highest for the normal-tubercular group (9.78), and lowest for the reactive schizophrenics (9.33). These results appear not only to support Goldstein's (1944) concept of concrete thought as the most salient dimension in schizophrenia, but they also indicate that process schizophrenics are closer to brain damaged patients, whereas reactive schizophrenics are closer to normals.

Sturm's experiment has its problems, however. A very important one, which confounds the results of many studies on schizophrenia, consists of the fact that a large number of patients in the sample were given tranquilizing drugs. Sturm tells us that 80 percent of his schizophrenic population received drugs. In a valiant attempt to measure the effect of this drug, he compared the performance of the patients on the drug with those few who were not. He found no difference between the two groups of schizophrenics on the number of concrete responses and slightly more overinclusive responses in the tranquilized group than in the untranquilized group. The only difficulty with such an analysis is that drugs are, after all, not administered at random and we have no estimate of the extent to which schizophrenics on drugs differ from those who are not, prior to drug intake. In comparing these results to those obtained by other investigators using other populations we would have to know whether the same drugs were administered according to the same criteria and in the same dosages. This is a very important source of disagreement in the schizophrenia literature.

In reviewing this article, Payne (1968) suggests that the Epstein inclusion test may, because of its correlation to vocabulary level, not be the best concept formation test for overinclusiveness (Sturm did, however, match the groups for vocabulary). A more critical problem with Sturm's experiment is his definition of "concrete" and "overinclusive." The subject's task is best explained by giving an example of one of the items. He is instructed to select, from among the following, those words that are "absolutely necessary to make a complete house": walls, curtains, telephone, bricks, roof, none. If the patient included only the words "walls" and "roof," he was scored correct. If he chose those two words plus any others he was scored overinclusive for that item and, finally, if he left out any of the essential words, no matter how many others he included, he was scored concrete for that item. Thus, the concrete score was arbitrarily given precedence over the overinclusiveness score. Whether one agrees with Sturm's definition or not is less important, however, than the disagreement in results arising from different operational definitions of what various investigators believe to be the same concept. Furthermore, the fact that schizophrenics tend to form concepts sometimes smaller and sometimes larger than those that normals do, suggests a difference at least worthwhile theorizing about.

Payne (1968) points to the lack of knowledge about the interrelationship of the various techniques used to measure overinclusion as the barrier to its further usefulness. He concludes tentatively, however, that overinclusiveness seems to characterize acute or reactive rather than chronic patients, while underinclusion, which he accepts as one aspect of concrete thinking, seems to characterize process schizophrenics.

Construct Deficit. Bannister (1962; Bannister and Fransella, 1966; Bannister and Salmon, 1966) asserts, making use of Kelly's (1955) Personal Construct Theory, that the thought-disordered patient lacks the notion of concept (Bannister prefers the word "construct") as a way of predicting regularities in the events surrounding him. A patient who construes another person to be loving should be able to predict other characteristics about him, such as being kind, honest, and helpful. Failure to show such consistencies forms one aspect of the thought-disordered schizophrenic's problem. The test Bannister uses consists of a series of photographs of persons that he requires the patient to sort in terms of the constructs, "kind," "stupid," "selfish," "sincere," "mean," and "honest." The patient is tested for two kinds of consistency: one of sorting the constructs in such a way as to retain their interrelationship over two different sets of persons at the same testing time, for example, if kindness and honesty went together in one set, consistency would have them relate in the other also), and the other to retain the interrelationship for the same set of persons at different times. This test differentiates thought-disordered schizophrenics from other pathological groups and normals. Most important, it differentiates the thought-disordered schizophrenic from the schizophrenic who is not so clinically characterized. The designation of thought disorder is, of course, the result of a subjective judgment and, despite Bannister's precaution of having three different psychiatrists making the judgment of thought disorder, we still have no guarantee that this measure is valid.

To take but one set of variables that influence such judgments, let us look at the effect of the types of verbal behavior that the psychiatrist must judge. Campbell, Hunt, and Lewis (1957) showed that the extent to which vocabulary definitions are considered to manifest schizophrenic disturbance varies as a function of the context of other vocabulary definitions. Judges called vocabulary responses of medium disturbance less disturbed when they were presented in a context of high disturbance (that is, among word definitions that are highly disturbed) than when presented in a context of low disturbance. This effect, predictable on the basis of psychophysical experiments, was also accompanied in some judges, however, by exactly the opposite effect, that is, a judgment of greater disturbance of the same item when in a context of items of great disturbance. We are led, therefore, to question Bannister's insistence on testing for thought disturbance when the only criterion for it is a subjective one.

Bannister and Salmon (1966) assert that schizophrenic thought disorder is more pronounced with respect to the judgment of persons than of objects. Unfortunately, the comparison made does not involve events of equal familiarity, nor do the judgment dimensions have equally agreed upon referents. Thus, in the case of people, subjects are required to judge such dimensions as kindness and stupidity, while for the judgment of objects, including such items as a bowler hat, a loaf of bread and a washing machine, they are asked to judge dimensions of size, and weight, for example. The differential deficit between people and objects could then be attributable to the other differences as well. The degree of difference within a patient might, however, be used as a sign of the severity of the disorder because a patient who fails to retain the same general relationship among physical dimensions might have more difficulty in getting along than an individual who has simply a more fluid way of combining character traits of people.

Unlike other investigators in this area, Bannister relates the patient's current behavior to a theory of how he got to be that way. Bannister maintains that schizophrenic thought disorder (he asserts that thought disorder is not characteristic of all schizophrenics) is the end product of serial invalidation in which the patient has repeatedly predicted the behavior of other people incorrectly. As a result of this misprediction, he falls back upon amorphous conceptions of people which cannot as easily be mispredicted since the predictions are vague to begin with. The description of the schizophrenic patient's thinking as a way of avoiding something else is a fairly common way of theorizing about the disorder and we will have occasion to return to it in Chapter 6.

Miscellaneous Concepts of Deficit. Carson (1962), also speaks of avoidance of an important variable, in his case it is the schizophrenic's avoidance of *unambiguous* statements. He constructed a multiple-choice proverbs test in which the alternatives were another proverb having the same meaning, an abstract interpretation of the proverb, a literal interpretation of the proverb, and an irrelevant proverb. The patient was required to rank the adequacy of the four alternatives as an interpretation of the proverb. The performance of the schizophrenics was compared to that of another psychiatric nonschizophrenic patient group. Schizophrenics chose the unambiguous abstract interpretation significantly less frequently than did the other patients. They did not, however, choose the literal alternative more frequently, nor did they choose the other ambiguous abstract alternative (the proverb choice) less frequently than the other patients. These results contradict the notion of a deficit in abstraction since literal interpretation was not preferred. When the schizophrenic makes an unambiguous statement he expects to get into trouble, as in the past, when his schizophrenogenic (producing schizophrenia) mother found fault with his communications. Only the emission of ambiguous statements allows him to avoid the negative reinforcement from his mother. This interpretation is based on the theory of Bateson, Jackson, Haley, and Weakland (1956), and will be fully explored in Chapter 6.

Another interpretation of the cognitive deficit of schizophrenics has differentiated it into two types of errors, *plausible* and *implausible*. Feinberg and Garman (1961) hypothesized that schizophrenics make more implausible or random responses than either normals or organic patients. These investigators modified the progressive matrices test (a nonverbal test) in such a way as to obtain both plausible errors (using geometric configurations that could easily be confused with the geometric pattern called for) and implausible errors (using configurations that, because of gross differences, could not be easily confused with the pattern called for). The results showed that the acute schizophrenics, but not the chronic schizophrenics, made a larger number of implausible errors than any other group, including the organic group.

Some investigators have explained the cognitive deficit in terms of a greater schizophrenic distractibility than in others. As Payne (1968) points out, the tests used to examine distractibility are conceptually similar to overinclusiveness tests but no empirical correlations have been obtained. Furthermore, overinclusiveness, according to Payne, characterizes the acute schizophrenic whereas distractibility appears to characterize the chronic schizophrenic. Chapman (1956) constructed a sorting test containing a number of distracter elements that had to be ignored to achieve a correct sort. The difference between the chronic schizophrenics and normals increased as the number of distracting elements on each card increased, that is, the number of errors for the normals remained much the same, but increased for the schizophrenics. Downing and his colleagues (Downing, Ebert, and Shubrooks, 1963a, 1963b; Downing, Shubrooks, and Ebert, 1966) found that those distracters more strongly associated to the stimulus words resulted in greater conceptual errors than more weakly or nonassociated distracters. The authors concluded that schizophrenics do not suffer from a loss in abstract attitude, but rather from a pathological distractibility.

Thought disorder in schizophrenia has also been related to the patient's difficulty with emotional stimuli. Deering (1963) compared schizophrenics and normals on the number of different responses that so-called emotional versus neutral stimulus words evoked in a word association test. Schizophrenics emitted a larger number of different responses to the emotional words than do normals but the same number in response to neutral words. De Wolfe (1962) set up groups based on the process-reactive distinction and a normal control (a physically ill) group. In a task where the subject had to construct a sentence by combining one of four pronouns (he, she, they, I) with a past tense verb (neutral for some and emotional verbs for others), only the reactive schizophrenics took a longer period of time to construct sentences with emotional verbs than with neutral verbs. The schizophrenic's exaggerated responsiveness to emotional stimuli interferes with his cognitive functioning.

I have already mentioned Cameron's (1944) interpretation of the schizophrenic's thought disorder as a social deficit. Flavell (1965) examined the relation of performance on a multiple-choice vocabulary test to the effectiveness of social behavior on a hospital ward. The vocabulary performance of schizophrenics was inferior to that of normals in that the schizophrenics selected the abstract meaning of the word less frequently than did the normals. More interesting, however, was the correlation between number of abstract responses and adequacy of social relationship (+.60). Furthermore, McGaughran and Moran (1956) showed that schizophrenics differ from normals in social communicability even on a sorting test designed to show the abstraction deficit. Sturm (1964), however, failed to confirm that finding.

Whiteman (1954) investigated the social-communicability deficit directly by having the schizophrenics perform concept tasks involving social, as contrasted with formal, nonsocial concepts. Schizophrenics showed a greater deficit for social concepts than for formal concepts. He concluded that social withdrawal is critical in the cognitive functioning of the schizophrenic. Davis and Harrington (1957) used human abstract stimuli in a comparison of problem solving ability in schizophrenics and normals. The inclusion of human stimuli significantly disrupted the performance of schizophrenics. They concluded that schizophrenics do not have a general intellectual deficit; the deficit is specific to human stimuli. Finally, Pishkin (1963) showed that the presence of the tester, while the patient is mechanically reinforced in a concept identification task, reduced the effectiveness of the reinforcement, thus furnishing more evidence for a special deficit in schizophrenia.

Word Association

The regulatory function of verbal behavior is carried out, in part, through the association of words. Different paths of association make possible creative solutions and, no doubt, explain peculiar logic as well.

Word association also enters into the definition of thought disorder as a process of disassociation, although this is to be construed as a change in what is associated rather than in a lack of association.

Many studies show that schizophrenics emit a larger number of idiosyncratic responses than do normals (Deering, 1963; Johnson, Weiss, and Zelhart, 1964; Moran, Mefferd, and Kimble, 1964; Sommer, Dewar, and Osmond, 1960; Storms, Broen, and Levin, 1967). Storms, Broen, and Levin (1967) also find more instability in the word associations from one day to the next. Faibish (1961) using words of multiple meaning, finds that schizophrenics have longer response latencies than normals. These results can be ascribed to the conflict among the different potential responses to each stimulus word. Thus, the longer response latency reflects the fact that such conflict produces vacillation.

Assuming that schizophrenics (at least in their early stages) suffer from high anxiety, Mednick (1958) has postulated it as the central problem in his theory. Anxiety is assumed to act as a drive in the same way as food deprivation. High drive has the effect of increasing the probability of all associates in proportion to their initial probability of occurrence. If the associate "table" is initially highly probable to the stimulus word "chair," an increase in drive level will soon bring it to its maximum. If the drive level goes up sufficiently then even generally lower probability words, such as "petunia," for example, will become likely and thus account for idiosyncratic associations (Storms, Broen, and Levin, 1967).

Measures of commonality (frequency with which a word is associated by a standardization group) of word association have been related to two different patient variables, one chronicity (length of hospitalization) by Higgins, Mednick, and Philip (1965), Higgins, Mednick, Philip, and Thompson (1966) and Higgins (1968), and the other the process-reactive distinction by Dokecki, Polidoro, and Cromwell (1965) and Dokecki, Cromwell, and Polidoro (1968). Higgins' group has consistently found the chronicity dimension related to the degree of commonality of the word associations; Dokecki's group has found only the process-reactive dimension consistently related to degree of commonality. The differences between the studies are not immediately reconcilable, although some differences in procedure can be implicated. Thus, the two groups employed different hospital populations, different (though related) methods of arriving at premorbid status, somewhat different word association instructions, and differently derived commonality-of-association scores. We do not have enough information to judge the validity of the two studies. They do, however, bring to our attention some of the difficulties involved in dealing with contradictory results on schizophrenia.

Utilizing a communication task, Cohen and Camhi (1967) investigated the way in which schizophrenics regulate their verbal behavior through the use of word association. The task consists of the following: the speaker is given a series of cards, each of which contains two words, one underlined. He is told to give a listener a one-word clue for guessing the underlined word. Some of the word pairs are synonyms (for example, pretty-beautiful); others are unrelated (for example, entertain-believe). Listeners and speakers were combined in schizophrenic-schizophrenic pairs, normal-normal pairs, schizophrenic-normal pairs, and normal-schizophrenic pairs. The results indicated that schizophrenic listeners are as good as normal listeners, but that schizophrenic speakers are less effective in communicating the right kind of clue than the normal speakers. These results show the schizophrenic's faulty selection process of verbal responses rather than a basically deviant associative repertory. As we shall see in our general discussion of thought disorder, this constitutes but one bit of evidence that the schizophrenic thought disorder is not a basic but a secondary deficit because of a more general fault in schizophrenia.

Finally, Skinner's (1936) verbal summator has been applied to schizophrenics by Trussell (1939) and Shakow, Rosenweig, and Hollander (1966). A number of different vowel combinations are presented to subjects with the instruction that someone is speaking unclearly and that they should try to reconstruct what he is saying. Trussell does not find the summator very useful as a research instrument, but Shakow et al differentiate schizophrenics from normals in terms of such characteristics as the schizophrenic's larger number of remote responses and fewer first person responses. A significant negative correlation between number of common responses on a word association test and number of human references in statements "heard" from the verbal summator shows that the association test can predict verbal behavior under different conditions.

Verbal Learning

The studies cited above assayed the strength and type of existing verbal associations in schizophrenics. The studies in this section either make use of these associations, assumed to have been learned by all speakers of English in a new learning situation, or teach the subject new associations to be used in a new learning situation. These experiments use two general paradigms to get at the associative process, serial learning (items are presented in a fixed serial order with each serving first as response and then as stimulus for the next item), in which the amount of intralist similarity determines the degree of associative interference, and paired associate learning (items are presented in pairs, whose positions are rotated from trial to trial, and one member of each pair serves as stimulus, the other as response) in which the transfer from one list to another determines the amount of interference that old learning exerts on the learning of new material.

As already mentioned, Mednick's (1958) learning theory of schizophrenia postulates that the schizophrenic functions, at least during the beginning of his disorder, under high anxiety drive (or high state of arousal as Mednick now puts it). This high drive makes simple response learning faster since the drive combines with the general probability of response (habit strength) in a multiplicative way. In the case of complicated learning where interfering responses (different responses evoked by the same stimulus) are evoked, the high drive makes these more probable as well as the appropriate response, thereby producing a conflict situation and poorer learning. In a test of the theory by Mednick and De Vito (1958), schizophrenics learn faster than normals when the paired associates are of high probability and more slowly when the paired associates are of low probability, with the interfering responses of relatively high probability.

A number of experiments followed, but not all replicated the original finding. Spence and Lair (1964) found no difference between acute schizophrenics and normal controls in the decrement in performance of a paired associate task when there was interference built into it. Using a paradigm according to which associative interference was produced during the course of the experiment rather than relying on the assumed interference based on word association norms, Kausler, Lair, and Matsumoto (1964) found the learning of schizophrenics more affected by interference than that of normals. Two experiments making use of the method of serial learning (Carson, 1958; Donahoe, Curtin, and Lipton, 1961) found no significant difference in response to different degrees of intralist similarity or to different degrees of interference produced by interpolated lists (a different list is learned between initial learning and final recall of the first list.)

Results of other experiments using the paired associate paradigm supported Mednick's hypothesis. Lang and Luoto (1962) found schizophrenics to be more interfered with by the learning of old responses than either neurotics or normals. Spence and Lair (1965), in a replication of their earlier study referred to above, investigated the effect of dividing the schizophrenic group into remitted and nonremitted subgroups. The nonremitted schizophrenics showed more associative interference than either the remitted schizophrenics or the normal group, suggesting again the advisability of speaking of at least two types of schizophrenics. Finally, Stedman (1967) studied the effect of interference on two subgroups of schizophrenics (acute and remitted) and a group of normals; both groups of schizophrenics showed the effects of interference more than the normals, with the greatest amount for the acute, next greatest for the remitted schizophrenics, and least for the normals. It is interesting to note that the schizophrenics forgot the responses of the first list (the list learned before the interpolated list) to a greater degree than the normals, making the potential mediator for learning less available to the schizophrenics than the normals. Thus, what first looks like inter-ferencc of associations that are present is apparently actually differential forgetting (or extinction). This result can be more easily explained in terms of a theory of the prepotency of immediate stimuli rather than one of interference.

The immediacy theory (Salzinger, 1971a, 1971b) states in very general terms that schizophrenics have a greater tendency to respond to those stimuli which are temporally and spatially immediate than those which are remote. The various implications of this theory will be discussed at length in Chapter 6, but here it predicts faster forgetting in schizophrenics than in normals, since with time the verbal stimuli to be remembered become more remote and new immediate stimuli take over control. Evidence for faster forgetting of a first list was obtained in the experiment by Carson (1958) with schizophrenics. Retention intervals were measured in an experiment by Gladis (1967) who found that, one week after learning, the schizophrenics recalled 33 percent of the words against 53 percent for the normals. At two weeks, the schizo-phrenics recalled 29 percent against 52 percent for the normals, and at four weeks the schizophrenics recalled 16 percent against 37.5 percent for the normals. Relearning data at each of these intervals gave rise to the same relations. Nachmani and Cohen (1969) showed that schizophrenics recall less verbal material than normals. The words were presented one at a time and the subject's task was to recall as many of them as possible. They were also given a recognition task. The schizophrenics were clearly inferior to the normals in the number of words they recalled correctly, but showed only a similar trend for the recognition data. Again, the immediacy of the stimuli appears to explain these results, since the stimuli that were present during learning and recognition were not during recall.

Higgins, Mednick, and Thompson (1966) made a test of the postulated stages of Mednick's (1958) theory of schizophrenia by assuming equivalence of process and late stage of schizophrenia and of reactive and early stage of schizophrenia. Mednick's theory suggests that when the patient has reached a late stage of schizophrenia, he has learned to make remote-associative responses because they are more likely to be anxiety-removing responses. Such patients will, therefore, be less subject to interference by close associates than reactive patients who are still learning to make such avoidance res-ponses. The results of the experiment bore out this part of the theory in that the process schizophrenics showed superior retention of the remote asso-ciates than did the reactive patients. The authors do admit, however, that one could equally well interpret the results to show that since reactive schizophrenics are under a higher drive or arousal level, the close associates interfered more with their learning than with that of the process schizo-phrenics who, according to Mednick's theory, are under less drive or arousal.

It is possible to interpret the results as showing that the immediate stimuli, that is, the words that the subject has to learn in the paired associates situation, have a greater effect on the behavior of the process schizophrenic than on the less ill, reactive schizophrenic. The fact that the process schizophrenic performs better than the reactive schizophrenic (instead of the more usual relationship in which the reactive does better than the process schizophrenic) makes the notion of the deficit less easily attributable to a potential artifact, that is, a general lack of cooperativeness.

Some Criticisms of the Concept of Thought Disorder

Several questions must be raised about the concept of thought disorder. Is it really a basic trait of schizophrenia, or is it an expression of maladjustment found in many disorders of behavior? Is schizophrenic thinking very different from normal thought? Can schizophrenic thinking be modified? That it is possible to view schizophrenics' problem-solving behavior in terms of other concepts, such as a deficit in communication, for example, has already been touched upon. The importance of the social competence variable in schizophrenia was suggested by Schwartz (1967) who found a cognitive deficit only in noncollege remitted schizophrenics.

Perceptual Deficit. Moon and others (1968) directed their attention to the word association test that, as has already been indicated, shows that schizophrenics emit more idiosyncratic responses than normals. Since this has for a long time been considered important evidence for a basic thought disorder, Moon and others tested an alternative possibility of viewing it as a perceptual aberration. Twenty male schizophrenics and 20 normals were first given a standard auditory acuity test to insure that all had normal hearing. The experiment included such words as "bit" and "pit," which can be easily mistaken for each other. Each subject was given one list of words that he was instructed to repeat as soon as possible after hearing it, and another list to which he was to respond with the first word that occurred to him. Five scorers judged a given response as a close or distant association; subsequently, they judged whether the distant response was actually a response made to a stimulus word that was misheard. None of the scorers knew which subjects had given a response. The results were as follows: schizophrenics emit a larger number of distant responses than the normals; they repeat a significantly larger number of words incorrectly than do normals; finally, when the word associations scored as distant because they were misheard were removed from the comparison of word associations, the difference in distant responses between normals and schizophrenics was no longer statistically significant. The results strongly suggest that schizophrenics have a basic deficit in perception at least in addition to, if not instead of, an association deficit.

Seth and Beloff (1959) have also implicated a perceptual rather than an associative process. Using a battery of verbal tests including word association, sentence construction, reading speed, size estimation, and verbal IQ, they found that the small difference along the abstract-concrete dimension, was attributable to a lesser *tendency* to attend to abstract concepts rather than to a deficit in *ability* to do so.

Similarity of Associative Process in Normals and Schizophrenics. Other studies have shown that the associative process is similar in normals and schizophrenics. Johnson, Weiss, and Zelhart (1964) showed a correlation of $+.76$ between the number of associations normals and schizophrenics emit to the same stimulus words, a correlation of $+.74$ for the number of nonidiosyncratic associations, and a correlation $+.73$ for the number of common associations given by the two populations. Moran, Mefferd, and Kimble (1964) concluded, on the basis of a factor analysis of word associations given by schizophrenic and normal populations, that subjects of both groups made use of the same idiodynamic sets, that is, they instructed themselves in the same general ways, and that, therefore, the two populations can be said to share a common associative structure. Cohen and Camhi (1967), as already mentioned, showed that the associative repertories of normals and schizophrenics are substantially the same; schizophrenics functioned as well as normals in the role of listener in the word communication task, showing a deficit only when they acted as speakers. In accordance with the immediacy hypothesis, schizophrenics were able to function as well as normals because the clues given to them constituted effective immediate stimuli for the evocation of the correct answer. When the schizophrenics had to function as speakers, however, all the relevant stimuli were not immediate and they functioned less well than the normals. Miller and Chapman (1968) showed that schizophrenics have stronger response biases (a predisposition to make one of a number of possible responses) than normals when asked to rank order the same items on a number of dimensions. They concluded that at least some of the erroneous beliefs that schizophrenics have may be viewed as an accentuation of normal response biases. The fact that schizophrenics are not as reliable in their judgments as normals, a finding already discussed with respect to Bannister's work, was taken into account by Miller and Chapman by matching the two groups on that variable.

Specificity of Thought Disorder. Salzman and others (Salzman et al, 1966; Goldstein and Salzman, 1967) tested for abstract thinking by using a vocabulary and proverb interpretation test. They found a deficit in conceptual functioning in a number of different diagnostic categories and suggested impairment in conceptual behavior as a general index of maladaptation rather than as a specific index for schizophrenia. Nevertheless, the performance of the schizophrenic patients is significantly inferior to that of other diagnostic patient groups. Thus, while other patient groups show the same type of disturbances as do schizophrenics, the amount of disturbance of the latter is greater.

Modifiability. Thought disorder has been challenged as a valid characterization of schizophrenia because it can be easily modified. Cavanaugh (1958) administered a concept formation test to schizophrenics and normals under two different conditions of feedback: in one, the experimenter told the subject when he made an incorrect response; in the other, white noise at 116 decibels (a very loud noise) was terminated upon the correct solution or upon the expiration of the maximum time allowed for solution of the problem. Although the schizophrenics performed worse than the normals under the verbal reinforcement condition, they performed equally well under the white-noise escape condition.

Another procedure employed in the modification of thought disorder is the enriched input condition. Blaufarb (1962) presented proverbs to schizophrenics and normals for interpretation under two different conditions. In one condition, subjects were asked to give the meaning for single proverbs; in the other condition, they were required to give the meaning for a set of proverbs, members of each set having the same meaning. Although the schizophrenics performed worse than the normals when only one proverb was given for each meaning, they performed equally well when proverbs were presented in sets. The schizophrenics improved significantly from the single to the set proverb condition, while the normals behaved in the same level for both conditions.

In a replication of the Blaufarb experiment, Hamlin, Haywood, and Folsom (1965) compared the ability to interpret proverbs for schizophrenics differing in degree of pathology. They compared closed ward schizophrenics, open ward schizophrenics, former schizophrenics in remission, and nonpsychotic patients (including neurotics, personality disorders, and medical patients without psychiatric diagnosis). The open ward and former schizophrenic patient groups showed a significant increase in the proverb interpretation score that replicated the Blaufarb experiment. The nonpsychotic group, like the normal group in Blaufarb's study, showed no gain from the enriched input situation. The severely schizophrenic group (closed ward), also showed no improvement. Hamlin et al argue that the mildly schizophrenic groups demonstrate an input deficit that the proverb set procedure overcomes, while the closed ward schizophrenics demonstrate an abstracting deficit to which a continued input deficit inevitably leads. This set of experiments shows that, at least for one group of patients, it is inappropriate to talk of a thought disorder on the basis of the proverb test. The importance of stimulus input will continue to arise with respect to other experiments, particularly the experiments in perception and we will have occasion to further discuss it in Chapter 6.

Attempts to modify word association behavior have also been made. Sommer, Witney, and Osmond (1962) conditioned common associations in schizophrenics by using cigarettes as reinforcements, followed by the use of verbal reinforcements. Although the schizophrenics emitted a significantly larger number of common associations, they did not improve as much as alcoholic patients, nor did they generalize to a new word association list. In a followup experiment, Ullmann, Krasner, and Edinger (1964) successfully conditioned common associations in 20 long-term schizophrenics by using verbal reinforcement. Like Sommer et al, they found no generalization of the increase in common associations; they looked for generalization in a task in which subjects were required to describe stick-figure line drawings of people by selecting one of five adjectives. The failure to show generalization of the conditioning effect must be ascribed to the relatively brief period of conditioning in both experiments. Furthermore, degree of generalization depends on the way the response is conditioned. On the other hand, success at even partial modification of a primary symptom of schizophrenia certainly raises a question concerning its importance.

Investigators have developed many techniques to measure the concept of thought disorder or, as I prefer to call it, the regulatory function of language. I advise the interested reader to look at Zubin and Burdock (1960) and Payne (1960, 1968) for a more general description of some of these techniques. The results of many of the techniques described lend themselves to explanations in terms other than that of thought disorder (for example, in terms of stimulus input); furthermore, even when they seem to be correctly interpreted as thought disorder, the results are, in some cases, unreliable and not replicated, in other cases not very striking, and in still others relatively easily modified.

THE COMMUNICATIVE FUNCTION

The oft-related but rarely occurring anomalies of "schizophrenic language" have challenged many to construct theories purporting to explain these anomalies but few to collect the data necessary to test their validity. Nevertheless, an increased sophistication in the study of verbal behavior in general has brought with it a corresponding improvement in the methodology used to study schizophrenic language. The many and still current clinical descriptions of schizophrenic language have encouraged psychologists to examine it indirectly solely by the methods described in the first section of this chapter (see Cromwell and Dokecki [1968] as an example). The emphasis has most often been on anomalies of speech that occur only in very isolated instances. Clinically derived descriptions of schizophrenic language include such characterizations as word salad (where words are emitted in almost telegraphic style) and opposite speech (where the patient says "yes" when he means "no" and vice versa). Woods (1938) provides a large number of examples of abnormalities of speech based upon clinical examination of the verbatim reports of conversations with 125 schizophrenics. He tried to keep examiner influence on the speech sample to a minimum but he did not specify the exact procedure for accomplishing this end. As an example of a speech segment showing poverty of ideation, Woods (1938, p. 297) supplied the following :

"Well, the reason I, this is, you, this going to be something, this is what I thought afterwards, I figured out about going with this girl, probably I was, I would, I figure, I say, well, I know from the way I, it's been since that I really just thought and forgot about it and this is one reason why, that really isn't my trouble, though. My trouble is, well, it's that's what I want to know, why I, I know I had this breakdown and what I want to know is what's after that, see?"

The confusion of this passage, the continuous repetition of words and phrases, and what Woods calls the difficulty in forming concrete ideation are sufficiently dramatic to convince many that schizophrenics have difficulty in communicating. Nevertheless, the fact that at least some normal individuals talk in a similar if not equally confused, roundabout style, with as many interruptions, makes the detection of a communication difficulty a more than routine matter. Let us look at other equally dramatic examples of communication difficulties in schizophrenia; most notable perhaps are the phenomena of muteness and echolalia, the former being no speech at all and the latter consisting of literal repetition of everything the patient hears, at least within certain limits of utterance length. The phenomenon of neologisms (new words) is also widely reported in the schizophrenic literature. Woods (1938, p. 303) presents the following conversation as an example of impromptu neologisms :

PATIENT : "I have seen you, but your words alworthern."
EXAMINER : "What does *alworthern* mean?"
P.   "Ashens. Guiding the circumfrax."
E.   "What does *alworthern* mean?"
P.   "Alworthern? Al-" (seems to be thinking).
E.   "Can you tell me what love is?"
P.   "Love? Gians ... vitruous of the vein and rhenebal of wehlein."
E.   "What does that mean?"
P.   "Vaigs."
E.   "That isn't very clear to me yet. How is your husband?"
P.   "He is hopeful."
E.   "What about?"
P.   "What is hopeful about? of the fuch."

Woods also supplies an example of tangential remarks that schizophrenics are likely to make (Woods, 1938, p. 308) :

EXAMINER : "Can people receive messages from others when these people are not near?"
PATIENT : "Yes."
E. "How?"
P. "By radio, telephone."
E. "Any other way?"
P. "By writing letters, by wire, by water."
E. "Did you say water?"
P. "By some code or by, or by flowers, by old plays, by true lovers."

Woods quotes additional excerpts from his speech samples, including such statements as "about five" in response to "what is your name?" and "third degree" in response to a question about what grade the patient was in. On the basis of such examples, Woods characterizes the speech of schizophrenics as suffering from a poverty of precise ideational thought, as being egocentric, metaphorical in an eccentric way, and as demonstrating a tendency to slip from one category of meaning to another.

Many students of schizophrenia have characterized the primary problem as one of communication. Ferreira (1960, p. 134) says the following: "... the patient who speaks in a secret code does so *not to communicate* his thoughts for, in fact, he much fears to be understood." Bateson, and others (1956) developed this idea more fully, using it to explain the genesis of schizophrenia in terms of what they call the "double bind" situation. They explain it as follows: as a child, the patient receives one message that threatens to punish him unless he does as told, and another in direct conflict with it, in which he is told (either by the tone or gesture of the same speaker or the other parent) not to regard the threat as coming from a punishing agent. Confusion generated by such repeated exposures results in a disinclination to communicate because the patient's experience with his clear communications is that they are punished no matter which way he responds to the injunctions made by the schizophrenogenic mother.

A note of caution is in order concerning the examples of schizophrenic speech given above. They are not typical of schizophrenic speech in general. Nevertheless, some of the characteristics outlined in such glaring clarity in these cases can be identified to a lesser degree in the speech samples of many schizophrenics by means of objective and quantifiable procedures. Furthermore, the pathology of even the average schizophrenic's speech can be detected by undergraduates (Cohen, 1961). These students attributed the same ratings of pathology to the patient's speech as did clinical criterion judges.

Before leaving this general introduction to the communication deficit in schizophrenia, it might be well to hear a dissenting voice (Goffman, 1964). He believes that the notion of communication has been used excessively for behavior that could be more profitably described as being in accord with, or deviant from, some social rule in a public place. However, whether we view communication as a class in and of itself or merely as a member of a more general class of behavior, it does make sense to examine the communicative function in schizophrenia in some detail.

Content Analysis Studies

Content analysis, in its classical mode, consists of an independent count of different classes of verbal behavior. Content analysts draw their conclusions about a passage on the basis of statistical indices of covariation of the various categories (classes of verbal behavior). In order to determine whether a particular speaker tends to think of two people together, the analyst compares a count of the number of times that each person is mentioned alone in a sentence and the number of times that they are mentioned together. He would use the same approach to investigate the relation between the expression of aggressive attitudes, as evidenced by a particular set of words, and the particular people towards whom such attitudes are expressed.

Meadow and others (1952) constructed the discomfort-relief quotient (DRQ) in an early attempt to classify the verbal behavior of schizophrenics. They obtained continuous verbal behavior samples by asking each patient to tell what "was on his mind." The verbatim speech samples were unitized and each unit classified as showing discomfort, comfort or satisfaction, or neutrality. The DRQ is computed by dividing the number of discomfort statements by the total number of units. Although initially described as a measure of tension, the DRQ failed to relate to a direct rating of tension by a psychiatrist. The DRQ did relate significantly, however, to the schizophrenics' performance on a proverb interpretation test and to a measure of looseness of association derived from the same speech samples. Since the higher DRQ related to better performance, it was concluded that the expression of discomfort signified relatively good adjustment. The more seriously ill patients' lack of insight into their discomfort and their inability to express it in such a way as to be understood corroborated this conclusion.

Gottschalk and his colleagues (1967; Gottschalk and Gleser, 1969) have constructed a more extensive content analysis system. They (Gottschalk and Gleser, 1964; Gottschalck et al, 1958) elicited speech most commonly by asking the patient to talk about anything for a period of three and sometimes five minutes. Using the grammatical clause as the unit to be scored, they assigned weights to each clause. The weights were empirically derived on the basis of how well each category differentiated schizophrenics from others.

The units were classified in terms of social integration and well being or personal malfunctioning and social alienation. The categories included in the schizophrenia scale of this content analysis were unfriendly interpersonal references, helpful interpersonal references, interpersonal references to self as getting better, and denial of feelings. This system of content analysis is limited by the subjectivity involved. Nevertheless, the scoring system is reliable and has had some success at differentiating schizophrenics from normals and medically ill subjects. The fact that a basically subjective method of content analysis, applied to very short samples of speech, is able at all to differentiate schizophrenics from others augurs well for the examination of speech for this purpose.

Laffal (1960, 1961, 1965) developed a technique called the analysis of contextual associates. He content-analyzed the speech of a schizophrenic during the course of months of psychotherapy. Using a list of 94 categories, each containing words of similar meaning, he showed that the relative frequency of occurrence of the categories varied from the early and middle stages to the late stages of therapy. According to Laffal's subjective judgment, the late stages represented new and more integrated behavior on the part of the patient. Laffal used correlations over categories to examine the similarities among different patients. Such a technique had earlier proved its usefulness in demonstrating the similarity between disturbed children and their friends and relatives (Salzinger, 1958), based upon an analysis of their correspondence. Furthermore, Laffal used an information theory measure to examine the variation in the occurrence of different categories at various stages of therapy and found a reduction in the use of diverse categories with improvement in the state of the patient. Finally, by studying the contexts of the various categories, he demonstrated different patterns of association among them. Although not widely used, this technique gives promise of proving useful.

Analysis of the Production of Speech

Sequential Influence of Responses. Basic to the production of speech is the fact that responses made sequentially influence each other. There are some disagreements on the nature of this influence, that is, whether it depends upon some superstructure (such as a set of rules prescribed by the grammar) or whether the interdependency can be explained by the recurring sequences of the responses themselves. Whatever the interpretation, however, investigators agree on the existence of the interdependence. Since schizophrenic speech is described as tangential, that is, relatively free of this interdependence, a number of studies have made an effort to quantify this effect with a restricted set of responses. Yacorzynski (1941) investigated the patterning of binary guesses (the order in which subjects guess the occurrence of one of two events) and concluded that symmetrical patterns of responses are preferred by psychotic patients but that normals prefer nonsymmetrical patterns. Skinner (1942) reanalyzed Yacorzynski's data and concluded that the schizophrenic's tendency to alternate guesses is not differentially influenced by his prior alternation. He claims that psychotic individuals are relatively uninfluenced by their own past behavior. Such a characterization is consistent with the immediacy hypothesis that states that the behavior of schizophrenics is controlled by the most immediate events in their environment. Thus, the patient's last response influences him to emit the alternate response but the rate of the alternation remains the same independent of what he did before.

Zlotowski and Bakan (1963) had subjects generate a series of random guesses of heads and tails. Comparing process to reactive schizophrenics, they found that process schizophrenics displayed a greater than chance tendency to alternate, and more of a tendency to alternate than the reactive schizophrenics whose alternation performance did not differ from chance. Their experiment confirmed Skinner's hypothesis, at least in process schizophrenics.

In another study of the "random" generation of binary guesses, Weiss (1964) found that schizophrenics had greater tendency to alternate their responses especially when they were given more time between successive guesses; he also found other biases, such as a preference for one response.

Yavuz (1963) examined the interdependency of successive responses in a task requiring subjects to generate random letter sequences. Although the finding was not statistically significant, the small sample of schizophrenics tended to repeat pairs of letters more often than normal subjects.

In 1968, Ramsay and Broadhurst compared the behavior of 72 paid normal volunteers with that of 12 chronic schizophrenics. Subjects were required to say the numbers 1 through 10 in time to a metronome set at one per second in any order they desired. The schizophrenics' behavior was not random. They tended to emit certain numbers and certain pairs of numbers more frequently than the normals.

These studies have shown, with a restricted number of responses, some of the tendencies that have been postulated for language. Meadow, Greenblatt, and Solomon (1953) used the same method of evoking speech samples as did Meadow et al (1952) in the study mentioned above. The typed verbatim manuscript is divided into independent clauses or as close to that as possible. The investigators then examine the typescript, one pair of units at a time, for looseness of association by determining whether there is an abnormal shift ("a break in the stream of associations which the scorer judged would not occur in nonpsychotic subjects"). The looseness of association in schizophrenic speech correlated significantly with measures of abstraction ability, particularly with regard to a proverb interpretation test and a similarities test derived from the Wechsler–Bellevue intelligence test, but only to a small degree (+.27) with an object sorting test.

Formal Measures of Speech. Whitehorn and Zipf (1943) applied an entirely objective technique to schizophrenic speech in a classic study. Their measure is based on the rate of repetition of different words (types, which are words having identical orthography) relative to the total number of words (tokens). These investigators examined long written samples of verbal behavior of a few patients of various diagnoses and suggested the hypothesis that schizophrenics tend toward more repetitiousness than normals. Such repetitiousness constitutes an example of a tendency toward autism (an extreme form of self-interest), since it demonstrates little concern in communicating for the sake of the receiver of the message and more interest in communicating for the speaker's convenience. Following the work of Mandelbrot (1953), Parks (1961) derived a rigorous mathematical description of this relationship to evaluate schizophrenic speech.

The year following publication of the Whitehorn–Zipf study, Johnson (1944) edited a monograph including two studies concerning this question with more subjects and a simple, direct quantitative index of repetitiousness. The index was the type–token ratio; it is the number of different words (types) divided by the total number of words (tokens) considered. It varies from close to 0 (1 divided by the total number of words considered, in the extreme case when a person uses the same word to convey all the different meanings) to 1 (in the extreme case in which the subject never repeats a word within the sample of words considered). In fact, of course, the typical TTR (Type–token ratio) varies between these extremes. Mann (1944) compared written material, while Fairbanks (1944) compared speech obtained from schizophrenics and normal college students. As pointed out by these investigators, their major interest was in finding two contrasting groups to provide empirical data concerning the variation of the index rather than in schizophrenia. Nevertheless, the fact that they obtained statistically significant differences between the groups has been viewed as evidence for the greater repetitiousness of speech in schizophrenics.

Some 15 years later, Seth and Beloff (1959) in a better-controlled study recorded conversations between patients and examiner. TTR's were then obtained on these speech samples of 100 words each, using ten 100-word samples for each subject. The schizophrenic and the control samples were matched in terms of hospitalization and for equivalence of socioeconomic and geographical variables. The schizophrenic patients differed from the normals significantly in that they had lower TTR's. Thus, using better control groups, these investigators found schizophrenics to be more given to repetition than normals.

In 1962, Feldstein and Jaffe also tried to replicate the original Fairbanks study using control groups more closely matched in schooling. They found no significant difference between normals and schizophrenics. However, their study differed in two significant ways from the original study. The speech samples used for the computation of TTR's consisted of only 25 words each, a number of such samples being averaged to obtain the TTR employed for the comparison of schizophrenics and normals. The use of smaller numbers of tokens for computation of the TTR might not differentiate groups as well as larger word samples because of the greater opportunity for repetition in larger samples than smaller ones. In addition, there is some empirical evidence that shows that better differentiation of groups can be achieved by considering longer speech samples (Hammer and Salzinger, 1964). The Feldstein and Jaffe study also differs from the Fairbanks study in that the schizophrenics of the former were under the influence of tranquilizers. Salzinger, Pisoni, Feldman, and Bacon (1961) showed, albeit in a study using a single subject only, that an increase in dosage of chlorpromazine causes an increase in TTR that brings it closer to the normal's (the TTR was based on thousands of words obtained during each of several 30-minute monologues), thus suggesting a second reason for the negative results obtained by Feldstein and Jaffe. Mittennecker (1951, cited by Brengelmann, 1960) investigating the rate of repetition of syllables and the mean distance between repetitions, found that schizophrenics repeat more and have shorter distances between repetitions than normals.

Finally, Hammer and Salzinger (1964) found, on a small sample of subjects matched for ethnic background and education, that schizophrenics had lower TTR's than normals. In fact, the differences in TTR's found were greater for the ethnic group comparisons than for the pathology comparisons. On the other hand, a related index of repetition (Yule's Characteristic K) was less affected by the background factors and more influenced by pathology. This index takes into account not only the total number of words repeated, but also the number of times each is repeated. It seems fair to conclude that schizophrenics repeat words more than normals, a finding that is further bolstered by the previously cited results showing that schizophrenics also tend to repeat other verbal patterns, such as binary guesses and letter sequences.

There are other formal measures of deviance used in the study of verbal behavior of schizophrenics. Hammer and Salzinger, for example, examined the extent to which schizophrenics shared the same vocabulary, the extent to which normals did, and the extent to which they shared vocabulary between the two groups. The results showed more sharing of vocabulary among the normals than either among the schizophrenics or between the schizophrenics and normals, thus supplying additional evidence for the idiosyncracy of the speech of schizophrenics already demonstrated in the word association studies above. Other investigators have applied grammatical analyses to schizophrenic speech. Both Mann (1944) and Fairbanks (1944) found a higher verb-adjective quotient for schizophrenics than for normals. Brengelmann (1960) interprets these results, along with some additional findings on other abnormal groups, to mean that psychological abnormality increases the use of "activity" (verb) language and reduces the use of "qualitative" (adjective) language. High-anxiety patients and manic patients are some of the groups that also show the larger verb-adjective ratio.

Temporal Measures. Some investigators have turned their attention to temporal characteristics of schizophrenic speech. Beginning with a behavioral approach to verbal interaction, Chapple (1953) created a standard interview that consisted of five different periods. The first period is stress-free and the behavior of the interviewer is limited to encourage the patient to continue talking by means of five-second responses that consist essentially of asking the patient to go on. The second period contains a stress, silence on the part of the interviewer. The third period is another nonstress period identical to the first one. The fourth period is another stress period in which the interviewer deliberately interrupts the patient. The fifth period is another nonstress period identical to the first and third periods. The dependent variable (response) is measured in terms of the length of the patient's utterances, silences, latencies between the interviewer's remarks and his statements, and the length of time that the patient speaks while being interrupted.

Saslow and Matarazzo (1959) showed that this interview procedure is reliable. Chapple and others (1960) used the interview to show that schizophrenics are more variable in terms of the periods of silence and in terms of periods of activity. Furthermore, they derived a maladjustment measure from the patient's reaction to being interrupted (length of time before he stopped talking when being interrupted) plus the length of time between the last interviewer remark and his first response. The average duration of maladjustment was significantly longer for the schizophrenics than for the normals. In a similar study, Matarazzo and his colleagues (1957) also found that schizophrenics manifested the latency maladjustment. The consistency of this finding is interesting in relation to the reaction time studies in which schizophrenics are typically slower to respond. Also interesting in this regard is the fact that schizophrenics take longer to emit a given speech sample than do normals (Seth and Beloff, 1959). Feldstein (1962) used Mahl's (1956) speech disturbance measure (based on hesitations and pauses in speech) and found that schizophrenic speech contained more disturbances than the controls' speech.

Comprehensibility. Many of the studies cited so far, as well as many of the conjectures about schizophrenic speech, suggest that schizophrenics are difficult to understand. The search for a more rigorous test of this basic hypothesis led a number of investigators to the cloze procedure (Taylor, 1953). In this procedure, every nth (usually every fifth) word of a verbal behavior sample is deleted and a blank is substituted for each. Subjects must then guess the word they think the speaker had used for each blank. In this way, the speech sample of the patient is used as a message; it is transmitted in such a manner that the receiver of that message must guess every once in a while before he can understand the content of the entire message.

Salzinger, Portnoy, and Feldman (1964b) used some typed 200 word samples of speech, taken from monologues of schizophrenic patients

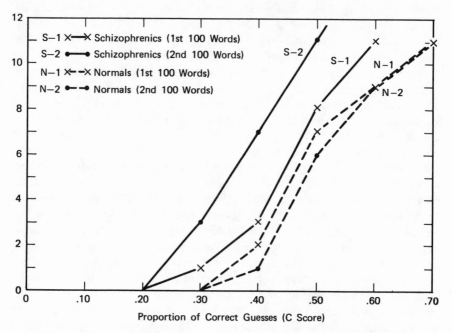

FIGURE 2–1. Cumulative frequency of schizophrenic and normal subjects as a function of proportion of correct guesses to total guesses (C score). The two chronic schizophrenics and their normal matches are not included. S-1 and S-2, and N-1 and N-2 refer, respectively, to the first and second 100 words of the schizophrenic and normal passages. (Courtesy of K. Salzinger, S. Portnoy, and R. S. Feldman, "Verbal behavior of schizophrenic and normal subjects," *Annals of the New York Academy of Sciences, 105,* **1964, pp. 845–860. Reprinted with permission.)**

(Salzinger, Portnoy, and Feldman, 1964a) and from a control group of physically ill hospitalized patients. The two groups were matched as closely as possible in terms of age, sex, education, and ethnic background; groups of college students (all native speakers of English) had the task of guessing the missing words of the cloze passages based on the speech samples of the two groups. Of the 11 male pairs compared, all schizophrenics were more difficult to understand (using the number of correct guesses for the blanks as the index of understanding or communicability) than the matched normals. Of the two female pairs, only one yielded a greater communicability for the normal than the schizophrenic. It is also interesting to note that the difference between the normals and the schizophrenics increased from the first 100 words to the second 100 words. This was due to the fact that the schizophrenic speech became more difficult to understand in the second than in the first 100 words, while the speech of the normals showed a nonsignificant trend in the direction of greater understanding from the first to the second 100 words. Inspection of Fig. 2-1 shows this effect even when considering the patients and normals as groups and not as matched pairs (only 11 acute patients were plotted here, leaving out the two chronic patients that also showed the effect in the predicted direction).

Salzinger, Portnoy, and Feldman (1966) confirmed these findings in a later paper. They obtained cloze scores on 23 acute schizophrenics and related them to short term outcome of illness. Using the number of correct guesses as the communicability score, they found a correlation of $-.47$, that is, the smaller the number of correct guesses, the longer the stay in the hospital. This means that patients who communicate effectively approximately one week after coming to the hospital are able to leave the hospital earlier than those who communicated poorly at that time.

The same authors described two other methods of measuring communicability. One of these, the method of reconstruction, consists of the following: a 200-word sample of speech is divided into 10 successive 20-word segments that are typed on white cards without any punctuation. The experimenter shuffles the cards and gives them to a subject to put into the order in which he thinks the speaker emitted them. This method leads to a number of scores to estimate the communicability of speech. One score is the length of time it takes normal subjects to reassort the speech segments until they are satisfied that they have achieved the correct order. A comparison of the 11 male pairs of the cloze procedure study showed that in all cases the subjects took longer to rearrange the schizophrenic than the normal passages. In the two female pairs, one schizophrenic speech passage took longer than the normal match and one took less time.

The sequence error score (a score that takes into account all the consecutive pairs) showed the schizophrenics to be less understandable than the normals, particularly when comparing the second 100 words. When the sequence error score was related to short-term outcome, there was a correlation of $+.66$ for the total passage, $+.21$ for the first half of the passage, and +.88 for the last half. This finding, along with the prior result that the second half of the speech sample distinguishes normals and schizophrenics better than the first half, led the investigators to posit the immediacy hypothesis. Since each speech sample used for the study came right after the experimenter's instructions and the first half of the speech sample is closer to those instructions (in which topics of discussion were suggested), the latter can be assumed to predominate as the immediate stimulus for the first half of the sample; for the second half, the immediate stimulus is the subject's own last verbal response; with only his own verbal behavior to guide him, the patient apparently speaks in a less comprehensible manner than he does when guided by external instructions.

The third approach to the study of communicability of schizophrenic speech is the method of unitization. The same schizophrenic and normal speech passages as used for the cloze procedure (but with no words deleted) was presented without punctuation to college students. They were instructed to divide the material into sentences without rearrangement, crossing out only those words that they could not fit into the sentences. The students crossed out more words from the schizophrenic than from the normal samples in 9 out of the 10 pairs considered for this measure. All in all, these measures suggest that communicability is better for normals than for schizophrenics.

Cheek and Amarel (1967) used 100-word speech samples from 10 alcoholics and 10 chronic schizophrenics; the schizophrenics had lower scores than the alcoholics but the difference only approached statistical significance. Since they compared only the first 100 words and found more of a trend for the second than for the first 50 words, and since these investigators did not match the two populations in terms of sex, age, and education, as was done in the Salzinger, Portnoy and Feldman (1964b, 1966) study, it is perhaps not surprising that they obtained no statistically significant results. Furthermore, alcoholics might also be somewhat less comprehensible than normals due to the neurophysiological effects of drinking.

In 1963, Honigfeld showed that the administration of a psychotomimetic (producing psychoticlike behavior) agent (psilocybin) engenders first an increase, then a reduction, and finally a restoration of the communicability of the normal subject. Fig. 2-2 demonstrates the trend over time. Thus, summarizing this section, we have good evidence for the disturbance in communication of the schizophrenic. More precisely, we can attribute the difficulty in communication to interference in interresponse dependencies. In terms of Mednick's (1958) anxiety-learning theory, patients demonstrate their tangential (anxiety avoiding) responses in a gross way in speech. In terms of Salzinger's immediacy hypothesis (1971a, 1971b) we have another demonstration of the schizophrenic's preponderant response to stimuli that

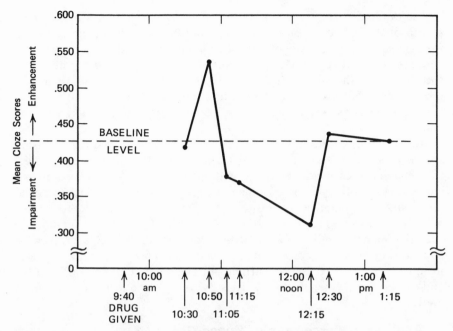

FIGURE 2–2. The effect of psilocybin on "understandability." (Reprinted with permission of author and publisher. Honigfeld, G., "Effect of an hallucinogenic agent on verbal behavior," *Psychological Reports*, 1963, *13*, pp. 383–385.)

are immediate in his environment. In order to communicate, a speaker must respond to the beginning of his sentences, or for that matter, to the topic of discussion he begins with; in other words, he must respond to remote stimuli. Thus, the schizophrenic's tendency to respond preponderantly to stimuli immediate in time and space results in a loss of communicability.

Hallucinations. Before leaving the topic of production of speech, we will look at hallucinations that are verbalized, even if they are not to be construed solely as a verbal behavior phenomenon. Gould (1948, 1950) presents some cogent arguments for the verbal nature of hallucinations, emphasizing that they are not due to auditory imagery, but rather to subvocal, whispered, and sometimes even shouted speech by the patient himself. He adduces evidence for this point of view from physiological sources and from the patient's own descriptions. His experiments on the physiology of hallucinations consisted of the measurement of the muscle potential from the vocal organs. Eighty percent of the schizophrenics suspected of hallucinating demonstrated increased muscle potential, while 90 percent of a group of patients without hallucinations showed no increase in muscle potential.

In one dramatic case, Gould (1949) was even able to amplify the subvocal speech of the hallucination so that he could hear the "hallucination." As for evidence from the patient himself, Gould reports that many patients describe their hallucinations spontaneously as being related to their own speech, that is, they sometimes report their voices to come from their own mouths first. He also cites observations by outsiders that hallucinating patients can be observed to move their lips and whisper to themselves during hallucinations.

In closing this section, I would like to mention the advantages in using speech production as an avenue to learning about schizophrenia. Unlike test behavior, speech can be evoked with little difficulty from schizophrenic patients (the only exception being mute patients); it is critical in social intercourse and therefore constitutes a good index of how well an individual will get along in society if he is returned to it; finally, a patient requires no special training to emit a speech sample, nor does it induce a problem in cooperation between the patient and examiner since almost any speech, including that of a refusal to participate (as long as that refusal is verbal and extensive), is amenable to analysis by some of the techniques outlined above.

Analysis of Perception of Speech

It is hard to imagine a deficit in the production of speech without a corresponding deficit in the perception of speech. Evidence for a deficit in perception comes both from the proverb interpretation test, which shows that schizophrenics have difficulty in responding to the general content of the proverb, as well from the word association test. We will consider first the perception difficulties evoked by language samples varying in degree of organization. In this way, we will be able to determine the extent to which schizophrenics as opposed to normals can respond to different amounts of organization.

Statistical Approximations to English. A technique for generating sequences of words differing in amount of organization was created by Miller and Selfridge (1950) after Shannon (1948). It consists, essentially, of the generation of passages, in each of which a different number of words is related. Thus, in a third order approximation to English any three successive words are related (make sense together), but sequences of words longer than that may sound very peculiar indeed because they are not, in fact, related to each other. An example of a second order passage is, "Was he went to the newspaper is in deep and." An example of a seventh order passage is, "Recognize her abilities in music after he scolded him before." Notice in the second order passage that all of the pairs of words make sense, but many of the sequences beyond that do not, thus, demonstrating that this passage has less organization for the hearer to take advantage of than the seventh order passage.

Cloze procedure analysis (Salzinger, Portnoy and Feldman, 1962) of these passages (using normal subjects) showed a regular increase in the proportion of correctly guessed words with an increase in statistical approximation. Moreover, the increases in ability to understand the passages are small through second order, becoming sizeable only after third order. At the same time the proportion of guesses of words in the same grammatical class as the original words begins to increase at second order, reaching a maximum at third and staying there for all the other orders. Lewinsohn and Elwood (1961) presented these passages on tape to test their subjects on immediate recall. A normal control group, an acute schizophrenic, and a nonschizophrenic psychiatric group recalled approximately the same amount. However, a chronic schizophrenic group recalled significantly less on all passages, benefiting least from an increase in statistical approximation to English.

In another experiment making use of the statistical approximations to English, Lawson, McGhie, and Chapman (1964) presented 10- and 20-word passages to test recall in schizophrenics (in this case a specially selected group known to be cooperative on other tasks) and normals. The schizophrenics performed more poorly than the normals and also made significantly less improvement with increasing approximation to English. It is of interest to note that the schizophrenics ceased showing any improvement in their performance after third order approximation (fourth degree of organization in Fig. 2-3). The reader will recall that this is the point at which no further

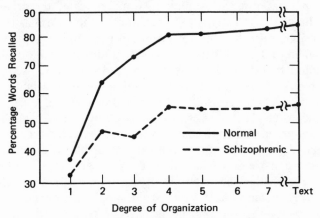

FIGURE 2–3. Relationship between organization and recall score (different length scores combined). (Courtesy of J. S. Lawson, A. McGhie, and J. Chapman, "Perception of speech in schizophrenia," *British Journal of Psychiatry, 110,* **1964,** pp. 375–380. Reproduced with permission.)

improvement took place in guessing words of the same part of speech as the word called for in the passage in the Salzinger study. It suggests that while the schizophrenics can take advantage of some of the grammatical properties of connection among the words, they are less able to take advantage of the content connections in recall.

Raeburn and Tong (1968) reexamined the findings of the above experiment. In an exact replication they found that in general schizophrenics do improve as much as normals with increasing approximation to English. Nevertheless, 6 of the 14 schizophrenics did show the effect demonstrated for the entire schizophrenic group in the Lawson study. A further comparison of the two studies shows that the schizophrenics in the Raeburn study do better than the Lawson schizophrenics, but that the Raeburn normals do less well than the Lawson normals, thus reducing the difference between the two groups. The schizophrenics who showed the Lawson effect of a dropoff in performance with an increase in statistical approximation to English had a relatively low vocabulary score. Although the authors discarded the process-reactive dimension as an explanatory factor (since they found length of stay in the hospital unrelated), the disparity in vocabulary can be considered to reflect differences in social competence, that is, high vocabulary scores imply high social competence and reactive schizophrenia, and low vocabulary scores imply low social competence and process schizophrenia.

Two months after this study, Levy and Maxwell (1968), apparently independently, tried to replicate the Lawson study also. Using a population of schizophrenics of relatively short duration of illness and no behavior disorders before the current hospitalization, and a group of depressives, plus a control normal group, these investigators replicated the original Lawson finding, showing better overall performance for the normals than the schizophrenics, and also less improvement with increasing approximation for the schizophrenics than for the normals. In addition, however, these investigators found that depressed patients yielded even lower scores than the schizophrenics, suggesting the possibility that the recall deficit is not specific to schizophrenia but reflects a general maladjustment.

In conclusion, these studies provide some evidence that schizophrenics have a diminished ability to take advantage of greater degrees of context.

Honigfeld (1967) found that schizophrenics fill in fewer correct words when doing a cloze procedure than do normals. Furthermore, they do equally worse whether the material they are filling in is a newspaper article, a schizophrenic speech sample, or a speech sample of a normal subject under the influence of an hallucinogenic agent.

Williams (1966) had schizophrenics generate statistical approximations to English and found that the resulting passages had an agrammatical quality about them in that the schizophrenics tended to respond to single words rather than to whole grammatical constructions. Pearl (1963) utilized the Shannon (1948) guessing game (subjects must guess the content of a sentence, letter by letter) to determine the effect of context on the verbal behavior of process and reactive schizophrenics. The normals required a smaller number of guesses to emit a particular short sentence than the two schizophrenic groups. When the groups were divided into high and low vocabulary levels, only the low vocabulary schizophrenics differed from the low vocabulary normals, with the normals requiring the smallest number of guesses, the reactive schizophrenics the next highest, and the process schizophrenics requiring the largest number of guesses.

Psycholinguistic Approach. Following some of the newer approaches of psycholinguistics, Gerver (1967) tested schizophrenics, nonschizophrenic psychiatric patients, and a normal control group on a memory task for three types of sentences under different noise conditions. One type of sentence was meaningful and grammatical, one was grammatical but meaningless, and one was both meaningless and ungrammatical. All three groups performed best on the grammatical meaningful sentences, next best on the grammatical but meaningless sentences, and least well on the ungrammatical and meaningless sentences. The schizophrenics performed worse under greater noise and did particularly badly with the last sentence type. They came closer to the performance of the two control groups when they had to deal with meaningful and grammatical sentences, suggesting that they can take advantage of at least some response interrelations subsumed under the heading of grammar and meaning. The relatively poor schizophrenic performance on the sentences that are both ungrammatical and meaningless might well be because the strong immediate associations in schizophrenics interfere most under those conditions whereas, in a short grammatical and meaningful sentence, they are sometimes the same as those produced by long range constraints. As to the differential effect of the noise, we can infer that the schizophrenics are more controlled by the immediacy of the noise than are the two control groups.

Feedback. Levitt (1965) showed that schizophrenics learn better when the stimulus material presented to them and the feedback of their learned responses are louder than when they are relatively quiet. This finding holds only for the learning of nonsense syllable material; the learning of meaningful material produces more errors for schizophrenics than for normals, but no differential performance as a function of the loudness of the stimulus or the response feedback of the subject. Levitt interprets the findings in terms of an altered attention function in schizophrenia. The immediacy hypothesis seems very relevant to the results of this experiment. In the first task, subjects learned to associate two nonsense syllables, thus taking advantage of the short range associations that for the schizophrenic are relatively effective;

also the increased loudness draws the schizophrenic's attention to the task, whereas a lower intensity allows his attention to stray to irrelevant but equally immediate stimuli. The schizophrenic has difficulty in learning the meaningful passage because the response interrelationships he has to learn are in many cases remote: consequently, the increased loudness that makes the immediate and the remote stimuli more prominent offers no appreciable advantage to the schizophrenic learner.

Three groups of investigators studied the effect of delayed auditory feedback (the speaker hears what he says a fraction of a second later than he ordinarily world). Although their general technique was the same they used different response measures, thus making comparisons difficult. Sutton, Roehrig, and Kramer (1964) found that delayed feedback slowed the speech of male and female schizophrenics more than that of normal males, but not more than that of normal females; on the other hand, male and female schizophrenics enunciated fewer words correctly than the normal females but not fewer than the normal males. Apparently, male normals respond to delay more in terms of poor enunciation of words while female normals more in terms of taking more time, that is, reading more slowly. Spear (1963) also found more slowing of speech in females than males in response to delayed auditory feedback. The experiments by Spear (1963) and Spear and Bird (1963) found significantly less change in loudness of the speech of the schizophrenic under delayed auditory feedback than of the normal and other nonschizophrenic control groups. Finally, Ludwig, Wood, and Downs (1962) found that schizophrenics take a longer or a shorter time than normals, in reading under delay. These findings are not very clear. Evidently the schizophrenic response to delayed auditory feedback is influenced by the way the speaker escapes the aversive condition of hearing, not what he is currently saying, but what he said a while ago. Since the speaker has a number of alternative routes of escape, such as speaking slowly, loudly, or quietly, only simultaneous consideration of a number of indices of changes in speech will bring order to this area.

On Conditioning of Verbal Behavior

Studies in conditioning have shown that the speech of schizophrenics is indeed conditionable: mute patients can learn to speak again; experimenters can directly influence the patients' classes of verbal response; in fact, conditioning takes place in all human interactions with schizophrenic patients (as it does, of course, also with normals), and investigators must therefore take it into account when obtaining information from them in order to construct a theory about the disorder. I will take up these studies in detail in Chapter 5. Here, I will merely supply one demonstration of how a particularly dramatic finding with respect to the speech of one schizophrenic can be interpreted in terms of learning theory.

Laffal, Lenkoski, and Ameen (1956) presented a case of opposite speech, where the patient says "no" when other aspects of the conversation clearly indicate that he means "yes." This patient showed other such examples of opposite speech, as "right" for "wrong," "like" for "hate," and "always" for "never." Laffal et al interpreted this language aberration in terms of psychoanalytic theory to mean that the patient suffered from unacceptable aggressive impulses. In a subsequent article, Staats (1957) suggested that the patient's usual speech made him feel anxious and that his opposite speech consisted essentially of avoidance responses to this anxiety. The question remaining is why the avoidance responses consist of opposites. The explanation comes directly from word association data such as that collected by Carroll, Kjeldergaard, and Carton (1962), who found that contrast or opposite responses often have the greatest strength. Thus, learning theory would explain opposite speech by hypothesizing that the avoidance response that has the greatest strength (given the fact that the patient is inclined to emit a word like "yes") is, in fact, "no."

SUMMARY

Language studies in schizophrenia were presented in two parts: the regulatory function and the communicative function. Experiments dealing with the former used sorting tests, intelligence tests, word association tests, and verbal learning experiments. These experiments were directed at the concept of thought disorder that has been described in many ways: concrete thinking, splitting of associations, tangential thinking, and overinclusiveness thinking (bringing into consideration factors not relevant to the task at hand).

The first approach to the problem of quantifying thought disorder, or, in more concrete terms, dysfunction in the regulatory behavior of language, consists of the assessment of the state of schizophrenic intelligence and its change through the course of the disorder. Since Kraepelin originally ascribed intellectual deterioration to schizophrenia, psychologists naturally sought to quantify this effect by using their standardized intelligence tests. Although some studies show lower intellectual functioning in schizophrenics than in normals, the question of deterioration in the course of the disorder was studied by examining preschizophrenic functioning. These studies have found lower intellectual functioning in preschizophrenics as early as in the second grade. In general, good evidence for deterioration in the intellect of schizophrenics is largely absent. Instead, the evidence points to a lower level of intellectual functioning in the preschizophrenic child than his siblings and his classmates of the same socioeconomic level.

Schizophrenics suffer from a cognitive deficit as usually measured by sorting tests. Various investigators attribute different interpretations to this difficulty, such as concrete thinking, overinclusive thinking, avoidance of unambiguous statements, distractability, and social deficit.

Studies are fairly consistent in showing that word associations given by schizophrenic patients are marked by their idiosyncrasy.

Experiments in verbal learning indicate that schizophrenics have greater difficulty in learning associates of relatively low probability when associates of high probability interfere. These findings are not as consistent as one might wish, however. Evidence of faster forgetting in schizophrenics is stronger and was shown to be consonant with the immediacy hypothesis that states essentially that schizophrenics are prone to be controlled by stimuli more immediate in their environment.

After discussion of the various types of evidence for the concept of thought disorder, a number of criticisms were taken up. Data often given in support of a thought disorder can sometimes be seen as evidence for a perceptual disorder related to the schizophrenic's distribution of his attention, rather than to his associations. Other studies have shown that schizophrenics' tendency to emit idiosyncratic associations is outweighed by the number of ways in which they resemble normals, and that it might be useful to view the schizophrenic disorder in terms of an exaggeration of normal tendencies. The so-called thought disorder also characterizes other diagnostic categories, thus suggesting that it may reflect a general difficulty in getting along with society. While it is relatively easy to demonstrate a deficit in schizophrenic performance, a number of investigators have shown that, given the appropriate conditions, they can improve the functioning of the schizophrenic so that he no longer differs from the normal.

The second part of this chapter took up the communicative function of language. It should be clear that separate discussion of the two functions of language does not imply that they are independent of one another. In fact, a number of the experiments cited showed that the problem-solving dysfunction could be interpreted as a problem in communication between the examiner and the patient, while the problems in communication have often been described in terms of the subject's disordered thought processes. After providing some dramatic examples of schizophrenic speech, I took up a number of objective techniques for the study of schizophrenic speech. The first of these was the method of content analysis that asks whether the patients' utterances or combinations of utterances are diagnostic of schizophrenia.

The second section dealing with schizophrenic speech asked a more basic question about the nature of the responses: Do schizophrenics show less interrelation among their responses than do normals? Such a deficit expresses itself in relatively simple response situations and in the more complicated response sequences of speech. The techniques used to establish this finding include formal analyses such as word sequence and repetition patterns, temporal analysis of patient-examiner interaction and finally, the direct testing for the schizophrenic's ability to communicate by way of the cloze procedure. The last topic in the analysis of speech production dealt with hallucinations and stressed the importance of the patient's own sub-vocal speech in their generation.

The next topic was the analysis of the perception of speech. Again the importance of the sequential response effect was demonstrated. The general findings in this area are that the schizophrenic is unable to take advantage of long-range response-response interrelations. Variation of the physical parameters of the speech to which the schizophrenic had to pay attention, including his own feedback, gave rise to interesting, but not altogether clear results.

Finally, I mentioned the topic of the conditioning of verbal behavior as another approach relevant to the communicative function of speech but postponed detailed discussion to Chapter 5.

CHAPTER THREE

STIMULUS CONTROL

At least two considerations justify the study of sensation and perception in schizophrenia. First of all, it is only logical that psychologists, who traditionally study the effect of stimuli on the responses of normals, should determine the contribution of the stimulus in producing the responses of schizophrenics. The tempting question with regard to schizophrenia is whether the disorder can (or the extent to which it can) be explained on the basis of a defect in the way in which the stimulus is received and/or processed. Second, experiments have suggested that the schizophrenic does not perceive stimuli in the same way as does a normal. In fact, investigators have interpreted the results of many nonperceptual experiments in terms of the way in which schizophrenics respond to stimuli. The notion of overinclusivity, mentioned with respect to the concept of thought disorder, states that schizophrenics respond to more stimuli than do normals.

As we shall see in Chapter 6, the schizophrenic's reaction to stimuli has often been used as a basis for the explanation of the disorder. Salzinger's (1971a, 1971b) immediacy hypothesis assumes that schizophrenics respond to a certain type of stimulus with a higher probability than to others (to temporally and spatially immediate stimuli). Silverman (1964a), reviewing some of the literature relevant to stimulus input, proposes that differences in scanning behavior (sometimes measured by eye movements), could explain the difference between schizophrenics and normals with regard to perceptual tasks. Venables (1964) speaks of two different kinds of stimulus input dysfunctions in schizophrenics, one consisting of a restriction in the attentional field and one consisting of a flooding by many stimulus inputs. Yates (1966) proposes the existence of a basic defect in the *initial* stimulus processing system of the schizophrenic. The stimulus is also important with respect to other theories that will be taken up in Chapter 6.

STIMULUS ATTRACTION

The stimuli to which an organism responds are not a random sample of the environment; on the contrary, the organism orients itself toward or away from stimuli. The frequent description of the schizophrenic as a withdrawn individual suggests that this dimension deserves study.

Silverman (1964a), as already mentioned, posits scanning as the mediating behavior that explains the differences found between schizophrenics and normals in perceptual constancy experiments (see "Perceptual Constancies" below). He claims that the schizophrenic who scans extensively is more likely to underestimate the size of an object whereas the one who scans little tends to overestimate the size. Interesting as this explanation is, Neale and Cromwell (1968) found differences in size estimation in the absence of scanning, under stimulus presentation conditions too short for eye movements to take place.

McReynolds (1963) studied the way in which schizophrenics expose themselves to stimuli. He first showed the patients a series of slides; at a later time he showed some of the same pictures along with a new series of pictures, allowing each subject to determine the length of time he viewed each slide. The most withdrawn schizophrenics spent almost the same amount of time viewing the novel as the familiar pictures; for the other patients, the less withdrawn they were, the greater the length of time they viewed the novel pictures. McReynolds interpreted this to mean that the withdrawn schizophrenic inhibits the input of novel stimuli with a consequent restriction of his range of behavior. Although not statistically significant, the withdrawn schizophrenics tended to make more errors in recognizing which pictures they had viewed previously than the less withdrawn, suggesting a deficit in memory for pictures like that found for verbal behavior (see Chapter 2).

Sidle, Acker, and McReynolds (1963) used a paper and pencil maze as a way of measuring the stimulus-seeking behavior of schizophrenics, normals, and nonschizophrenic psychiatric patients. The subject was given the task of repeatedly going from one point of the maze to another, with alternative routes equally long. The larger the number of different pathways a given subject took, the more stimulus-seeking he was assumed to be.

Schizophrenics showed the least amount of stimulus-seeking, nonschizophrenic patients showed more, and the normals showed the most. This result, like the one above, shows that schizophrenics, or at least some of them, tend to avoid novel stimuli; the schizophrenic's repeated use of fewer different routes is also comparable to the higher rate of repetition of words or guesses in simple guessing situations discussed in Chapter 2.

PERCEPTUAL CONSTANCIES

The concept of constancy described the fact that normally we respond to objects as if they did not change, even though our senses tell us that they do. For example, whether you see a person across the table or at a great distance your judgment of his height remains the same. Given that the basic sensory equipment of schizophrenics appears to be intact and that preservation of constancy is critical to life, investigators have looked for a dysfunction in the more complex perceptual phenomenon of constancy.

Physical Variables

The particular methods used to obtain data on psychophysical functions may relate importantly to the findings made. They may reflect not the subject's sensitivity to the physical stimulus but rather his response bias as controlled by the experimenter and/or self-instructions (Clark, 1966; Clark, Brown, and Rutschmann, 1967). In 1955, Gilinsky had already demonstrated the importance of instructions in perceptual constancy experiments with normals.

Rausch (1952) did the first study in the area of size constancy. He found that paranoid schizophrenics show more constancy than normals (are less influenced by the physical stimuli) while nonparanoid schizophrenics show only a tendency to underconstancy (tend to be more influenced by the physical stimuli) by comparison to the normals. A later study by Hartman (1962) found evidence for overconstancy in delusional schizophrenics, using the apparent size of after-images (an effect that persists after the exciting stimulus is withdrawn, as when you see a bright spot after viewing an intense light for a while) as stimulus material. Lovinger (1956) showed no difference between paranoid and nonparanoid schizophrenics but did demonstrate less constancy for schizophrenics in "poor contact." Still another experiment (Crookes, 1957) found evidence for underconstancy in schizophrenics as compared to normals, neurotics, and psychopaths. The constancy findings in schizophrenia led Weckowicz and Blewett (1959) to investigate the relation of size constancy to abstract thinking; the two types of faults correlate positively. The investigators interpreted the correlation to mean that both tasks reflect a schizophrenic deficit in selecting relevant from irrelevant information.

Johannsen, Friedman, and Liccione (1964) found a deficit in depth perception only in extremely chronic schizophrenics. Two other studies examined constancy from the point of view of distance. Weckowicz, Sommer, and Hall (1958) found that schizophrenics tend toward retinal image perception with respect to distance as they do with respect to size. Furthermore, Kidd (1964) made a similar finding with respect to distance perception through monocular regard (viewed with one eye). Weckowicz (1964) also found that schizophrenics had less constancy than normals and nonschizophrenic psychiatric patients with regard to shape. The results on under-constancy are in agreement with the immediacy hypothesis, assuming that retinal image stimulation is a more immediate stimulus than the more remote stimulus provided by the subject's experience with object constancy.

The constancy effect is not, however, restricted to schizophrenia. Harway and Salzman (1964) found that both schizophrenics and psychotically depressed and hysterically character-disordered patients had more constancy than normals. This experiment also provides evidence for a loss in constancy in the behavior disorders, however. The subjects had to judge the size of a stimulus by comparing it to a standard stimulus. The size judgments for matches that start far below or far above the standard stimulus produced greater discrepancies than those starting closer to the standard. The initial matching stimulus acts, as these authors point out, as an anchor stimulus much as in the weight judgment experiment (Salzinger, 1957) to be described below. The average results of the constancy determination experiments may not adequately reflect this "local" inconstancy. The particular experimental procedure must therefore be examined closely in order to define the exact nature of the determining variable.

Leibowitz and Pishkin (1961) found no difference in size constancy for schizophrenics and normals. Furthermore, Jannucci (1965) compared paranoid, catatonic, and undifferentiated schizophrenics with a normal control group and found the same negative results. How do we explain the discrepancy between these findings and those above? Part of the answer may lie in the population tested, part can be attributed to the experimental techniques used. Apparently, the schizophrenic fault is largest under conditions of minimal cues. This may be the condition in which the schizophrenic's control by immediate stimuli is most damaging to his performance; the maximal cues condition which appears to characterize the negative studies may supply enough immediate stimuli to guide the schizophrenic to make the normal judgment.

Social Variables

Size estimation depends not only on the physical energy variables imping-ing on the subject's sense organs, but also on his past experience with other people. Harris (1957) had normals and two groups of schizophrenics estimate the size of a number of stimuli. He showed each subject a picture and then asked him to adjust the size of a comparison picture to match it, beginning with a larger or smaller initial stimulus. The subject adjusted the size of six different pictures: a "neutral" picture consisting of a tree and a bush, a "dominance" picture, showing the mother telling the boy to do something, an "acceptance" picture, showing the mother giving the boy his favorite drink, an "ignoring" picture showing the mother refusing to read to the child, an "overprotection" picture, showing the mother taking the boy away from what she considered a dangerous game and, finally, a picture of a plain square. The poor premorbid (process) schizophrenics *overestimated* the size of the pictures, including the neutral picture of tree and bush but excluding the square, while the good premorbid (reactive) schizophrenics slighty *underestimated* the size of all the pictures except the neutral one and the square. The normals slightly overestimated the size of all the pictures except the square.

The fact that the neutral picture evoked as much overestimation as the relevant pictures suggests that the mere complexity, rather than the subject matter of the pictures may be the critical variable in the experiment. The complexity hypothesis is also corroborated by the patients' having the same reactions to the mother-child interactions regardless of their positive or negative content. Although the results do not clearly attest to the significance of the social variable, they do provide evidence in favor of the process-reactive distinction: when viewed as one group, schizophrenics do not differ from the normals; when they are divided into process and reactive schi-zophrenics, then these groups differ from the normals, each in a different direction.

A number of studies followed the Harris experiment (Davis, Cromwell, and Held, 1967; Webb, Davis, and Cromwell, 1966; Neale and Cromwell, 1968) and found, like him, that poor premorbid schizophrenics tend to overestimate the size of objects while good premorbids tend to underestimate. Furthermore, the paranoid-nonparanoid classification adds yet another dimension on which it is possible to separate schizophrenics with respect to size estimation, with paranoids tending toward underestimation and nonparanoids toward overestimation. Results related to the content of the pictures being judged for size, however, are less reliable, with various studies finding different pictures leading to significant differences. Since the basic experiment has not been checked with pictures other than those first constructed by Harris, by varying the physical aspects of the pictures while keeping the content the same we cannot determine the exact contribution of the content of the pictures.

The fact of overestimation by one group of schizophrenics and underestimation by another is explained by Silverman (1964a, 1964b), (as mentioned above) by the notion of scanning. The study by Neale and Cromwell (1968), however, showed that the differences in size estimation occur in the absence of possible differences in scanning. Furthermore, Pishkin (Pishkin, 1966; Pishkin, Smith, and Leibowitz, 1962) found no differences between normals and schizophrenics when they controlled the number of illuminations of the stimuli they had to judge in size. Schizophrenics required a larger number of illuminations than normals before they made their judgment. Pishkin suggests that the schizophrenics would have shown a profound deficit in size judgment had they not been given the opportunity for an indefinite number of illuminations. If we view the illuminations as equivalent to the scanning responses, then the lack of difference in size estimation in the face of differences in number of illuminations constitutes added refutation of the importance of scanning behavior.

In a more direct assessment of the social variable, Pishkin (1966) used a stooge to measure the effect of the judgment of another individual. Both normals and schizophrenics were influenced by the stooge, and both more so when the stooge was presented as an aide than as a patient. Schooler and Spohn (1960) showed, using the Asch (1956) procedure (a group of stooges all make obviously incorrect judgments of the same stimuli the subject judges), that even "regressed" schizophrenics were influenced by the judgments of others; however, the schizophrenics' judgments conformed to neither the physical stimulus nor the judgment of the other individuals.

In a study of the accuracy of distance estimation, Kidd (1963) found that schizophrenics place pictures of food and animals as far away from themselves as normals, but place pictures of human beings further away and pictures of nature closer to themselves than do normals. Although holding pictures of human beings at a distance seems to be easily reconcilable with what we know of schizophrenics, it is not equally easy to explain the closer placement of nature pictures. Blumenthal and Meltzof (1967) also employed distance placement as a way of studying perception in schizophrenics. The experimenter placed pairs of cutout figures, pictured in neutral and hostile relationships at different distances from each other, and required normals and schizophrenics to match the distances with the same figures. The nature of the objects and the relationship between them had no *differential* effect on the accuracy with which the schizophrenics placed them. On the other hand, schizophrenics matched all the distances less accurately than normals for immediate recall, with even more inaccuracy for the delay condition.

The authors interpreted the findings as demonstrating the patients' greater degree of influence by contemporary stimuli (see the immediacy hypothesis). In general, we are led to the conclusion that social stimuli in perceptual experiments do not differentiate schizophrenics from normals more clearly than do stimuli in general.

COMPLEX STIMULI

The basic question with respect to complex stimuli is no different than it is with respect to simple stimuli: Is there something about the input of these stimuli which is peculiar to the disorder of schizophrenia?

Physical Stimuli

Brengelmann (1958) asked this question about the schizophrenic's ability to reproduce the location of five different geometric shapes around a central reference point. He also posed the additional question of whether the length of exposure makes a difference. The results demonstrated that schizophrenics make a larger number of errors in reproducing these stimuli than neurotics, when the stimulus is exposed for 30 seconds, but not when exposed for two seconds. Brengelmann explains the different findings by positing an inability in the schizophrenics to maintain a level of preparedness that Shakow (1962) has described as a major set. For the short period of exposure, such a set need not be kept for long and thus the schizophrenic deficit does not show up. This finding also lends itself to interpretation by the immediacy hypothesis, namely that the long exposure allows more opportunity for other immediate stimuli to engage the attention of the schizophrenic than does the short exposure.

Johannsen and Testin (1966), apparently unaware of Brengelmann's experiment, had subjects reproduce the location of a single dot located in a matrix with the aid of grid lines in one condition but not in the other. They found no significant differences between the schizophrenics and normals (with the exception of long-term schizophrenics who differed only on the no-grid lines condition) as would have been predicted by Brengelmann, since they used an exposure time of a fraction of a second only. Johannsen and Testin conclude that the schizophrenic process does not influence this basic kind of perceptual functioning except in extremely chronic patients; they may be right since their stimulus situation was simpler than Brengelmann's, but it would be interesting to repeat their experiment with longer durations.

Gestalt psychology had had a profound influence on the field of perception and even though some of its theoretical implications are no longer the focus of research today, many of its techniques and some of its concepts still inspire experiments. Weckowicz (1960) tested the schizophrenic's ability to separate figure from ground, to use Gestalt theory language. The actual task consists of finding a hidden figure in a drawing, the rendering of which contains extra lines serving to obscure the object being sought. The pictures to be identified in this way included such objects as a glass, a human figure, a clock, and a cup. The experimenter compared the following groups: chronic schizophrenics, acute schizophrenics, nonschizophrenic and non-organic psychiatric patients, organic psychiatric patients, and normals. Normals and nonschizophrenic–nonorganic patients did not differ in ability to find the hidden figure; schizophrenics performed better than the organic patients, but worse than the normals and nonschizophrenic-nonorganic patients; the chronic schizophrenics performed worse than the acute schizophrenics. Differences in intelligence test performance could not account for the differential performance. Weckowicz concluded that schizophrenics are unable to disregard irrelevant information, an effect we have previously noted in other functions as in size constancy and verbal behavior.

Another concept in Gestalt psychology, that of closure, is the tendency to organize perceived objects into "good figures," that is, to see things that are incomplete as whole or complete. McReynolds, Collins, and Acker (1964) presented a group of delusional and nondelusional schizophrenics a series of incomplete pictures and asked the subjects to identify them. Since these pictures not only had some lines left out, but also some additional ones put in, the stimulus material somewhat resembles that of the previous experiment. The results showed that delusional patients attempt to identify a larger number of pictures and are correct on a larger number than the nondelusional patients. The investigators concluded that delusional schizophrenics tend to integrate ambiguous stimuli more than nondelusional schizophrenics. Unfortunately, no data were obtained on normals, thus making it difficult to compare with the above study. It is of interest to note, however, that the acute schizophrenics tested by Weckowicz did have a slightly larger proportion of paranoid schizophrenics and the delusional patients in the Mc-Reynolds study did tend toward a shorter stay in the hospital, tentatively indicating agreement between the studies. Along similar lines, Draguns (1962, 1963) found that schizophrenics tend to make quicker judgments of the identify of blurred pictures than normals and a heterogeneous institutionalized sample of nonpsychotics.

Snyder, Rosenthal, and Taylor (1963) studied closure by having subjects reproduce drawings containing gaps. The schizophrenics showed less closure on the reproduction of the figures than the normals, indicating again that the patients were paying attention to small details, in this case to the gaps, rather than to the whole figure. The authors explained the difference in terms of a deficit in arousal systems of the brain or in reflecting an inability to maintain a major set (see Shakow in Chapter 6).

Verbal Stimuli

Another group of studies deals with the reaction to verbal stimuli. Before asserting that the complexity of the stimuli is responsible for the defect in schizophrenia, we must show that simpler stimuli do not reveal differences between schizophrenics and normals. Ludwig, Wood and Downs (1962) found no difference in pure tone thresholds, although they did find a difference in a tone decay test that determined the lowest intensity a subject can *continue* to hear for a period of one minute. The schizophrenics had a larger percentage of abnormal responses to the decay, that is, the tone had to be raised more than five db (decibel—a unit of loudness) beyond the original threshold value for the subject to hear it for a full minute. This particular finding is interesting, in that it shows once more the schizophrenic's inability to keep his attention directed at a given stimulus (see Brengelmann above). Apparently, giving the schizophrenic a relatively long time period is similar to presenting him with many stimuli and in that way time resembles complexity in effect.

McGhie, Chapman, and Lawson (1965) report schizophrenics to be more distracted than normals by irrelevant stimuli both auditory and visual, when having to listen for digits or letters. In addition, Rappaport (Rappaport, Rogers, Reynolds, and Weinmann, 1966; Rappaport, 1967, 1968) found that interfering voices distract schizophrenics more than normals. Simultaneous voice messages distracted acute schizophrenics most, then chronic schizophrenics, with nonacute schizophrenics almost as little as normals. The defect in acute schizophrenics is attributed to a short-lived acuteness of the disorder, but the lower performance in chronic schizophrenics is attributed to the effect of hospitalization itself.

Another technique for testing the effect of distractability on auditory perception consists of presenting verbal stimuli in the presence of speech noise, a technique that is analogous to the figure ground problem in vision. The results here show that normals withstand the intereference of such speech noise to a greater extent than schizophrenics (Ludwig, Woods, and Downs, 1962; see Fig. 3-1 below). This finding is confirmed by Stilson, Kopell, Vandenbergh, and Downs (1966).

Experiments using simple verbal stimuli in the visual modality arrived at the same general conclusion as the above experiments. McGhie, Chapman, and Lawson (1965) found, with digits and letters as stimuli, that perception could be differentially influenced in schizophrenics by auditory distraction, but not significantly by visual distraction. With respect to the recognition of geometrical forms, however, Stilson and Kopell (1964) and Stilson et al

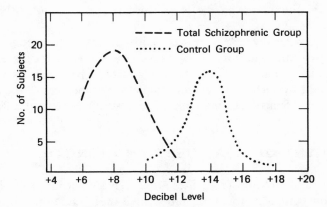

FIGURE 3–1. Signal-to-noise ratios. (Reprinted from A. M. Ludwig, B. S. Wood, and M. P. Downs, "Auditory studies in schizophrenia," *The American Journal of Psychiatry,* volume 119, pp. 122–127, 1962. Copyright 1962, the American Psychiatric Association.)

(1966) found that schizophrenics are more distractable than normals by visual noise.

Using the notion of perceptual defense (essentially avoiding sensing an aversive stimulus), McGinnies and Adornetto (1952) compared schizophrenics and normals on their visual recognition thresholds. They used as stimuli a set of neutral words and a set of taboo words approximately matched in frequency of occurrence in the English language. Both normals and schizophrenics had higher thresholds for the taboo than for the neutral words; schizophrenics also had higher thresholds for both types of words than did the normals. While normals are likely to guess the correct word on the basis of a few letters recognized, the schizophrenics apparently need more of the word before recognition. Of special interest is the schizophrenics' tendency to guess nonsense words more frequently than the normals' and to perserverate with wrong responses.

Orbach (1952) used a similar method with pictures as stimuli. He found that longer exposure times resulted in greater accuracy of description of the pictures for both normals and schizophrenics. However, only the normals continued to increase in detail of description when exposure time reached one second. The schizophrenic's inability to take advantage of this longer exposure time is apparently due to his reaction to repeated presentation of the same picture as if it were new each time. This is so despite having been told the same picture is being shown. Orbach also found that the normals left out significantly fewer details of description than the chronics at all the exposure times; in relation to the acutes, this was true only for the longer exposures. Given enough time for the schizophrenics' attention to be drawn to another stimulus, even the less disordered show their pathology (see Brengelmann above).

Finally, Wilensky (1952) showed that schizophrenics become less accurate in visual and auditory perception following a frustrating experience, while normals remain unaffected by it. The fact that perception is differentially influenced by such variables means that experimenters in the area must rule out possible artifacts in seemingly exclusively perceptual differences.

JUDGMENT OF HEAVINESS AND LENGTH

The visual and auditory modalities are clearly significant in our lives. Less obvious but equally, if not more, important is the modality of proprioception that refers to our perception of movement and location in space. We generally test perception in this modality using the psychophysical method of single stimuli or absolute judgment, and it is thus appropriate here to mention, in addition, some experiments on the absolute judgment of space or length of line.

Rosenbaum (1971) has suggested that a disturbance in proprioceptive feedback underlies the schizophrenic disorder. Poor feedback of this kind might well serve to interfere with so-called central integrating systems. Rado (1953) put forth a form of this hypothesis and Salzinger (1957) tested it finding no evidence in favor of it, at least in acute schizophrenics. Rosenbaum, Flenning, and Rosen (1965) retested the hypothesis on two groups of chronic schizophrenics; one was kept on maintenance medication and the other, somewhat more disturbed, was without drugs for six months. These investigators tested the proprioceptive deficit hypothesis, using light weights, on the assumption that the heavier weights in the Salzinger study might have obscured the proprioceptive deficit through the input of more intense stimulation. Rosenbaum et al's data bear out this explanation in that the performance of the chronic schizophrenics approaches that of the normals when subjects are presented with the heavier weights but is very much worse when the weights are lighter (see Fig. 3-2). As further evidence for the proprioceptive deficit hypothesis, Rosenbaum (1971) states that other sensory modalities, such as audition, do not differentiate schizophrenics from normals at either high or low intensity levels. A forearm flexion test, developed by Wayne Herron (and reported by Rosenbaum), showed that the schizophrenic has greater difficulty in flexing his arm at an angle to match the flexing of his other arm than does the normal. Rosenbaum's proprioceptive hypothesis is certainly very interesting; however, the fact that schizophrenics show deficits in other sensory modalities (see Ludwig et al, 1962, for their differences in the tone decay test) and that they show improvement in those other modalities as a function of increase in the

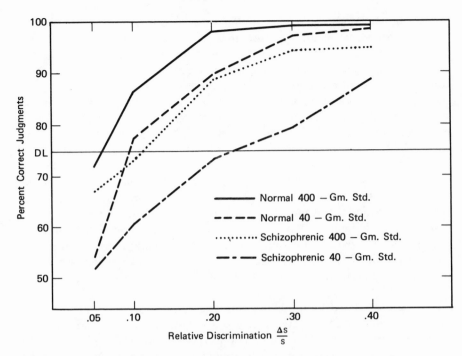

FIGURE 3–2. Weight discrimination of normals and schizophrenics at two intensities. (Courtesy of G. Rosenbaum, F. Flenning, and H. Rosen, "Effects of weight intensity on discrimination thresholds of normals and schizophrenics," *Journal of Abnormal Psychology, 70,* **1965, pp. 446–450. Copyright 1965 by the American Psychological Association and reproduced by permission.)**

intensity of stimulation (for example, King, 1954) suggests that the proprioceptive deficit is merely one deficit belonging to a more general class; that deficit relates to the amount of control that stimuli exert over the behavior of schizophrenics.

Salzinger (1957) examined the ability of schizophrenics to retain constancy in weight judgment. It is well known that the judgment of heaviness of weights shifts in reaction to an anchor weight, that is, the same weight judged after lifting a very heavy weight (anchor) feels lighter than when judged after lifting a very light weight (anchor). In the experiment, Salzinger instructed the schizophrencis and normals to resist the effect of the anchor when making their judgments. The results shows that the schizophrenics shifted more in response to the heavy anchor than did the normals, that is, they were not able to retain object constancy as well as the normals. In terms of the immediacy hypothesis, the schizophrenic responded more to the immediate stimulus of the anchor weight than the remote stimulus of the experimenter's instruction.

A followup study by Wurster (1965) replicated the effect of the anchor, with schizophrenics shifting more than normals. In another condition, however, he substituted an illusory weight for one of the stimuli in the series. This weight produces a feeling of greater heaviness than the standard weight in normals. The anchor stimulus used in the first part of the experiment was paired with each stimulus to be judged; the illusory weight, on the other hand, occurred as often as the other weights, and therefore had to exert itself through its pooled effect over time. The results showed that the schizophrenics, like the normals, were affected by the illusion, thereby overestimating the heaviness of the weight, but that they were not, unlike the normals, affected in their judgment of the remaining stimuli. We can summarize these results as follows: when the anchor stimulus precedes each stimulus to be judged, it interferes with the schizophrenic's ability to retain constancy of judgment; when the anchor stimulus (the illusory weight) appears only as part of a series of stimuli by changing the appearance of one of the stimuli only, it evokes a different judgment while other, more remote, stimuli remain unaffected. This result is consonant with the immediacy hypothesis.

Using a modified method of limits technique, Boardman et al (1962) compared schizophrenics' and normals' ability to judge the length of lines as a function of the initial comparison stimulus. They found that acute and, to a lesser extent, chronic schizophrenics were affected by the anchor of the initial comparison stimuli, again providing evidence for the power of the immediate stimulus over the behavior of the schizophrenic.

A number of investigators (Chambers, 1956; Cooper, 1960; Dillon (1961a) have used length of line as stimulus material. According to the three studies, normals are more accurate than schizophrenics. In addition, Dillon (1961b) found that the Mueller-Lyer illusion affects schizophrenics more than normals. On the other hand, Orme, Smith, and Berry (1968) showed that schizophrenics did not differ from psychiatric nonschizophrenics in the degree of the illusion; furthermore, hospitalized schizophrenics and hospitalized nonschizophrenics differed significantly from a group of nonhospitalized nonschizophrenics. They concluded that the greater susceptibility to the illusion is attributable to the severity of the illness, rather than to schizophrenia in particular. The effect of hospitalization could also play a role in all of this, although in a recent study by Johannsen and O'Connell (1965) perception of schizophrenics did not vary with length of hospitalization.

TEMPORAL DISCRIMINATION

The dimension of time has always been of special interest in psychopathology;

the patient's orientation with respect to time is used as one criterion for the severity of illness. The experimental approach has yielded both successes and failures with respect to the differentiation of schizophrenics from normals and from other types of patients. In 1950, Clausen failed to differentiate schizophrenics from normals, even though he used three different methods of measuring time judgment. More recently, Warm, Morris, and Kew (1963) failed to find differences in time estimation among normals, neurotics, and schizophrenics.

Beginning in 1956, Lhamon and Goldstone began a formidable research program on the "internal clock" of the schizophrenic. The first finding was one of overestimation in the schizophrenic. Later studies (Lhamon, Goldstone, and Goldfarb, 1965; Goldstone, 1967; Webster, Goldstone, and Webb, 1962; Wright, Goldstone, and Boardman, 1962) showed that schizophrenics underestimate time intervals under some conditions, and under others their estimates do not differ from those of normals. In a summary of these studies, Goldstone (1968) concluded that no systematic alteration in time estimation per se could be demonstrated for schizophrenics. The results could, however, be explained along the same lines as those used for the estimation of length of lines or heaviness of weights in that the schizophrenics proved to be more susceptible to anchors than normals. Goldstone (1968) also viewed the temporal data he collected over the years in terms of intra-subject variability and found schizophrenics to be consistently more variable than normals and than other patients. Of interest in the context of anchor effects is his finding that extraserial anchors not only reduced the variability of the schizophrenic, but did so to the normal level.

Estimation of long time intervals showed that schizophrenics over-estimate the length of their interviewing time (Rabin, 1957). A later study (Orme, 1966) however, found a trend in the opposite direction. A closer analysis showed that paranoids tend to overestimate whereas nonparanoids underestimate the time interval. Since the first study provided no breakdown into subgroups, no further comparisons of the studies are possible. Estimates of filled-time intervals, however, are clearly sensitive to a larger number of extraneous variables than estimates of short intervals (discussed above), the exact content of which can be more easily controlled.

SUMMARY

Investigation of the kind of stimulus control that is effective with a schizophrenic is basic in the search for the cause of the peculiarity of his behavior. Psychologists using this approach have often assumed that unusualness in the response to stimuli implies a biological deficit; in fact, however, peculiar responses to stimuli may be caused by environmental as well as biological causes. In any case, many theories of schizophrenia have appealed to the aberrant reception of stimuli.

Schizophrenics differ from normals in terms of the kinds of stimuli to which they expose themselves. Furthermore, unlike normals, schizophrenics fail to discriminate between new and old stimuli; they act as if all stimuli were new to them.

Given the fact that schizophrenics have no basic sensory deficit, the question has been raised as to whether they have a deficit in perceptual constancy. Although the evidence is not as consistent as desirable, it does indicate that schizophrenics have difficulty in retaining constancies, showing either too little constancy or too much depending, apparently, on the particular subgroup of schizophrenia being tested. Since the subgroups are not always reliably identified, these results cannot be wholly accepted without further verification. The investigation of social variables with respect to the perceptual constancy experiments has not proved to be particularly helpful in differentiating schizophrenics from normals.

Complex stimuli proved particularly useful in differentiating schizoprenics from normals, the complexity apparently revealing the schizophrenic's basic distractability or tendency to respond to the most immediate stimuli independent of their role in the task at hand. Experiments in this section also showed that schizophrenics have more difficulty in responding correctly on a perceptual task when given a longer period of exposure to a stimulus. They also have greater difficulty in finding a hidden figure and they pay more attention to details unrelated to the whole configuration. Furthermore, while they show no difficulty with pure tone thresholds, they show a deficit in ability to continue hearing the same low level tone. Further experiments show that schizophrenics are unable to concentrate in the face of different types of visual and auditory noise.

Experiments on the judgment of heaviness and length exposed the schizophrenic's tendency to be controlled by immediate anchor stimuli. Data on proprioceptive stimulation were interpreted as being due to control by the interaction of the immediacy and the intensity of stimuli.

The final topic dealt with temporal discrimination. Although early studies found different time estimation behavior in schizophrenics and other populations, this difference was partly a function of the particular experimental procedures employed rather than simply a function of a schizophrenic-normal difference. Nevertheless, these procedures corroborated the schizophrenic's susceptibility to the influence of immediate temporal stimuli in the form of anchors. With respect to long-time interval estimates, the literature is too sparse to come to any definite conclusion.

CHAPTER FOUR

PSYCHOMOTOR BEHAVIOR

The study of psychomotor behavior represents the other term of the stimulus-response equation that we began to examine in the preceding chapter.
The basic assumption underlying much, if not most, of the research in this
area is that the basic biological deficit in schizophrenia will show itself in the
behavior that King (1968) tells us lies somewhere between reflex behavior,
which interests the neurologist, and more complex perceptuomotor behavior, which is influenced by perceptual and verbal factors and is typically
of interest to the clinician. King claims that behavior belonging to this class
is relatively uncontaminated by cultural and social factors. His emphasis
is on fine motor behavior, making it possible to measure the speed and
accuracy of movement in preference to its strength.

SOME VARIABLES THAT AFFECT PSYCHOMOTOR
BEHAVIOR

Here we will assume that psychomotor behavior is relatively independent
of cultural factors, learning, intelligence, and socioeconomic status, and
present some of the data and arguments demonstrating the influence of
biological factors. King (1954, 1960, 1968) is the principal source for the
material in this section. Psychomotor behavior is said to depend upon age,
sex, and a rather large genetic component as shown by McNemar (1933).

Simple psychomotor functioning presents signs of brain injury even when neurological motor tests do not. Motor responses, such as simple reaction time and tapping rate, reveal a slowing down in such individuals. Brain damage appears to affect speed of response more than does depressive mood in patients. Brain operations such as frontal and nonfrontal lobectomy, and superior and orbital topectomy cause some retardation in speed of movement. Separation of the two cerebral hemispheres by sectioning the corpus callosum in human beings has resulted in a profound increase in reaction time. Electrical stimulation of the human septal brain, on the other hand, has resulted in the speeding up of such basic psychomotor functions as tapping rate. It is interesting to note that while the psychomotor tests are sensitive to these brain injuries and operations, the more complex psychological tests such as the Rorschach and word association test are not. King (1968) also presents some interesting data on social delinquents who volunteered to be injected by taraxein, (Heath, et al, 1958) a substance said to induce schizophrenialike behavior. He found that a perceptual threshold, critical flicker fusion (the rate at which an intermittent light appears to fuse), was insensitive to taraxein while fine psychomotor behavior, which requires no less cooperation than the critical flicker fusion test, was very sensitive to it. Furthermore, the psychomotor behavior did not change in response to a saline solution placebo condition.

The use of psychomotor behavior to assess the effect of drugs has been a rather fruitful area of research. To take but one example (Orzack, Kornetsky and Freeman, 1967), regular administration of carphenazine, a phenothiazine, reduced the number of errors that chronic schizophrenics made on a continuous performance test. In that test, the subject must react as rapidly as possible to the occurrence of "0" inserted at random among the flashing of other numbers. As in the case of brain injury, a cognitive task, involving the coding of symbols, did not show the effect of the drug. One final piece of evidence for the association of psychomotor behavior with the biology of the organism comes from Callaway (1965). The latency of brightness judgments varies with the EEG alpha cycle (brain wave type). Furthermore, the autonomic cardiovascular cycle influences reaction time independently of the stimulus modality by affecting the response itself.

REACTION TIME

The history of psychomotor studies of schizophrenia is long indeed, going back to Kraepelin who studied the so-called work curve of the schizophrenic. Donders worked with the reaction time of normals as far back as 1865. With respect to schizophrenia, experiments in reaction time began a steady flow of papers when Huston, Shakow and Riggs (1937) found that schizophrenics are slower in responding to stimuli than are normals. Such findings have been confirmed repeatedly since then (for example, by Rodnick, and Shakow, 1940; Shakow, 1946) and the deficient behavior in reaction time has been interpreted in terms of the concept of set, that is, readiness to respond. The theory holds that the schizophrenic suffers from an inability to hold his set longer than a few seconds, with the consequence that he is less ready to respond when the time comes. King (1954) discovered the basic finding to be as true of simple reaction time as of disjunctive reaction time (where the subject had to respond to one key when one stimulus is sensed and to another key when a different stimulus is sensed). Normals respond much faster than chronic schizophrenics and somewhat faster than the so-called subacute schizophrenics (pseudoneurotic schizophrenics). Of added interest is the fact that the simple and the disjunctive discrimination tasks distinguished the groups equally well from each other. Karras (1967) found that both types of reaction time to visual stimuli (King employed auditory stimuli) were slower for schizophrenics than for nonpsychiatric patients. Because the schizophrenics' performance is not proportionately worse for the two-choice than for the single-choice situation, Karras concluded, as did King before him, that these data contradict the hypothesis that schizophrenics are particularly slow at processing stimulus data.

Physical Variables

Since reaction time is a response to a particular stimulus, an important question to ask is what happens if that stimulus is varied in intensity? King (1962) compared schizophrenics with normals on tones varying from 25 through 35 to 50 db. Normals' reaction time decreased with an increase in intensity, but the schizophrenics' decreased even more. Grisell and Rosenbaum (1964) obtained a similar result for a series of tones ranging from 15 db to just below the pain threshold (approximately 90 db). In neither case did the schizophrenic reaction time drop to the normal level. In an effort to determine whether a combination of intensity of stimulus and a massing of trials could speed up reaction time, Crider, Maher, and Grinspoon (1965) used tones ranging from 75 to 95 db, presenting them from once every 15 seconds to once every 5 seconds. These investigators presented stimuli at three sensory input levels (low input = 75 db at 15 second intervals, medium input = 75 db at 5 seconds or 95 db at 15 seconds, and high input = 95 db at 5 seconds). Although good premorbid schizophrenics (reactive) did not differ from normals at any sound intensity, poor premorbid schizophrenics (process) were slower in their response at the lower input levels, improving sufficiently at the high input level, so that they no longer differed significantly from either good premorbids or normals (see Fig. 4-1).

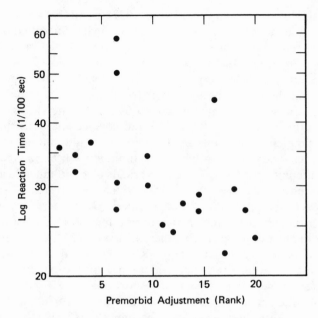

FIGURE 4–1. Relationship of reaction time scores to level of premorbid adjustment. (Courtesy of A. Crider, B. Maher, and L. Grinspoon, "The effect of sensory input on the reaction time of schizophrenic patients of good and poor premorbid history," *Psychonomic Science, 2,* **1965, pp. 47–48. Reprinted with permission.**)

Another variable related to reaction time is the preparatory interval— the time from the warning signal to the presentation of the stimulus to which the subject must respond. Rodnick and Shakow (1940) found for schizophrenics that shorter preparatory intervals produced faster responding when embedded in regular rather than irregular series of intervals but that the reverse was true for longer intervals. Normal subjects, on the other hand, were consistently faster on the regular series, with the exception of preparatory intervals of very long duration. The authors took these differences into account in devising a set index that discriminated, *post hoc,* perfectly between a group of schizophrenics and normals. A later study (Rosenthal et al, 1960) successfully related the same set index to a rating of the relative mental health of a group of schizophrenics.

In a followup of the finding on preparatory intervals, Zahn, Rosenthal, and Shakow (1961) found that at least two factors determine reaction time, the actual length of the preparatory interval, and the order in which other intervals are presented. They therefore presented the preparatory intervals in ascending or descending order of duration. The ascending series of preparatory intervals shows the earlier reported effect for schizophrenics, that longer preparatory intervals cause longer reaction time when part of a regular series. The descending series of preparatory intervals, however, gave rise to much longer reaction times in schizophrenics for the long *and* the short preparatory intervals, suggesting that the longer preparatory intervals not only interfered with the functioning of the schizophrenic on those specific trials, but that the effect of the slow reaction times for the longer preparatory intervals carried over to the shorter preparatory intervals.

The same investigators (Zahn, Rosenthal, and Shakow, 1963) examined the effect of the longer preparatory intervals directly upon the succeeding shorter preparatory intervals' reaction times and found that, indeed, the effect of the preceding preparatory interval was greater for schizophrenics than for normals. This showed itself through a greater lengthening of reaction time in schizophrenics than in normals because of the preceding preparatory interval. The preparatory interval prior to the immediately preceding one had no discernible effect, indicating again the importance of immediacy in accounting for schizophrenic responses.

Another interesting parameter of reaction time is the phenomenon of modality shift (change of stimulation from one sensory organ to another). Sutton et al (1961) had subjects (normals and chronic schizophrenics) respond to whichever of four stimuli occurred (red light, green light, high tone, or low tone) by lifting a finger. In addition to finding the usual slower reaction time in chronic schizophrenics, they came across a further slowing down of reaction time when the preceding stimulus differed from the current one in modality. In a followup of their experiment, Sutton and Zubin (1965) replicated the findings on modality shift with a group of recently hospitalized schizophrenics, although the significant differences were limited to the reaction times to sound. They extended the finding to a choice reaction time experiment; again they found, for sound stimuli, that a stimulus following a stimulus of another modality caused further slowing down of reaction time in schizophrenics than in normals. Finally, Kriegel and Sutton (1968) equated the light and sound intensities on a response criterion and found a slower reaction for both light and sound stimuli that follow a stimulus of a different modality.

In a modification of the original modality shift experiment, Kristofferson (1967) presented sound and light stimuli simultaneously and had subjects make a simple response to whichever of the two terminated first. Normals and schizophrenics were significantly different from one another both in conditions when subjects were informed which stimulus would stop first as well as when they were not given this information. Furthermore, schizophrenics reacted more slowly when uncertain than when certain about which stimulus was going to go off first in comparison to the normals, thus again showing the schizophrenic's greater difficulty in switching between modalities. Finally, she made the same comparisons as Sutton et al, that is, reaction times to stimuli the same as those on the preceding trial with reaction times to stimuli different from those on the preceding trial. She found the same results, although the modality shift did not as effectively distinguish normals from schizophrenics as did the certainty-uncertainty difference.

Reinforcement Effects

Despite our earlier claim about the relative imperviousness of simple psychomotor behavior to influences such as learning, given the proper circumstances, we can demonstrate the effect of reinforcement. King (1954) showed that the little learning that takes place does not differentiate the chronic or the acute schizophrenic from the normal. Furthermore, the learning necessary to do the task takes place in a few trials. However, King's learning situation actually occurs under conditions of extinction, that is, all the subject gets is practice; he receives no explicit feedback that might serve as a reinforcement, either positive or negative. Furthermore, Shakow (1946) related such variables as degree of cooperation on the task to a simple auditory reaction time task, obtaining a correlation of $+.45$, and to a discrimination task using visual reaction time, obtaining a correlation of $+.61$. In other words, variables in addition to psychomotor ability are involved in psychomotor behavior.

In 1957, Stotsky tested the extent to which the deficit in reaction time (slower responses in schizophrenics) is an organic aspect of schizophrenia, and the extent to which it is a motivational deficit or an inability to retain set as Shakow views it. The reaction time tasks were the ones used by King (1954), with the exception that the experimental group of schizophrenics received a special motivational session with their therapist (having first established that the patient in question had a positive relationship with his therapist). In that session, the therapist praised the patient's performance in the first part of the experiment, and urged him to do still better in the next part of the experiment. During the course of the experiment, the investigator told these patients that they were doing well 10 times. He gave the control subjects no feedback, nor did they have a special session with their therapist. The experimeter who knew the normal subjects before the experiment took experiment took place, gave them direct encouragement in addition to the 10 positive reinforcements. Positive reinforcement improved the performance of both the normals and the schizophrenics in excess of that produced by practice without the explicit reinforcement and motivating session. Nevertheless, the improvement of the patients did not bring their performance up to the level of the normals. These results suggest that even if there is an important organic base to schizophrenia it is not the only factor deter-

mining the performance deficit since a relatively short period of encouragement and a small number of reinforcements can significantly attenuate this
deficit.

Berkowitz (1964) followed up Stotsky's experiment by preceding the
experimental situation with three different types of conditions: in the first,
the experimenter tested the patient immediately after meeting him; in the
second—the "rebuff" situation—the experimenter held three interview
sessions before the experiment and acted in an aloof manner, keeping his interactions with the patient to a minimum; finally in the third—the "warmth"
condition—he acted in a warm manner and did all he could to encourage
interaction of a friendly kind in the course of the three interviews. He reinforced all subjects by praising their performance every four trials. Only
the schizophrenics who had been in the warmth condition had a significant
deficit in reaction time performance. They differed not only from the normals
in the same condition but also from other schizophrenics who were tested
after the rebuff or the no-contact condition. Berkowitz explained that the
warmth condition is like the satiation condition in the Gewirtz and Baer
(1958) study. The patients were essentially satiated by the warmth condition
but put on social deprivation under the other conditions. The Berkowitz
experiment suggests that the previous studies might have produced the
deficits they were trying to measure. Stotsky demonstrates that the performance of the schizophrenics was improved because of the direct reinforcement given for appropriate behavior, and that reinforcement was more
effective when given after a period of deprivation of social reinforcement
than when given after a period of social reinforcement satiation.

Fontana and Klein (1968) conducted a further experiment supporting
the motivation explanation. These investigators attributed the increase
in reaction time to the interaction of the hospital atmosphere and the way
in which the patient presents himself to the staff in order to stay or leave the
hospital. They demonstrated the effect by using an explicit evaluation condition in which patients were compared to other patients in their performance
with the result that the deficit increased or decreased depending on the
particular conditions.

In a review of studies of schizophrenia, Garmezy (1966) concluded
with two generalizations: schizophrenics appear to have a greater sensitivity
to psychologically noxious stimuli and a lessened sensitivity to positive
social reinforcements. A number of experiments on reaction time relate to
these generalizations. Rosenbaum, Mackavey, and Grisell (1957) compared
schizophrenics and normals on a task in which the subject had to depress
a key as fast as possible on seeing a light signal and to release it on hearing
a buzzer. In the group given negative reinforcement, the key that had to be
released was electrified when the buzzer sounded, thus setting up essentially

an escape conditioning paradigm. The schizophrenics were consistently slower in their reaction times when the buzzer alone was used (the so-called social motivation situation); the introduction of the negative reinforcement, however, reduced the reaction time for all groups and, in the case of most male schizophrenics, brought their performance to the normal level; a similar but not statistically significant trend pertained to the females.

Goodstein, Guertin, and Blackburn (1961) found that social motivation (despite Garmezy's statement to the contrary) in the form of verbal praise or rebuke influenced the reaction time of schizophrenics (and of normals); the failure condition (where the experimenter told the subject he is doing badly) caused the largest improvement. Klein, Cicchetti, and Spohn (1967) tested the effect of negative reinforcement in the form of evaluative comments made by the experimenter contingent on the patient's behavior. The schizophrenics did not differ at all from the normals, thus showing that, at least under some conditions, reinforcement can completely attenuate the reaction time deficit. Of added interest is that these investigators found no evidence for differential response patterns as a function of the different premorbid histories when the negative reinforcement contingency was effective (see Chapter 1 for the discussion of process versus reactive schizophrenia).

I shall refer to one other set of studies in this context. The issue concerns itself with whether the effect of aversive stimulation in reducing the reaction time of schizophrenics is due to arousal or reinforcement. Lang (1959) concluded that the improvement of performance of schizophrenics depended upon the dynamogenic effect of aversive stimulation, that is, on its increasing the arousal or alertness of the patient. Karras (1962), in a clear contrast of the two interpretations, concluded that reinforcement was the correct interpretation. He demonstrated that those patients who were given an opportunity to escape an aversive stimulus (a very loud sound) had the shortest reaction time, those who could escape a less intense sound had a longer reaction time and did not differ significantly from the control group that had no aversive stimulus, those in a noncontingent, high stimulation group (the loud sound was on throughout the experiment and subjects could not escape it) reacted more slowly than the above mentioned groups and, finally, those in a noncontingent medium-sound group were the slowest of all. In other words, schizophrenic reaction time improves when the patient can escape an aversive stimulus, that is, when the reinforcement is contingent on his reaction time. The effect of aversive stimulation per se, without the possibility of escape, increases the reaction time.

In a rejoinder, Lang and Buss (1965) make the point that since Karras' noncontingent medium stimulation group performed worse than his noncontingent high stimulation group, the stimulation by itself did have an arousing function. Furthermore, they contend that Lang's (1959) pairing of the stimulation sound with the light stimulus, to which the subjects had to respond, focused their attention appropriately, thus improving reaction time. These discussions show that one cannot talk of a general arousal function but that one must talk specifically about particular contingent stimuli; stimuli may evoke an observing response (the way in which the Lang experiment used the aversive stimulus) or may reinforce a response (the way in which Karras used the aversive stimulus).

We are led to the conclusion that testing under one set of conditions does not insure against the possibility that a different set of conditions might produce different results. Thus, the general finding that schizophrenics have longer reaction times than normals is correct only under the condition of no feedback, the condition that investigators most frequently assume allows the measurement of the biological substrate of schizophrenia. This is actually a condition of extinction. Many investigators who have found an improvement from this extinction condition to a reinforcement contingency condition have assumed that the schizophrenic needs some *extra* motivation in the form of reinforcement to reach a normal level of performance.

Another explanation is also possible, however. Given the fact (to antici-pate the chapter on behavior theory) that schizophrenics extinguish faster than normals (Salzinger and Pisoni, 1960), we would expect faster extinction in schizophrenics than normals in reaction time as well. In other words, longer reaction times reflect differences in rate of extinction. Furthermore, on the basis of the immediacy hypothesis, when immediate guiding stimuli in the form of feedback or reinforcement are lacking, the schizophrenic's behavior is guided by other, probably unrelated stimuli that would then, of course, interfere with his efficient performance.

Correlates of Reaction Time

Investigators using psychomotor tests, and particularly reaction time tests, are of course interested in relating their data to other aspects of schi-zophrenic functioning. Goldberg, Schooler, and Mattson (1966) found that reaction time measures were significantly correlated to symptoms of with-drawal but not to paranoid symptoms. Nevertheless, auditory hallucinations, which are often viewed as paranoid symptoms, correlated quite consistently with reaction time measures. Raskin (1967) also showed positive correlations between the magnitude of auditory hallucinations and reaction time during a distraction condition, for example, a tape recorded conversation playing in a low volume could be heard by the patient while he was responding in the experiment. The conversation acted either to distract the patient directly or possibly to produce some hallucinations that, in turn, distracted him.

Using a reaction time situation without any special feedback, Crider,

Grinspoon, and Maher (1965) found a correlation of + .62 between ranked premorbid adjustment and log reaction time (reaction time decreased with an increase in premorbid adjustment). The reader should take note that this finding is not at variance with the Klein, Cicchetti, and Spohn (1967) study cited above, since the relationship between premorbid history and reaction time was eliminated only when a reinforcement contingency was in effect. This is but another bit of evidence showing that we can attenuate psychopathological behavior by the use of immediate feedback contingent on the behavior of the schizophrenic.

Finally, some investigators have used psychomotor tests in an attempt to predict outcome of illness. To take but one example, Weaver and Brooks (1964) showed consistent differences in the reaction times of patients who were in the hospital and those who were out of the hospital by the end of a two-year study. Weaver and Brooks rank-ordered the reaction times of four groups of chronic schizophrenics in the following way: those out of the hospital and not chosen for rehabilitation performed best; those who were out of the hospital and were chosen for rehabilitation were next best; those who were chosen for rehabilitation but who were still in the hospital were next; and those patients not chosen for rehabilitation and who were still in the hospital performed worst. This experiment thus provides the possibility of using a reaction time measure for predicting the schizophrenic's performance through the course of a rehabilitation program.

OTHER PSYCHOMOTOR TECHNIQUES

Yates (1960) and King (1960, 1968) provide more extensive descriptions of the measurement of psychomotor behavior in schizophrenics. It might be well to mention two other measures, however. King (1954) used speed of tapping as a measure of psychomotor dysfunction and, like Shakow (1946) before him, found this particular technique to distinguish schizophrenics from normals; in addition, he found that this task distinguished different degrees of psychopathology. The simplicity of the test, requiring only a stereotyped wrist movement makes it a good candidate for use as a diagnostic instrument.

Using the Purdue Pegboard as a test for manual and finger dexterity, he obtained a measure relatively independent of reaction time and tapping speed. The three measures together permitted him a means of describing a general motor deficit in schizophrenia. Stotsky (1957) also used the Purdue Pegboard. It is of interest to note that the effect of practice (without reinforcement) improved the performance of schizophrenics on the Purdue Pegboard more than that of normals, but that practice with reinforcement produced a smaller increment of performance in the schizophrenics than in the normals, suggesting the importance of the complexity of the response variable. It is possible that with a more complex task, the experimenter must administer the feedback more carefully, that is, he must make it contingent on particular parts of the performance or he will condition inappropriate aspects of the behavior, with the result that reinforcement might be counterproductive. The fact that the schizophrenics improve less than the normals under these conditions suggests that the immediacy of the reinforcement effect on complex behavior is such as to leave the patient open to the conditioning of inappropriate responses.

SUMMARY

Although the assessment of the psychomotor behavior of the schizophrenic does not constitute a common approach to such patients, some very interesting research has been done in this area. Generally, the research may be considered to revolve about the question of the extent to which the abnormality can be ascribed to a basic psychomotor deficit, and the extent to which it can be ascribed to a stimulus or a motivational deficit producing a motor deficit as a secondary effect only.

Although investigators working in this area have emphasized physical variables as most critical in determining psychomotor behavior, other investigators have pointed out the importance of motivational factors. In fact, some of these motivational variables have turned out to be so important that they have modified the classical finding of a slower reaction time in schizophrenics.

Most of the discussion of this chapter dealt with the reaction time technique reflecting not only its simplicity but also its popularity. In addition to the success of psychomotor techniques in distinguishing schizophrenics from normals, they have enjoyed at least some success in differentiating among various kinds of schizophrenics. Motor tests have been shown to reflect premorbid history, to be potentially useful as a prognostic index, and to relate as well to some specific symptoms.

|| *CHAPTER FIVE* ||

THE BEHAVIOR THEORY APPROACH

In the past, a chapter such as this would have been entitled "Learning," and the material would have consisted of comparisons of the rate of acquisition and extinction of different types of responses in schizophrenics and normals. Since then, however, research in learning has extended its province to the problem of the maintenance of behavior. One of the complicated issues that we must keep in mind in the investigation of schizophrenia is that the process of acquisition and the process of maintenance need not be a function of the same mechanism. In other words, the issue is no longer only whether, or even to what extent, schizophrenic behavior is learned but instead how this peculiar behavior is maintained, independent of its beginning (whether it be by learning, by neurological insult, by single traumatic experience, or by biochemical dysfunction).

In addition, it has recently become clear that a large number of types of responses formerly thought to be unmodifiable are conditionable (Miller, 1969). Heart rate and evoked potential (brain waves in response to a particular stimulus) number among these physiological responses. Under these circumstances it is difficult to continue to talk of a physiological substrate of behavior when that very substrate can itself be modified by the same variables as the behavior it is supposed to underlie.

112

THE PLACE OF BEHAVIOR THEORY IN THE STUDY OF SCHIZOPHRENIA

Behavior is a function of its consequences, that is, it varies as a function of the consequences produced by that behavior in the past. It is reinforced in the presence of certain stimuli called discriminative stimuli and is left unreinforced in the presence of certain other stimuli. This means that given stimuli become the occasions for the emission of various classes of behavior and, therefore, certain kinds of behavior are more likely to occur in some experimental situations than in others. Idiosyncratic life histories contribute further to response variance since different people (independent of whether or not they are schizophrenic) have been conditioned in different ways to different stimuli. Finally, to take but one additional important aspect of behavior theory, stimuli formerly neutral become conditioned reinforcers through their association with primary reinforcers. What constitutes a conditioned reinforcer for one person may not function in that way for another, and what functions as a positive reinforcer for one person may function as a negative reinforcer for another. Any attempt to discover a difference between schizophrenics and normals or between schizophrenics and other abnormal behavior groups must take into account the effect of the variables of behavior theory. In the last chapter, we pointed out the folly of viewing schizophrenic responding on a reaction time task as a basic motor deficit without considering the exact conditions under which the measurement is taken. A difference between normals and schizophrenics was absent when a powerful reinforcement contingency was in effect and appeared only when the reinforcement contingency was eliminated. This is the methodological rationale for taking into account behavior theory variables.

The second set of reasons for looking into behavior theory with respect to schizophrenia is substantive: Is there a basic learning defect in schizophrenia? How can one best measure it? Do schizophrenics react differently to schedules of reinforcement than do normals? What is the effect of the delay of reinforcement gradient for schizophrenics as compared to normals? What single learning task or group of learning tasks is best suited to answer these and other questions concerning behavior theory variables?

The third reason for looking at behavior theory in relation to schizophrenia is that we cannot ignore it. We do not yet have enough information to determine whether schizophrenia is a product of learning, disease, or both. If we suspect learning, then surely we must look to behavior theory. If the original cause is a disease process, then we must still look to behavior theory, for behavior is multiply determined (variables that maintain behavior may differ from those that originate it), and an abnormality that is positively reinforced by the surrounding environment (society or family) will have a different fate from one that is not. No matter what the cause of schizophrenia, a full understanding of it will not be achieved unless we also understand the interaction of that cause and the laws of behavior theory.

Finally, behavior theory is relevant to schizophrenia in that it prescribes a therapeutic method. In recent years, behavior modification has been applied to good effect on the wards of state hospitals. In the past, such wards have given patients custodial care and prevented them from getting into trouble. Analysis in terms of behavior theory shows that the prevailing conditions on the wards have reinforced the pathological withdrawn behavior thought to be so characteristic of schizophrenia. By making desirable activities and objects, which used to be presented on an arbitrary basis, available on a contingent basis, investigators have shown that they can eliminate or at least modify abnormal behavior of long standing.

Modification of behavior takes place according to two conditioning paradigms. The first we have been discussing: it is called operant conditioning and is effective with behavior that operates upon the environment. The other design for the modification of behavior is called respondent or Pavlovian conditioning, and consists of the transformation of an initially neutral stimulus into a conditioned stimulus (a stimulus that elicits a response) by pairing it with an unconditioned stimulus.

OPERANT CONDITIONING

Methodological Studies

We have already reviewed methodological studies in Chapter 1. We will mention them here only to call the reader's attention to the importance of taking behavior theory variables into account when obtaining background information on a patient. Diagnostic procedures normally obtain information on the history of the patient either from him or from a relative or friend. The behavior that the interviewer reinforces positively is more likely to be emitted by the patient or by the normal informant. Furthermore, the fact that schizophrenics extinguish more rapidly than normals means that the same interviewer influences the schizophrenic differently from the way he does a normal and thus may be a cause of differential histories. These studies have been well summarized by Inglis (1966).

Basic Studies

Let us begin with a truism. No patient is equally psychotic under all conditions. Reinforcement contingencies act upon all individuals for given classes of behavior on particular occasions or in the presence of particular stimuli, and in accordance with specific schedules of reinforcement. The first job of the operant conditioning approach is to examine these conditions of behavioral control. Beginning in 1954 Lindsley and Skinner constructed a series of experiments with schizophrenics under the same kind of precise conditions as they utilized with animals lower in the phylogenetic scale. The response chosen had to be simple and easily repeatable, and the reinforcement had to be easily consumed, the subject had to be ready to make the next response right after he had made one or received a reinforcement and, finally, all of this had to be objectively (preferably automatically) programmed and recorded. By using a small experimental cubicle with very little furniture and with only those stimuli present to which the experimenter wished to obtain the patient's reaction, they reasoned it should be possible to chart the laws of behavior for the schizophrenic patient.

Lindsley (1956, 1960) and Inglis (1966) review much of this research. Sampling chronic schizophrenics who had been in the hospital for many years, Lindsley experimented with a great variety of potential reinforcers, such as candies, cigarettes, coins, food morsels, pictures of female and male nudes, and such ingenious reinforcing events as the opportunity to feed a hungry kitten. He studied the effect of drugs on various patients; he measured the effect of the presence of a stranger or a nurse-therapist on the patients' response rate while on a particular reinforcement schedule; and he charted the effect of various somatotherapies and psychotherapy. Since he monitored the patients' behavior regularly and over long periods (years) of time, Lindsley had the opportunity to observe the cyclical nature of phenomena such as psychotic episodes and study the effect on his response measure.

In an effort to relate these operant response rates to other measures of the functioning of patients, Mednick and Lindsley (1958) studied a group of male chronic psychotic patients hospitalized for periods of three to 47 years with a median of 16 years. They attempted to give these patients an intelligence test and the Rorschach test; they also rated the patient's behavior with King's (1954) behavior rating scale during the testing (see Chapter 4) and on the ward. When they compared testable patients with those who were not testable, they found higher operant response rates for the testable than for the nontestable ones with still higher rates for a group of normals. The two patient groups also differed in the distributions of pauses in responding. The testable patients had a larger number of short pauses in responding while the nontestable ones had a smaller number of long pauses. The behavior rating on the ward correlated + .81 with the response rate closest in time to it (the higher the rate of response the better the rating); interestingly enough, this correlation was only + .23 for the first 10 sessions of conditioning. Behavior ratings made during the test situation did not correlate significantly with the operant response rate although, as already stated, they did relate to the fact of testability.

A similar study on acute schizophrenics by King et al (1957) resulted in different findings: they obtained a curvilinear relationship between severity of illness, as defined by behavioral ratings, and operant response rate (low response rate occurring at both extremes of severity of illness and highest rate in the middle). For an acute schizophrenic, low rate of response for inanimate reinforcement apparently means either that he is in good control and finds the repetitive task too boring, or that he is too disoriented and responds at a low rate because he is generally not reacting to his environment. These authors question the assumption that commerce with the environment as depicted in the interaction with a machine reflects the most important aspect of the functioning of these patients. Nevertheless, we will see in the section on conditioning therapy, that control of behavior by inanimate reinforcement may have to precede, at least in some patients, the possibility of its control by social reinforcement. The basic operant conditioning paradigm uses different kinds of discriminative and/or reinforcing stimuli, and thus provides a technique for the precise study of the effect that such stimuli have on different behaviors.

Other experiments have made use of more complicated responses. Studies of the conditioning of verbal behavior have been stimulated by Greenspoon's 1955 work in which he showed that verbal behavior of a normal individual can be modified without his being aware of it. The obvious clinical implications of verbal conditioning inspired a great deal of research to determine how to utilize it in alleviating abnormal behavior. Salzinger and Pisoni (1958, 1960, 1961), Salzinger and Portnoy (1964), and Salzinger, Portnoy, and Feldman (1964a) applied the operant conditioning model to the conduct of the clinical interview with schizophrenics. They demonstrated that they could change the verbal behavior of such patients in the course of a ten-minute period, that they could use extent of conditioning as a prognostic index, and that schizophrenics extinguish more rapidly than normals. Since the patients did not know that they were taking part in an experiment, they could not, as they can in reaction time or perceptual experiments and the like, "decide to cooperate" or not. The extraneous variables of cooperation (whatever they may consist of—avoiding an aversive stimulus based on a previous history of conditioning in which any tests become aversive, or responding at a high rate because the examiner constituted a discriminative stimulus for such behavior) do not enter. This is a method of extracting from the patient a sample of typical behavior rather than a sample of his "best" or "worst" behavior. In the course of these experiments, the investigators were able to condition even those patients who spoke to their "voices" while being reinforced.

It is revealing to compare the conditioning of chronic patients during the interview (Salzinger and Portnoy, 1964) with the motor response conditioning done by Lindsley (1960). In both cases a low rate of response was found, which, in the clinical literature, had mistakenly been interpreted to mean that the schizophrenic patients were unable to emit affect when, in fact, it appears to reflect a low rate of emitting behavior in general.

The studies on conditioning during the interview or during a monologue made use of the response class of self-referred affect and, in one case, of speech in general. Other studies have used such response classes as emotional words (Weiss, Krasner, and Ullmann, 1963) in a story-telling situation and have also had success in conditioning the verbal behavior of schizophrenics. Even more interesting perhaps are the studies that have focused directly on such verbal behavior as delusional speech (of grandeur and of persecution) by reinforcing incompatible rational speech (Rickard, Dignam, and Horner, 1960; Ayllon and Haughton, 1964).

Theoretically Motivated Studies

The studies above were primarily empirical in that they provided data on how the schizophrenic reacts to the consequences of his responses and how conditioning and extinction rates (as well as other well known conditioning phenomena) apply to him as compared to normals. The studies in this section use learning experiments as a means for testing a particular theory of schizophrenia. As Garmezy (1964) points out, learning inadequacies are not viewed by these investigators as primary deficits, but instead as the consequences of other variables, such as states of the patient (anxiety being a favorite candidate for distinguishing schizophrenics from normals—see Mednick, 1958) lack of cooperation, attention deficit, and the aversiveness of stimuli.

Let us consider first the research revolving about the hypothesis that schizophrenia is characterized by a highly generalized withdrawal from the environment (particularly from aversive stimuli) and that schizophrenics therefore discriminate less among stimuli. Garmezy (1966) states that the withdrawal from aversive stimuli is accompanied by lessened responsiveness to conditioned reinforcement. Garmezy (1952) corroborated the above hypotheses in an experiment in which normals showed a steeper stimulus generalization gradient than schizophrenics. Incorrect responses (responses to the most different generalization stimulus) were punished by the appearance of the word, WRONG in a lighted box. It meant that the subject lost some points that he could otherwise have exchanged for candy or cigarettes. On the other hand, a comparison of the generalization gradients under conditions that used only rewards (points exchanged for desirable objects) yielded no difference between normals and schizophrenics.

Wiener et al (1965) criticized Garmezy's experiment because the punishment condition punished only some of the responses (responses to the original stimulus were rewarded; only responses made to the stimulus most different from the original stimulus were punished, with responses to the generalization stimuli in the middle of the range being neither rewarded nor punished) while the reward condition rewarded responses to one stimulus only. They maintained that this difference produced greater task complexity for the punishment condition and that the complexity rather than the aversiveness produced a deficit in the schizophrenics' performance. Furthermore, although not entirely conclusive, Mednick (1955) and Gaines, Mednick and Higgins (1963) produced more stimulus generalization in schizophrenics than normals under conditions of no negative reinforcement, thus questioning the enticing hypothesis that aversive stimulation produces greater stimulus generalization in schizophrenics. Gaines et al confirmed one aspect of Mednick's (1958) theory of schizophrenia—that the postulated heightened physiological arousal (or anxiety as he first thought of it) of the acute schizophrenic results in greater stimulus generalization for the acute schizophrenics than the normals. They did not, however, verify the hypothesized greater stimulus generalization in acute than chronic schizophrenics, who were postulated to suffer from hypoarousal (too little arousal).

Behavior Theory as Therapy

Since behavior theory deals with the variables that control the emission of behavior, that is, its acquisition, maintenance, and elimination, it follows that such a theory should have relevance for the problem of the modification of behavior, too. In 1953, Peters used a motivation condition consisting of subshock insulin plus deprivation of breakfast and demonstrated learning. Somewhat later, King, Armitage, and Tilton (1960) constructed what they called the operant-interpersonal method of therapy, a modification and extension of Lindsley's method. The procedure consisted of the following stages: first, the patients were reinforced by cigarettes, candy, and colored slides for making simple operant motor responses; then the response reinforced was made more complex by requiring problem solving; eventually appropriate verbal behavior, evoked by the therapist who was present during the sessions accompanied the problem solving behavior; then the patient was trained in cooperating with the therapist who had a response lever just like the patient's; after learning to cooperate with the therapist in problem solving, the patients were allowed to solve problems with one another. A comparison of this type of therapy with verbal therapy, recreational therapy, and no therapy showed it to be superior to all in producing favorable change, whether the evaluation was based on ward observations or interviews.

More sophisticated applications of behavior theory have dealt with social behavior rather than the more easily specificable and controllable simple motor responses. Verbal behavior is the prototype of such social behavior. Isaacs, Thomas, and Goldiamond (1960) reinstated verbal behavior in two psychotic patients who had been mute for 14 and 19 years respectively. They shaped speech by reinforcing ever closer approximations to the desired response and they also used imitation training. One patient was first reinforced for looking at the reinforcement (gum); then for moving his lips and looking at the gum; they gave the gum to the patient only if he looked at it and made a vocalization; and finally, the experimenter said say "gum" whenever the patient grunted and then reinforced gradually closer approximations to the word "gum." During the sixth session, when the experimenter said "say gum," the subject said "gum, please." After that, the patient answered direct questions in group sessions. Although he did not speak to ward personnel, he did to the experimenter when seeing him on the ward. To make the verbal behavior generalize to other people, the experimenter brought a nurse into the therapeutic room and worked with the patient until he began answering the nurse's questions as he did his. Other hospital personnel could get the patient to speak by withholding the objects he requested in a nonverbal way until he requested them verbally.

In a more recent study of the same problem, Sherman (1965) used imitation procedures along with fading of the discriminative stimulus to produce speech in three mute schizophrenics. The fading procedure can be demonstrated by quoting the successive instructions given by Sherman (1965, p. 158): "(a) 'Say food'; (b) 'Say foo—'; (c) 'Say f—'; (d) 'What is this? Say f—'; (e) 'What is this? Say——'; (f) 'What is this?'." The experimenter gave these instructions while holding up food in front of the patient. Sherman demonstrated that the reinforcement was the variable controlling the verbal behavior by reversing the reinforcement contingency such that the patient received food only if, after seeing the food and hearing, "Say food," he did not reply for 30 seconds; in other words, he was reinforced if he did *not* speak. The results showed that when the reinforcement was contingent on *not* speaking then he did not speak, if contingent on speech, then he spoke.

The applications of behavior to long and short-term schizophrenics have shown that it is possible to reduce such behaviors as hoarding, avoidance of self-feeding (Ayllon and Michael, 1959), and even delusions. The success of these procedures has led investigators to introduce what has come to be called a "token economy" into the psychiatric ward. According to this system (Atthowe and Krasner, 1968; Ayllon and Azrin, 1968) the the patient lives in a ward and receives positive reinforcements in the form of tokens for emitting various behaviors. The patient can then exchange the tokens for such desirable reinforcements as the following: cigarettes, money, passes, watching television, sitting on the ward, feeding a kitten, the privacy of a room, the choice of a bedspread, coat rack, placebo, a leave from the ward ranging from 20 minutes to a trip to town with an escort, private audiences with such staff members as the nurses, chaplains, ward physician, ward psychologist, social workers, the opportunity to go to religious services, movies, and commissary items, such as candy, milk, toilet articles, reading and writing materials, plants, and stuffed animals. The behaviors reinforced in this way have varied from self-grooming, bed making, serving meals, and cleaning floors on the ward to more complicated duties off the ward, such as six-hour daily jobs as clerk, dietary worker, and laboratory worker. Long-range followup periods are not yet available for full evaluation of this procedure. Nevertheless, the immediate results are dramatic changes in the behavior of patients who had long ago been given up for lost. The behavior modification procedures have implications not only for therapy, but also for theories of etiology. It is conceivable that even if the original cause of schizophrenia is biological that the behavior theory approach is powerful enough to overcome some aspects of it. In addition, we must take into account the fact that behavior is generally reinforced; it is no more possible to omit reinforcement from behavior than to omit oxygen from human life. This suggests that hospitals usually reinforce behaviors directly antithetical to improvement and may even maintain "sick" behavior. Since it is possible to modify behavior of long standing it is even more important that we take all measures of schizophrenic behavior under well planned and controlled conditions of reinforcement.

RESPONDENT CONDITIONING

As already mentioned, there are two paradigms for the conditioning of behavior and therefore both must be considered with reference to schizophrenia. Pavlov (Kaplan, 1966) was interested in the relation of respondent (or Pavlovian) conditioning to psychopathology and produced the first model of abnormal behavior through a behavioral procedure; he called it experimental neurosis. Essentially, it consisted of a discrimination in which the stimuli were made increasingly more alike until the subject (in this case a dog) could no longer tell them apart; at that point he engaged in some wild behavior—tearing at his harness and biting at the apparatus—behavior that he had not shown before. Furthermore, this irrational behavior was accompanied by a complete breakdown of the formerly effective discrimination.

Ban (1964) describes Pavlov's views on schizophrenia. Pavlov hypothesized schizophrenic behavior to result from a basic hypnotic state. He began with the observation that stuporous patients did not respond to questions under ordinary circumstances, but did respond to a soft voice in a very quiet environment. He interpreted that to be similar to the paradoxical response in animals at the beginning of experimentally induced sleep, in which they respond to weak stimuli but not to strong ones. He also discerned a similarity of the negativistic responses (such as refusal to eat) in catatonic schizophrenics to the negative responses to the positive stimulus in the ultraparadoxical stage of conditioning of the dog. Pavlov essentially interpreted schizophrenic behavior as caused by a general inhibition of the cerebral cortex, that, in turn frees the subcortex from its customary role of control and results in an excitatory chaotic condition. This point of view looks upon schizophrenia as a protective device against overwhelming surplus stimulation attacking the weakened nervous system (considered to be part of the basis of schizophrenia), particularly the cortical cells, and that prevents destruction by further overstimulation. In other words, schizophrenic symptoms are seen as a defense against further schizophrenic disorganization.

In a review of the application of respondent conditioning in schizophrenia, Ban reported the following general findings: catatonic schizophrenics occasionally show an inhibited unconditional defense (where the unconditional stimulus is aversive) reflex and, occasionally, absence of an orienting reflex (a sort of observation or startle response to the occurrence of a new stimulus); at the same time, Ban described an increased persistence in the orienting reflex in acute schizophrenics and, with the progress of the pathology, a reduction in conditionability and the internal inhibitory function as expressed in the processes of extinction, stimulus discrimination, and delayed and trace reflex formation.

In a series of conditional reflex studies, Astrup (1962) reported general confirmation of Pavlov's hypotheses. Astrup examined three different levels of functioning of the nervous system: subcortical activity that he measured through responses to unconditioned stimuli, cortical activity of the first signalling system that he examined through the conditioned responses to nonverbal stimuli, and the cortical activity of the second signalling system that he investigated through the conditioned responses to verbal stimuli. He found that deteriorated schizophrenics, unlike other types of patients, showed inhibitions and dissociations at all three levels of nervous activity.

In this country, studies of respondent conditioning have been relatively sparse. As a consequence, we have few studies with respect to schizophrenia. One study by an American investigator is of particular interest. Peastrel (1964) compared the generalization of words to one another in eliciting a galvanic skin response (essentially a sweating response) as a function of the relationship of the generalization stimulus with the conditioned stimulus. There were two types of generalization stimuli, homonyms and synonyms of the conditioned stimuli. Normals generalized more to synonyms and schizophrenics generalized more to homonyms. Apparently, schizophrenics have a greater tendency to respond to the sound of words, while normals tend to respond to their meaning. Although the author himself made no attempt to relate this finding to a Pavlovian model, it shows a deficit in the second signalling system. In addition, however, this finding also fits in well with the idea about schizophrenics having difficulties in communication, as already indicated in Chapter 2.

Research in the area of respondent conditioning has primarily concentrated, like the work in psychomotor and perceptual functioning, on uncovering the "basic deficit" presumed to be in the nervous system rather than in the environment. It has, however, been much more popular in Russia, in other countries in Europe, and even in Japan than in this country.

SUMMARY

The aim of this chapter was to make clear the ways in which behavior theory is useful in the study of schizophrenia. Behavior theory must be taken into account whether or not schizophrenia proves to be caused by some biological fault, since whatever the basic defect, it must express itself in terms of behavior and that, of course, is influenced by the laws of behavior theory.

Behavior theory is also found to be useful from a purely methodological point of view. It predicts that a test finding cannot be generalized from a condition of no reinforcement to one of reinforcement. Thus, the findings concerning the behavior of schizophrenics must include information on the reinforcement contingency. Many differences between normals and schizophrenics make their appearance only under conditions of no reinforcement.

Naturally, we must take behavior theory into account with respect to the question of a basic deficit in learning in schizophrenia. The evidence here suggests that learning deficits, like the other postulated deficits, manifest themselves when no appropriate reinforcer is used. We will explore this in greater detail in Chapter 6.

Furthermore, behavior theory offers a prescription for a method of therapy for schizophrenia as it does for other types of abnormal behavior.

The methodological studies have shown the necessity of keeping reinforcement contingencies well under control since even such procedures as diagnostic interviews are susceptible to the effects of reinforcement.

Basic studies have shown the feasibility of carrying on operant conditioning experiments with schizophrenics, using either simple motor responses or more complex verbal responses as the dependent variable. These measures have some face validity but, in addition, they have also been shown to relate to other measures of functioning.

As an example of theoretically motivated studies, we discussed Garmezy's deduction, based on the schizophrenic's hypothesized withdrawal from the aversive aspects of the environment, that schizophrenics have a more shallow gradient of stimulus generalization than normals.

Examination of the use of behavior theory to provide a method of therapy showed that it can be applied to some of the most chronic patients, and thus underlined the importance of reinforcement contingency with respect to any behavior measured in schizophrenics.

The last section of the chapter dealt with respondent (Pavlovian) conditioning. Following Pavlov's lead, a number of investigators have made inferences concerning the nervous system on the basis of the subject's responses to the unconditioned stimulus, the nonverbal conditioned stimulus, and the verbal conditioned stimulus. The results suggest that many schizophrenics have a deficit in all of these types of responses. Finally, we described a respondent conditioning experiment demonstrating that schizophrenics have a tendency to generalize to words that sound alike while normals have a tendency to generalize to words of the same meaning.

CHAPTER SIX

THEORIES OF SCHIZOPHRENIA

I will start this chapter by describing the general functions of theory. The first function of theory is to make the discovery of otherwise isolated facts yield more information. To take one example, the fact that reaction time of schizophrenics can be shortened by the application of a loud raucous noise after longer reaction times may merely suggest a methodological artifact. However, the way in which such a fact fits into a theory that postulates that schizophrenics have a motivational deficit, assuming the noise to be a negative reinforcement, increases the plausibility of that theory and makes the finding generally more interesting.

The second function of a theory is to give rise to new experiments. In the example given above, the research question that follows from the finding of improved performance is whether the noise stimulus acts to strengthen behavior (motivational interpretation) or simply to arouse behavior (physiological arousal interpretation—a controversy discussed in Chapter 5). In addition, experiments could determine more specifically the kind of reinforcement contingency that causes a change in the behavior of schizophrenics. Such experiments could deal with the following variables: type of reinforcement (positive versus negative reinforcement), magnitude of reinforcement, delay of reinforcement, primary versus conditioned reinforcement, schedule of reinforcement, and the combinations of types of reinforcement. On the other hand, the research could refine the idea of motivational deficit by examining the population of schizophrenics susceptible to the reinforcement contingency effect; we could investigate whether this effect holds equally for males and females, recently hospitalized versus chronic patients, and reactive patients versus process patients, in each case relating the finding to the theory that spells out the kind of effect particular reinforcement contingencies might have on given kinds of patients at particular stages of development of the abnormality.

A third function of theory is not often stressed. It is to promote related experiments in a particular area of research. In this way, a great deal of evidence pertaining to a single question or a single set of related questions becomes available. It encourages replication of experiments, which is, of course, the final arbiter of the validity of any finding.

We need to make another point before leaving this general discussion. To be useful, theories must contribute something beyond gratifying a particular investigator's intuition. The prediction must be part of an explicit system of viewing the behavior of the schizophrenic. Explicit deductions make possible checking the logic as well as the empirical validity of the statements.

Theories on the subject of schizophrenia can be usefully divided into two types, biological and environmental, even though no theory can deal exclusively with one type.

BIOLOGICALLY FOCUSED THEORIES

Genetic

No one who has studied schizophrenia can ignore the finding of genetic involvement since Kallmann's (1946) research. Nevertheless, as already pointed out in Chapter 1, the evidence is not as clear as was once thought. Figures of concordance with respect to schizophrenia in identical twins vary widely. On the other hand, Kety and his colleagues (1968) and Heston and Denney (1968) found that the children of schizophrenic mothers placed in foster homes at an age too early for any profound environmental effect by the biological mothers had a higher frequency of occurrence of schizophrenia than control children. The controversy rages on and the interested reader is advised to see the discussion of this issue by Rosenthal and Kety (1968). In any case, the evidence for a genetic factor in the etiology of schizophrenia has given impetus to the search for a biological cause of schizophrenia.

Even the studies of discordant (one twin having schizophrenia and one not) identical twins have suggested that a physical cause may be responsible for the disorder. In a review of studies of discordant twins, Pollin and Stabenau (1968) showed differences in such factors as birth weight, cyanosis at birth, and neonatal medical complications, all of which the authors attribute to a difference in the intrauterine environment of the twins. Thus, where genetic factors fail to explain the presence of schizophrenia, other biological events often do. These authors do, however, admit that the mechanism of transmission of schizophrenia need not be exclusively interpreted in terms of constitutional factors. In line with this, they posit the possible social effect of role conflict in which the constitutionally weaker twin suffers from being compared to his stronger twin. In either case, these investigators maintain that stress is necessary for schizophrenia to occur. The stress may release either a genetically controlled enzyme that produces the psychotic behavior or it may, in interaction with some genetically determined behavioral disposition, evoke the aberrant behavior directly.

Biochemical

The idea of a physical basis for schizophrenia is not new. Bleuler (1930) spoke of a number of physical bases for schizophrenia, including disturbances of the chemistry of the body with respect to abnormal protein content in the spinal fluid. Recent progress in the field of biochemistry and the ability of chemicals to simulate schizophrenic-like behavior have stimulated the investigation of biochemical hypotheses of schizophrenia. A chemical known to simulate schizophrenia is mescalin; derived from Mexican peyote, it resembles adrenalin, a substance readily found in the body, and it was, therefore, suggested that such a chemical might well be manufactured (metabolized) in the body and thus account for schizophrenia (Osmond and Smythies, 1952; Hoffer, 1964). According to this theory, adrenochrome, and later, because of its instability, one of its metabolites—adrenolutin—was held responsible for psychotic behavior. Research showed that more adrenolutin was manufactured from adrenochrome in schizophrenics while in normals it was metabolized into a dihydroxy-N-methyl indole. We have evidence to support this hypothesis in the occurrence of symptoms, produced by ingestion of adrenochrome, consisting of hallucinations and changes in thought and word association. In addition, incidental evidence for more adrenochrome in schizophrenics comes from the report that schizophrenics have fewer allergies than normals (adrenochrome is an antagonist of allergins). Nevertheless, some investigators have been unable to find adrenochrome either in normals or in schizophrenics (Holland, Cohen, Goldenberg, Sha, and Leifer, 1958).

Heath (1960) suggested a substance in the blood, taraxein, as the cause of schizophrenia. He maintains that it is qualitatively different from the proteins found in the blood stream of normals. A toxic compound that is formed as a result of the interfering presence of taraxein produces changes in particular areas of the brain and results in abnormal (schizotypal) behavior. He characterizes this schizotypal behavior as basically pleasure deficient. It makes the individual particularly sensitive to the stresses that assault his feelings of identity and reality. Other symptoms of schizophrenia are considered to be secondary to the disorder. This theory has some experimental support. Administration of taraxein produces schizophrenic behavioral symptoms and changes in the electrical activity of the lower brain centers. Nevertheless, such scientists as Kety (1960) have questioned this biochemical theory, along with others, because of inability to replicate Heath's findings. One attempted replication induced schizophrenic symptoms with saline or normal blood injection. Kety lists, among the possible artifacts in such studies, suggestion, nonspecific toxic reactions from contaminants, and reinforcement of these cues by the biases of subject and observer, particularly when assessment is based on an unstructured interview.

Let us look briefly at one other biochemical hypothesis. A drug that has become famous for its psychotomimetic effects (it produces some of the symptoms of schizophrenia)—LSD—has given rise to the serotonin hypothesis because its structure resembles that of serotonin and because serotonin is found in the brain, particularly in the limbic system where emotional behavior is assumed to be regulated. The similarity of chemical substances in the body increases the likelihood that some might take the place of others in necessary chemical reactions, thereby changing their course. It is also noteworthy that the structure of serotonin resembles the structure of adrenochrome (mentioned above) and reserpine, a tranquilizing drug sometimes helpful in alleviating schizophrenic symptoms. A description of the effects of excessive serotonin (causing agitation as produced by LSD) or of insufficient serotonin (causing suppression of activity, as in catatonia) is given in Wooley (1962). This hypothesis also has difficulties. For example, as Kety (1960) points out, chlorpromazine, whose effect on the behavior of schizophrenics resembles that of reserpine, has no known effect on serotonin.

We do not have enough space here to go into further detail on the above theories or on other less well-known biochemical theories. Nevertheless, it is important to point out other difficulties of such theories. Kety (1960) listed a series of methodological difficulties with which an investigator in this field must deal. They include the problems of diagnosis and other attempts at behavioral description, the special diets instituted by hospitals or resulting from the idiosyncracy of the individual patient, the effects of lack of exercise in institutionalized patients, the effects of long periods of hospitalization, the many and extreme types of somatotherapy applied to the typically chronic patients whose biochemistry is studied, and anxiety produced by the research procedures.

Neurological (Autonomic Nervous System)

Another source of biological theory stems from examination of the functioning of the autonomic nervous system and the endocrine system which it controls, since it is most closely related to emotion. Like the evidence concerning the biochemical theories, data in this area are confusing and contradictory. Buss (1966) summarized some of the findings concerning three measures of somatic arousal. All three measures (galvanic skin response, cardiovascular response, and muscle action potential) showed that schizophrenics are less reactive than normals when stimulated because of the initially higher level of arousal characterizing their unstimulated level. In other words, schizophrenics are physiologically both hyperactive and hyporeactive. Buss speculates that the hyperactivity can be related to a biochemical fault in neural transmission in the brain. In another discussion of this area, however, Maher (1966) warns us that these generalizations do not seem to hold for paranoid schizophrenics.

A number of interesting biological theories have been propounded to account for the etiology of schizophrenia. We need more data before we can accept any one theory. Furthermore, the solution of the problems of patient selection depends on the development of suitable techniques in the behavioral area and thus, at present, they represent stumbling blocks to progress in the biological study of schizophrenia. Biological theories must also deal with the problem of translating biological defects into behavioral abnormalities. They must do this, not in terms of symptomatic description as gleaned from uncontrolled interviews, but in terms of the objective measures of behavioral functioning described in the preceding chapters.

ENVIRONMENTALLY FOCUSED THEORIES

We have already indicated that social variables are inextricably involved in the disorder of schizophrenia. We do not recognize that a person is peculiar or psychotic or schizophrenic by a survey of the serotonin content in the structures of his brain. We are directed to a potential patient through his social behavior, that is, by the way he interacts with other people. It is not at all surprising, particularly in view of the long period of dependence of children on their parents—a period further lengthened in recent years because of society's demands for more education—that investigators should have looked to environmental variables for explanations of schizophrenic behavior.

Intensive study of the families of schizophrenic children has shown communication problems within this social structure; furthermore, the patterns of communication differ from those engendered in families having a neurotic or a normal child. Although uncertain that abnormal patterns of communication cause schizophrenia, Clausen (1968) maintains that such patterns interfere with healthy personality development. Family research has given rise to the concepts of "schizophrenicness" (signs of schizophrenia) and "schizophrenogenicness" (behavior that tends to produce schizophrenia in others through communication patterns that make it difficult for the listener to understand what is being said) to describe the parents of schizophrenic children. Wynne (1968), who posited these concepts, showed that the parent's degree of schizophrenogenicness is a better predictor of the child's becoming schizophrenic than the parent's schizophrenicness.

Let us look at a theory of schizophrenia that has come out of family research. In the original statement of the double-bind theory, Bateson et al (1956) viewed the schizophrenic as a person who has difficulty in communicating with others or himself, that is, in understanding what others say to him or what he himself says about his sensations and perceptions. The authors consider repeated interactions between two or more people, with one person the victim, as essential to the double-bind situation. These interactions consist of a primary negative injunction to behave in a particular way or take the consequences, a secondary injunction expressed at a more abstract level that conflicts with the first one but is enforced in the same way (a gesture or a tone of voice might convey this conflicting message but it may also be verbal, as in "do not view this as a punishment"), and finally a tertiary negative injunction that prohibits the victim from escaping the conflict set up by the first two injunctions (this is sometimes enforced by capricious promises of love). The double bind means essentially that the victim will be punished no matter what he does, and that he cannot escape except into a metaphorical (essentially disguised) kind of communication that even he could not recognize as a response to communications he receives. When he does not know that his statements are metaphorical, he has become pathological. After a long period of exposure to double binds, he might try to escape by one of a number of routes. Not understanding what a particular message meant anymore, he might become excessively concerned with hidden meanings (paranoid symptomatology), or accepting everything literally, he might laugh at everything people told him (hebephrenic symptomatology), or he might ignore the threatening messages by withdrawing from the environment (catatonic symptomatology).

Ringuette and Kennedy (1966) showed that experts on the theory of the double bind failed to find more double-bind statements in letters written by parents of schizophrenics than in a control group. Mishler and Waxler (1965) and Schuman (1967) pointed out ambiguities in the description and measurement of the concept. Intriguing as the theory is, it does not have sufficient empirical validation.

Although not going into enough detail to construct a theory, Hammer (1972) made some interesting points about schizophrenia from a cultural perspective. She assumes a genetic factor of social noncongruence that manifests itself in two ways: in terms of schizophrenia and in terms of creativity. She hypothesizes that the phenotypic route (the way the gene expresses itself) taken is determined by the structure of the group in which the particular person is a member, and by his being able to remain in the group. In migration, he must leave the group and this condition is associated with higher rates of psychopathology. The noncongruence may help the process of cultural change if accepted by the group or may result in the person being labelled by a system of psychopathology as a schizophrenic. Hammer bolsters her statement that creativity is caused by the same genotype as schizophrenia by showing that although both longevity and fertility are reduced in schizophrenia, its incidence has remained constant over generations, thus suggesting a compensating mechanism of this sort. The interesting implication from this is that the proper study of schizophrenia should be expanded to include the more creative individuals in our society. This approach to schizophrenia is an example of a productive combination of the findings from the area of behavioral genetics and social sciences.

Although the remaining theories in this chapter are also concerned with the inception of the disorder of schizophrenia, their major source of evidence comes from the regularities discovered by the different experimental methods used in describing schizophrenic behavior. We shall therefore refer to them as descriptive theories.

DESCRIPTIVE THEORIES

A descriptive theory is somewhat more closely anchored to behavioral data than an etiological theory, whether it is biological or social. The descriptive theories describe some regularity in the functioning of the patient that is relevant to a large number of schizophrenics or, at least, to a subgroup of them.

Thought Disorder

We need not say much about thought disorder in schizophrenia since we have described it in detail in Chapter 2. Not all experiments found evidence for it. Some questioned the validity of the concept, attributing the findings to other variables, such as differential reactions to stimulus input. Furthermore, some investigators have been unable to replicate the original, some have found evidence for thought disorder in other types of psychopathology, and, finally, some have been able to modify it.

Let us cite one more example of the alteration of thought disorder in the schizophrenic. Wagner (1968) demonstrated not only the direct modification of attending and abstracting responses in schizophrenics, but also a considerable degree of transfer to specific tests of abstraction in the proverbs test, similarities test, tests of vocabulary and short term memory, and the attention test. Operant conditioning brought about the change in what some investigators consider to be basic to schizophrenia; in the case of the attention responses, the experimenter used tokens as reinforcements for the correct matching of identical figures (simple geometric designs, pictures of common objects, nonsense syllables, and common words); in the case of abstracting responses, he reinforced the subject for selecting the stimulus of a choice display that resembled but was not the same as the sample stimulus. Wagner concluded that the attending and abstracting behaviors simply occurred among schizophrenics at a lower rate than among normals. The fact that the amount of change in the transfer tasks did not depend on the degree of learning in the conditioning situation suggests that the conditioning served merely to evoke certain rather well-established responses rather than to produce them in the first place. This kind of experiment suggests that the response mechanisms of the schizophrenic are intact, and that we should look for a deficit either in the way schizophrenics respond to stimuli on each occasion (attention deficit as evidenced by low operant rate of attending) or in the way schizophrenics respond to stimuli over a repeated series of trials (learning deficit).

Learning Theory Interpretations

Pavlovian Conditioning. We have already discussed Pavlov's theory in Chapter 5. We might add to this Bridger's interpretation: "... it is postulated that in schizophrenia, the limbic system is undergoing increased activation and simultaneously the neocortex is under a state of partial inhibition" (Bridger, 1964, p. 194). In this manner he seeks to implicate the relationship between the limbic system (first signalling system) and the neocortex (the second signalling system). This interpretation agrees with the findings that schizophrenics have a communication difficulty (the second signalling system) and that their emotional behavior is often excessive, that is, either too much or too little. The question one must ask is whether this kind of interpretation adds very much beyond applying physiological labels for behavioral findings.

Drive as Avoidance Producer. In 1958, Mednick articulated a theory of schizophrenia that he followed up by a number of experiments. Mednick's theory consists of a number of elements, but probably the most important one relates to the notion of anxiety that he has recently translated into the more contemporary concept of arousal (Mednick and Schulsinger, 1968). The idea of anxiety has a long clinical history in the description of schizophrenia. Mednick's idea was that the schizophrenic has a low threshold for eliciting anxiety, at least in the acute stage. He assumed that anxiety (or arousal) acts like a drive and, accepting Hull's law that drive interacts with a response in a multiplicative manner, he expects an increase in the likelihood of a response being evoked with an increase in anxiety. Such a higher drive state evokes responses in greater strength and produces faster conditioning when only one response can be evoked—as in the knee jerk—but causes slower conditioning when more than one response can be evoked—as in a paired associate task. In the more complex task, responses other than those considered correct would be evoked in greater strength for the schizophrenic than for the normal person and they would interfere more in the schizophrenic's learning than in the normal's.

Mednick also maintained in his earlier formulation that acute schizophrenics recover more slowly from anxiety, thus receiving prolonged exposure to it, and that they have a greater tendency toward stimulus generalization, thus having the same anxiety reaction to many objects, people, and events in their environment. In learning to avoid this anxiety, the schizophrenic makes responses that lead him away from the aversive stimuli; eventually he learns to have avoidance thoughts that are reinforced in that they successfully avoid the aversive stimuli. By making more tangentially related and eventually unrelated responses, the schizophrenic goes from the acute to the chronic stage where his most pronounced symptom, according to Mednick, is his flatness of affect.

We have already discussed the evidence for this theory in Chapter 5. Mednick himself has modified it in the face of some conflicting data. True to his own advice, Mednick (Mednick and Schulsinger, 1968) tested his theory on a population of high-risk children—children whose mothers had been diagnosed as schizophrenic. Here he found that the high-risk population (potential schizophrenics) showed faster conditioning and more generalization, but contrary to his prediction, faster recovery from arousal as shown in the galvanic skin response. Mednick changed his theory to conform to the new data. He also suggested that this new generalization was, in fact, more in keeping with his theory of the inception of schizophrenia than his older one because the rapid recovery from stress stimuli makes more certain that the avoidance responses are reinforced through the elimination of the anxiety response to the aversive stimuli.

This theory does not explain adequately the presence of various perceptual anomalies, such as those found in the constancy experiments. Furthermore, the assumedly larger degree of anxiety or arousal does not explain or predict performance in many other situations than those used by Mednick to buttress his theory. A number of experiments (in which patients participate without realizing that they are doing so) have shown that the behavior of the schizophrenic can be conditioned. It is considerably more modifiable with respect to complex response classes than Mednick's theory would lead one to suppose. Perhaps Mednick's verbal learning experiments are influenced by artifacts such as the patient's cooperativeness and thus reduce performance for that reason rather than because of anxiety. Nevertheless, Mednick's theory is one of the most serious attempts to integrate learning theory with the data on schizophrenia. It also has given rise to more experiments than we have room here to describe.

Drive as Activator. Another theory of schizophrenia that makes use of the drive variable was promulgated by Broen and Storms (1967; Broen, 1968). Like Mednick, these theorists used the concept of anxiety as a drive and then changed to the concept of arousal because of its physiological implications. Their theory differs from Mednick's in that they conceive of drive in terms of its activating or energizing property instead of in terms of its aversive quality. In this way, the theory is able to deal with the schizophrenic's responses to nonaversive stimuli also. In addition, although the theory postulates the same hierarchical order of responses in schizophrenics as in normals, it states that the response ceilings of the dominant responses are lower for schizophrenics than normals and thus closer to the lower level of strength of the competing responses. Under conditions of high arousal the dominant response cannot continue to rise as a function of increasing drive because of its relatively low ceiling while the competing responses still can, thus causing a collapse of the response hierarchy and the emission of the unrelated responses. They tested this ingenious explanation of the emission of tangential responses by schizophrenics under experimental conditions that manipulated arousal. Assuming that muscle tension represents arousal, they produced various degrees of it by having the subjects exert different amounts of hand-grip pressure. The results show that this muscular exertion interferes more with the responding of schizophrenics than that of normals in a discrimination task.

Closer examination of these experiments (Broen, Storms, and Goldberg, 1963; Broen and Storms, 1964) shows, however, that the hand-grip pressure response was controlled by a buzzer set to go off if the subject did not exert a sufficient amount of pressure; effectively, it put that response under a negative reinforcement contingency where the buzzer was the stimulus to be avoided. We can thus interpret this "arousal" effect as a distracting stimulus where increased pressure causes more distraction or where the pressure exerted by the hand acts as a more immediate stimulus for the schizophrenic than for the normal. In other words, these experiments do not show unequivocally that the different performances are due to differences in drive level (arousal). Another aspect of these experiments questions the drive difference interpretation. All subjects were originally trained under conditions of low drive (that is, they exerted no pressure). The low and high drive conditions that follow the training condition either resemble or are different from the training conditions. Since there is evidence that changes in stimuli influence schizophrenics more than normals, we need not invoke drive-level differences as explanations. Despite these ambiguities of interpretation of the experiment, statement of the theory in terms which are testable means that further tests will be done in the future.

As already indicated, many investigators have utilized the notion of anxiety with respect to schizophrenia. We shall mention two more. McReynolds (1960) related anxiety to perception, instead of to response interference, as did the above formulations. He states that anxiety results from a person's inability to assimilate an ever increasing number of percepts (new information as well as feelings) because of the incongruence of these new percepts with the person's past experience. In order to prevent too large an accumulation of unassimilated percepts, the person engages in such schizophrenic symptoms as withdrawal behavior, hallucinations, and delusions that may then allow him to make sense of the new and incongruent material. The major problem with this theory is that the basic concepts are not well specified, nor is there any good evidence for the dilemmas postulated by McReynolds.

Other Drive-based Theories. Epstein (1967) made an attempt to present a unified theory of anxiety. He postulates the basic defect in schizophrenia to be an inability to modulate initially excessive levels of arousal; the main problem is not one of over- or under-inhibition, but rather one of an inadequately modulated control system. He suggests that the cause of schizophrenia lies in a child's lack or excess of energy in responding to stimulation. He hypothesizes that the environment could produce schizophrenia by keeping a child in a constant state of high arousal. Such a state would occur if the mother supplied the child with a small number of positive reinforcements, a large number of negative reinforcements, and periods of no reinforcement scheduled in such a way that the child would not be entirely satisfied, yet satisfied enough to maintain his behavior. Keeping the child in a state of high arousal is doing effectively what Bateson et al (1956) called the double bind. Unfortunately, this theory predicts too many different things about schizophrenics. It predicts that some will suffer from too much arousal (overreacting to stimulation) others from underarousal (underreacting to stimulation), and still others from both, thus vacillating in their reaction to stimulation. It is very hard to show that such a theory is valid (or for that matter, that it is not), unless it predicts that over a long range of time the schizophrenic will show more extreme responses than the normal. The occurrence of extreme behavior (variability), however, might well be a function of many other considerably less important variables than the one postulated here. Clearly direct measurement of arousal would be useful; however, not enough agreement on measurement of the concept exists at this time.

The next theory limits itself to consideration of verbal behavior that is central in social behavior. It also derives its importance from the fact that it deals most directly with the problem of thought disorder in schizophrenia. Chapman's theory (Chapman, Chapman, and Miller, 1964) states essentially that schizophrenics make responses in the direction of their response biases to a greater degree than normals, that is, that they, like normals, have a response hierarchy (see Broen above) but that, unlike normals, they tend to emit the highest probability response independent of the particular context. He explains the schizophrenic's errors in word definition or proverb inter- pretation (most of his validating data stem from such experiments) in terms of such context independent but strong normal meaning responses. Although this theory summarizes much data in the area of verbal behavior, it cannot easily be extended to explaining the other kinds of phenomena, such as perceptual anomalies, in the behavior of the schizophrenic.

Aversive and Social Stimuli. Another learning theory (Rodnick and Garmezy, 1957; Garmezy, 1966) states that schizophrenics tend to with- draw from noxious stimuli in a persistent and inflexible manner and that they exhibit a lessened responsiveness to positive social reinforcements. These statements are based on experimental studies and are congruent with clinical descriptions of schizophrenics.

McReynolds and Guevara (1967) found evidence for the Rodnick- Garmezy theory in a success-failure inventory consisting of such items as, "I have a tendency to give up easily when I meet difficult problems." Fourteen percent of the normals and 46 percent of the schizophrenics responded "true", supporting the idea that schizophrenics avoid aversive stimuli. An item that differentiated the two populations in the opposite direction was, "I am ambitious." Eighty-eight percent of the normals and 58 percent of the schizophrenics responded "true" to it, suggesting that schizophrenics are less responsive to positive social reinforcement.

Goodman (1964) also investigated the Rodnick-Garmezy theory. He used performance on the digit symbol section of the Wechsler intelligence test as the dependent variable. Process schizophrenics showed an interference effect as the result of hearing a tape recorded conversation in which a mother censured her son, while reactive schizophrenics showed an interference effect after hearing a tape in which the father censured his son. Normals did not show these effects. This study indicates that the negative reinforcement is more effective in interfering in schizophrenic than in normal responding but that what is negatively reinforcing relates to the subtype of schizophrenia. These results, however, are limited to male schizophrenics since they were the only subjects in the study. In addition, the complexity of an experiment of this kind, which must use a particular manner of presentation of script to show the two types of parent behavior, inevitably involves extraneous variables whose full import is difficult to evaluate.

Not all the experiments concerning the Rodnick-Garmezy theory have confirmed it. Spence, Lair, and Goodstein (1963), using verbal discrimination tasks, found no differential reactions in schizophrenics and normals with respect to positive and negative reinforcement or with respect to social versus nonsocial cues. This negative result points out the importance of taking into account the particular task used to test a theory. Thus, while some experiments have suggested that positive social reinforcement is not effective in modifying the behavior of schizophrenics, others have shown that schizophrenic behavior could in fact be changed by means of positive reinforcement, particularly in situations that are not obviously experiments (for example, Ayllon and Azrin, 1968; Salzinger and Pisoni, 1958). Experimental control is critical in the investigation of behavior disorders; it is equally important to avoid those controls that inject irrelevant variables producing behavior quite atypical of behavior in general.

Although the area of motivation in schizophrenia has evoked a great deal of interest, it can be described here in small part only. The reader is referred to Johannsen (1964) for a more complete review.

Attending Responses. Ullmann and Krasner (1969) presented a theory of schizophrenia based on their view that we can eliminate or at least modify the deficit in schizophrenia by the proper reinforcement contingencies. Their basic assumption about the inception of schizophrenia is that the schizophrenic's attending responses, particularly those to social stimuli, have been extinguished.

These authors show how the symptoms of schizophrenia can be derived from this simple assumption. They also state, "While the null hypothesis can never be proved, and hence a physical basis can never be ruled out, it seems plausible that differences in reinforcing contingencies may account for differences in attentiveness between schizophrenics and normals" (p. 383). They explain shallowness of affect, for example, in terms of extinction of attending as follows: the person who does not attend will become sloppy in his work, in the way in which he listens to other people, and in the way in which he works for reinforcements, and thus may leave himself open to negative reinforcements from such persons as his boss, his wife and children, and his friends for not conforming to the rules of society. Ullmann and Krasner explain inappropriateness of affect and other behavior in terms of responses no longer under the control of appropriate discriminative stimuli. This may lead to a situation where the person no longer discriminates between self-generated stimuli and those in his external environment. Finally, the authors point to the effect of the hospital in providing the environment and the reinforcement contingencies for the learning of abnormal behavior that the patient did not emit before coming to the hospital. Ullmann and Krasner contend that attending behavior is reduced in frequency because of extinction in the hospital and before, instead of reflecting a lost *ability* to attend. We have discussed evidence related to this theory in Chapter 5.

Salzinger (1968) presents a number of behavior theory paradigms for the inception of abnormal behavior. We refer to them here to remind the reader that a sufficient number of paradigms for the acquisition of normal behavior exist so that no special mechanisms are necessarily required for the explanation of the acquisition of abnormal behavior.

Stimulus Theories

Of the theories so far discussed, the Ullmann-Krasner theory probably comes closest to considering stimulus input as crucial in schizophrenia. We shall now turn our attention to a number of other theories that focus upon a dysfunction in stimulus control as the basic deficit in schizophrenia. Since they are usually raised in the context of psychophysical experiments, we have already alluded to them, particularly in Chapter 3.

Stimulus Input Control. Let us look first at Silverman's attention theory (1964a; 1964b; 1967). Even more than the Rodnick-Garmezy theory, it is directed at differentiating several subgroups of schizophrenics from one another. Silverman accepts the reactive-process distinction, adding to it the symptom pattern dimension of paranoid versus nonparanoid and, finally, the length-of-hospitalization dimension. He then suggests that these categories of schizophrenia can be related to a number of sensory-perceptual response prototypes. We will take up each of his three main constructs: stimulus intensity control, scanning control, and a gating mechanism controlling sensory input versus ideational input. He views long-term hospitalized, process, nonparanoid schizophrenics as hypersensitive individuals who show marked stimulus intensity reduction as a kind of defense mechanism. With respect to scanning control, Silverman finds differences between paranoid and nonparanoid schizophrenics. In the early stages of the disorder, reactive paranoid schizophrenics manifest exaggerated scanning behavior. In contrast to this, withdrawn, process, nonparanoid schizophrenics manifest little scanning behavior. In other words, the manner in which patients react to defend themselves against the threat of the environment explains the difference in symptom patterns. The early-stage paranoid appears always to be looking for some relationship in the environment, while the later-stage paranoid has already learned to reduce the incoming stimulation by a lower rate of scanning of his environment. Silverman's third concept relates to symptom patterns as follows: the gating mechanism, which acts to screen out certain types of stimuli, brings a surplus of sensory aspects of the stimuli to the attention of chronic nonparanoid, process schizophrenics and keeps to a minimum the connotative attributes, particularly their aversive aspects.

This very detailed theory is buttressed by a good deal of data. Nevertheless, like many other theories, it suffers from the use of relatively unreliable systems of classification such as the process-reactive and the paranoid-nonparanoid categorizations. Furthermore, differences in scanning among the subgroups of schizophrenics are inferred on the basis of size estimation experiments instead of being directly measured. Stannard, Singer, and Over (1966) showed that they could eliminate the difference in performance between normals and schizophrenics on a size constancy task by reinforcing appropriately. This questions a basic tenet of the theory, because if mode of perception is that easily manipulable, it could not very well be responsible for the acquisition of so many symptoms; it suggests that scanning is a correlated factor produced by the differential response of schizophrenics and normals to reinforcement. (The reader should recognize the phenomenon of the elimination of normal-schizophrenic differences by means of alteration of reinforcement contingencies.)

McKinnon and Singer (1969) measured scanning behavior more directly by recording eye movements during the course of size-judgment experiments and during a so-called free-search condition. Paranoid and nonparanoid schizophrenics did not differ significantly from one another, from a normal control, or from psychotic depressives in degree of scanning. However, patients who were under the influence of tranquilizers showed a definite reduction in eye movements. Whereas the findings for size judgment were the same as those found in the Silverman study (1964b) *for the tranquilized subjects,* the opposite held for the schizophrenics without drugs. Furthermore, McKinnon and Singer found no significant correlation between eye movement scores and size judgments, contradicting Silverman's assumption that we can infer scanning behavior from such tasks. Finally, we must add that in this study, as in the previously cited one, conditioning eliminated the normal-schizophrenic differences in size judgment that were found under conditions of no reinforcement.

Venables (1964) promulgated another theory concerning the schizophrenic's reaction to stimuli. He characterizes chronic (possibly also process) schizophrenics as suffering from restricted attention resulting from activation of the sympathetic and cortical parts of the nervous system. The acute (possibly also reactive and paranoid) schizophrenic has a problem opposite to that of the chronic patient in that he has difficulty in restricting the range of sensory stimuli. Although not as detailed as Silverman's theory, Venables's certainly resembles it.

Stimulus Processing. Yates (1966) points out that the first task of a theorist in this area is to examine the four basic parts of the functioning of the organism where a breakdown could occur to produce the schizophrenic deficit. They are the input phase, the initial data-processing phase, the central processing phase, and the motor response. Yates locates the basic schizophrenic difficulty in the initial data-processing phase. He maintains that the schizophrenic processes data at a very slow rate. Since his short-term memory system holds information for a brief period of time only, he loses a good deal of it before it can get to the long-term memory store. The consequence is that the patient processes only some of the relevant information. After long periods of time, he begins to suffer from thought disorder and begins to emit bizarre behavior because he is responding to only part of the relevant stimulus information. Yates states that, unlike other theories, his avoids postulating the screening out of irrelevant information for the normal but not for the schizophrenic and, in that sense, is simpler. It does not, however, explain why schizophrenics respond to irrelevant stimuli.

No discussion of theories of schizophrenia would be complete without at least mentioning the work of Shakow (1962, 1963, 1967). According to him the schizophrenic's major difficulty is an inability to maintain a major set, that is, a state of readiness to make a response at some time in the future. Instead, he is controlled by minor sets with the result that he shows segmented patterns of behavior. Shakow rejected what he termed an overemphasis on cognitive functioning as the candidate for the basic deficit of schizophrenia. Instead, he concentrated on the function of attention.

Immediacy Hypothesis. Another theory describing the way in which the schizophrenic responds to stimuli can be summarized by the immediacy hypothesis (Salzinger, Portnoy, and Feldman, 1966; Salzinger, 1971a, 1971b): schizophrenic behavior is primarily controlled by stimuli that are immediate in the environment. Such a conceptualization explains the fact that schizophrenic behavior is often, but not always, controlled by irrelevant stimuli by showing that immediate stimuli are frequently, but not always, irrelevant. Furthermore, because it states that one class of stimuli is preponderant in controlling the behavior of schizophrenics to the relative exclusion of other stimuli, it need not postulate an additional special process for screening out stimuli that do not evoke responses. The control over his behavior by immediate stimuli makes it less likely that the schizophrenic will expose himself to aversive stimuli, particularly the conditioned aversive (social) ones, since these stimuli are aversive only when he responds to them in terms of their more remote conditioning history, instead of their immediate and unconditioned stimulus aspect.

This hypothesis shows how schizophrenics manifest a thought disorder because no one who responds primarily to the immediate aspects of stimuli can solve a problem of an even rudimentary level of difficulty. Furthermore, although the hypothesis says nothing specifically about language, the implication for language is clear: if only immediate stimuli control the words emitted by a speaker, he must become unintelligible because few sentences can be constructed that consist of relations only among pairs or triads of words; subject must agree with verb in number no matter how many words intervene; the beginning and end of a sentence, paragraph, chapter, and even book must agree at least somewhat in content. The hypothesis explains schizophrenics' deficit in object constancy by calling attention to the fact that the retinal image is more immediate as a stimulus than the history of the object being viewed. Although the theory states nothing specifically about slower reaction time in schizophrenics than in normals, it follows that a person whose behavior is controlled by immediate stimuli might show a slower response to a given stimulus if other stimuli are present to capture his attention. In the case of no special reinforcement contingency, the immediate stimuli are irrelevant and produce the typical schizophrenic longer reaction time; when there is a reinforcement contingency, then the immediate stimuli reinforce the shorter reaction times. This theory also predicts that the schizophrenic's behavior will last only as long as the immediate stimuli that control it. In general, the immediacy hypothesis explains the many experiments that demonstrate a deficit only in the absence of feedback (immediate stimuli).

We might define the concept of immediacy a little more explicitly here. When we require a subject to respond to a particular stimulus and other stimuli are present, produced either by the same external environment or by the subject himself, that stimulus will control the schizophrenic's behavior that is closest to the occasion for response emission. Such a stimulus would not depend on its history for evoking a response. It implies that a schizophrenic is more likely to respond to the sound of a word (in generalization experiments) than to its meaning (see Peastrel, 1964); it means that although schizophrenics might condition at the same rate as normals (given that the reinforcing stimulus is immediate), they will extinguish more rapidly (Salzinger and Pisoni, 1960); and it predicts that a token reinforcement system of running a ward will change the behavior of schizophrenics (Ayllon and Azrin, 1968), many of whom have not interacted significantly with their environment for decades, since the tokens are immediate stimuli that are changed only gradually into stimuli auguring more distant reinforcements.

An important aspect of this theory is that it relates the schizophrenic abnormality (independent of whether it results from a gene, prenatal environment, or learning) to the way in which an individual so afflicted might react given also the well-documented laws of behavior. In other words, the theory holds that whatever the normal-schizophrenic difference, we must explore how that difference interacts with the laws of behavior. Let us look at another kind of difference among individuals to clarify this point. We will compare people with and without sight. We can obviously predict that a blind individual is not stimulated by visual stimuli. In terms of behavior theory, it means that visual discriminative stimuli could not guide him and that visual reinforcements could not condition him. To predict his behavior patterns fully, we would have to determine exactly how our society relies on visual stimuli to guide and reinforce behavior. In addition, we would have to take into account how other individuals respond to a blind person and what kind of sensing devices such a person might have as substitute discriminative stimuli and reinforcers for his behavior.

We can do a similar kind of analysis with respect to schizophrenia. Assuming that preponderantly immediate stimuli control schizophrenics, we can determine how such individuals would respond to their environment. We could infer from such control that extinction should be more rapid in schizophrenics, and indeed it is (Salzinger and Pisoni, 1960; Dinoff, Horner, Kurpiewski, and Timmons, 1960). On the same basis, we would predict that schizophrenics show relatively little evidence for an intermittent reinforcement effect and we find such evidence in a verbal conditioning experiment (Rickard, Dignam, and Horner, 1960) and little differential effect resulting from different schedules of intermittent reinforcement, which we see in Wagner (1964) with respect to a motor response. Control by immediate stimuli would lead us to predict little generalization from one situation to another and, indeed, we find it so (Morris, Hannon, and Dinoff, 1963). When schizophrenics were conditioned to increase their verbal behavior (other-oriented speech) by one person, they failed to generalize the increase to other persons. Subsequently, the experimenters gave the schizophrenics a hearing-aid-like radio when other people interviewed them. The original experimenter then provided discriminative stimuli and reinforcers while the schizophrenic was being interviewed by another experimenter. This procedure produced some carryover of the conditioning effect and thus demonstrated the importance of the reinstatement of the original (immediate) stimuli.

Cromwell and Dokecki (1968) describe schizophrenic language by a disattention theory resembling the immediacy hypothesis. According to them, the critical dysfunction of the schizophrenic is his inability to disattend stimuli thus making it impossible for him to separate the relevant from the irrelevant. They also stress the importance of current and immediately recent events. However, their contention that the schizophrenic has difficulty disattending a stimulus makes it difficult to explain how a new current event comes to control behavior. Furthermore, the notion of disattention suggests a two-process theory that is more complicated and therefore less parsimonious than the theory of immediacy that requires only one process—that of a particularly strong attraction—to explain the behavior of the schizophrenic.

Comparison of the immediacy hypothesis with many of the other theories now extant shows that it does not contradict them but, instead, that it encompasses them. Thus, Mednick's (1958) theory states that simple responses can be as easily conditioned in schizophrenics as in normals while complex ones cannot. Yet complex responses make a demand on the person to react to stimuli that are less immediate. Furthermore, the faster recovery rate from aversive stimuli (a point that Mednick accepted in his reformulation of his theory in light of empirical evidence) also agrees with the idea that schizophrenics respond primarily to immediate stimuli because the results show that aversive stimuli control behavior only for brief periods, that is, until new immediate stimuli take over. Finally, the tangential responses that Mednick looks upon as avoidance responses can also be explained in terms of control by immediate stimuli, since conditioned aversive stimuli lose their aversive quality when viewed in their immediate aspect— their physical quality—instead of their conditioned association. The interference hypothesis (Buss and Lang, 1965; Lang and Buss, 1965) postulates that schizophrenic behavior is the result of the interference of competing stimuli; it is encompassed by the immediacy hypothesis but made more specific, in that it predicts the type of stimuli that compete.

The generality of the immediacy hypothesis allows us to apply it to a number of sets of data and to explain the kind of behavior now described by more specialized and less parsimonious theories. In a recent test of the immediacy hypothesis, Salzinger, Portnoy, Pisoni, and Feldman (1970) compared schizophrenic and normal speech samples on a modified cloze procedure (see Chapter 2). The speech segments sampled were of different lengths and the middle word was deleted in all of them. Normal subjects were required to guess the deleted words on the basis of different amounts of surrounding context. The results showed that at low degrees of context (when only two words surrounded the blank for which the subjects have to guess the word) the normal predictors guessed correct words equally easily for schizophrenics as for normals. However, as the context increased, it became considerably easier to predict the correct word for the normal speech samples, but only somewhat easier for the schizophrenic samples. In schizophrenic speech only the most immediate words are related to one another by response-produced stimuli, while in normal speech both immediate and remote words relate to one another. This result not only supports the immediacy hypothesis but it also makes clear why we do not understand a schizophrenic even though his speech does not appear to be altogether disconnected.

The immediacy hypothesis is not yet firmly established. It requires a large amount of research in defining more precisely some of its basic concepts. To begin with, it is important to have some physical specification of the time period involved in the word "immediate." It also requires a more precise investigation of the tradeoff we might expect between the intensity and the immediacy of stimuli. We also need experiments to specify more precisely the size of the unit of stimulus to take into account. And, finally, we must determine when the immediate stimuli in question are external and when they are response-produced as in language.

In general, we can characterize the new development of theories in schizophrenia as a healthy aspect of research, for theory is no longer sheer speculation. Theory now comes from data and is stated in such a way that large parts of it are directly testable. This means that theories are changeable as well as verifiable and thus are grist for the research mill.

We need to make another point about the new kinds of theories. If, as many investigators have suggested, there are different kinds of schizo-phrenics, different theories may not be conflicting, they may simply charac-terize different types of schizophrenics. Such theories can then be used to define a population of patients having the characteristics posited by the theory. In view of the bankruptcy of the current diagnostic procedures, methods that are objective and that can provide measures of basic processes in patients might well provide us with new methods of selection of patients who have in common characteristics so long sought after by the diagnosti-cians. They would, of course, have the advantage of being based on theory and thus would make it easier to select and treat such patients than is presently possible. We would suggest that theory stimulated by objective data gathering will provide us with the new methods of grouping patients into meaningful categories for purposes of classification and treatment and, eventually, prevention.

SUMMARY

The object of this chapter was to present a number of current theories of schizophrenia. They integrate the data described in detail in previous chapters in such a way as to do more than just catalogue normal-schizophrenic differences. These theories explain the various and varied differences by a small number of general statements.

First, we took up biologically focused theories. We pointed out the importance of somatic involvement in schizophrenia. Whether this involve-ment refers to a genetic effect, an intrauterine effect, or even a socially produced biological effect we must take it into account for a complete description of schizophrenia. The biologically focused theories we discussed were the biochemical ones and those that concentrate on investigation of the autonomic nervous system.

Next, we considered the environmentally focused theories. Environment was specified by social variables such as the family and the group to which a particular individual belongs. Theory described the complicated interactions between an individual's personal difficulties and his social milieu.

We labelled the last set of theories in this chapter descriptive because they stem primarily from consideration of behavioral data concerning the schizophrenic. Although ultimately interested in matters of cause, these theorists considered of primary importance the problem of describing how the schizophrenic or a subgroup of schizophrenics behave. Since thought disorder is considered to be part of the definition of schizophrenia, we touched upon theories related to that concept first.

We considered a number of learning theories. First, we took up Bridger's interpretation of Pavlov's inhibition theory. Then we described Mednick's anxiety or arousal theory with a number of relevant experiments. This was followed by consideration of Broen and Storms' nonaversive drive theory. Next, we turned our attention to McReynolds who related anxiety to perception rather than to response competition. We described Epstein's unified anxiety theory and Chapman's theory of verbal behavior in schizophrenia. We discussed Rodnick and Garmezy's theory in some detail since it speculates about both initial cause and current behavior. The last learning theory we took up was that of Ullmann and Krasner.

Finally, we dealt with stimulus theories of schizophrenia. These theories have in common the hypothesis that the schizophrenic has a peculiar way of responding to stimulus input. It is of interest in this context to point out that the stimulus is important in learning theories also, for example, in Ullmann and Krasner's theory which locates the schizophrenic's basic problem in his failure to attend to parts of his external environment.

Of the stimulus theories, Silverman's is surely most elaborately developed, not only stating what makes schizophrenics behave in particular ways but seeking to classify them into a number of subgroups, each with a particular description of the clinical behavior and the responses under experimental conditions. A theory similar to Silverman's is Venables' which also describes schizophrenic behavior in terms of the degree of attentional restriction (too much or too little). Yates promulgated a theory in which he implicated the initial data processing phase as the area of difficulty in schizophrenia. Shakow's theory of loss of major set was described only briefly since experiments testing this theory were discussed in preceding chapters. The final theory discussed was Salzinger's Immediacy Hypothesis, which states that schizophrenics owe their abnormality to a greater susceptibility to immediate stimuli and to the interaction (as specified by the laws of behavior) of this susceptibility with the environment.

In the final section of the chapter, we related some of the theories to each other to indicate in what ways they can be usefully integrated with one another.

EPILOGUE

In many ways, this book might seem to have taken an overly critical view of research in the area of schizophrenia. To the extent that it has been critical, the cause lies with the state of the field. Nevertheless, some hopeful developments are growing out of current work. We know much more about the artifacts in experiments and, because of our increased knowledge of social factors, we are now taking an entirely different tack in dealing with schizophrenics. The concept of community treatment has very much come to the fore. We no longer send patients to hospitals automatically. The advent of drugs, even though it has effected no cures, can often control the behavior of patients most difficult to deal with. Mental health workers are beginning to take advantage of the behavior theory approach in the management of the schizophrenic in the hospital and even at home.

Research has yielded significant consistencies about the behavior of the schizophrenic with respect to the importance of the concept of reinforcement contingency. In every chapter we have shown that deficits attributed to schizophrenia can be modified by the proper administration of reinforcement over surprisingly short periods of time. The implication is obvious. Behavior theory should be more widely applied to schizophrenics, whether the cause is biological or social. Prosthetic devices such as eyeglasses for the nearsighted and hearing aids for the hard-of-hearing can and should have their counterparts in the management of behavior. Independent of what a particular theory posits as an attribute of schizophrenics, behavior theory can provide the paradigm for therapeutic intervention, as well as for testing the validity of the theory.

Thus if it is true, as one theory has it, that schizophrenics are easily distractable, it is important to reinforce them for looking at single items at a time, perhaps in combination with the administration of drugs that reduce the variability in behavior, or to design behavioral prosthetic devices to make them pay more attention to particular items. This might take the form of reducing the number of objects around them so that at any given time only particular predictable stimuli control their behavior. We might also change the object of their attention by a device for presenting slides or tape-recorded messages for particular time periods, directing them to the next activity in a previously trained sequence without the presence of interfering stimuli. We might eliminate withdrawal from stimuli by having reinforcements available only if they make at least minimum contact with them. By training schizophrenics in the hospital before they leave for home, or possibly in some specially constructed homes, behavioral prosthetic devices could well come to control their behavior in the direction of better adjustment and to make them people who can function adequately in society.

One final point. Schizophrenia is basically a clinical area in which hunch and intuition govern the behavior of the clinician. It is precisely in such an area of less-than-adequate documentation that superstitious behavior is conditioned, strengthened, and maintained with the resulting reduction of further investigation. We are often told not to begin investigating a new area without familiarizing ourselves with what has been done in the past. In an area burdened with clinical "knowhow," however, we must also guard against the converse danger of being misled by generalizations that are old but quite unwarranted by fact. Progress in the area of abnormal behavior has, more often than not, been the product of work in other areas such as pharmacology, biochemistry, behavior theory, sociology, anthropology, and psychophysics. It is important that the area of schizophrenia continue to be a meeting ground of the sciences, which when fully brought to bear on this important problem, will finally free people of its deleterious effects.

APPENDIX

295 Schizophrenia[a]

This large category includes a group of disorders manifested by characteristic disturbances of thinking, mood and behavior. Disturbances in thinking are marked by alterations of concept formation which may lead to misinterpretation of reality and sometimes to delusions and hallucinations, which frequently appear psychologically self-protective. Corollary mood changes include ambivalent, constricted and inappropriate emotional responsiveness and loss of empathy with others. Behavior may be withdrawn, regressive and bizarre. The schizophrenias, in which the mental status is attributable primarily to a *thought* disorder, are to be distinguished from the *Major affective illnesses* (q.v.) which are dominated by a *mood* disorder. The *Paranoid states* (q.v.) are distinguished from schizophrenia by the narrowness of their distortions of reality and by the absence of other psychotic symptoms.

295.0 Schizophrenia, simple type

This psychosis is characterized chiefly by a slow and insidious reduction of external attachments and interests and by apathy and indifference leading to impoverishment of interpersonal relations, mental deterioration, and adjustment on a lower level of function-

---

[a]Reprinted with permission from DSM-II: The Diagnostic and Statistical Manual of Mental Disorders, the American Psychiatric Association, 1968, pp. 33–35.

ing. In general, the condition is less dramatically psychotic than are the hebephrenic, catatonic, and paranoid types of schizophrenia. Also, it contrasts with schizoid personality, in which there is little or no progression of the disorder.

295.1 Schizophrenia, hebephrenic type

This psychosis is characterised by disorganized thinking, shallow and inappropriate affect, unpredictable giggling, silly and regressive behavior and mannerisms, and frequent hypochondriacal complaints. Delusions and hallucinations, if present are transient and not well organized.

295.2 Schizophrenia, catatonic type

29.23* Schizophrenia, catatonic type, excited*
295.24* Schizophrenia, catatonic type, withdrawn*

It is frequently possible and useful to distinguish two subtypes of catatonic schizophrenia. One is marked by excessive and sometimes violent motor activity and excitement and the other by generalized inhibition manifested by stupor, mutism, negativism, or waxy flexibility. In time, some cases deteriorate to a vegetative state.

295.3 Schizophrenia, paranoid type

This type of schizophrenia is characterized primarily by the presence of persecutory or grandiose delusions, often associated with hallucinations. Excessive religiosity is sometimes seen. The patient's attitude is frequently hostile and aggressive, and his behavior tends to be consistent with his delusions. In general the disorder does not manifest the gross personality disorganization of the hebephrenic and catatonic types, perhaps because the patient uses the mechanism of projection, which ascribes to others characteristics he cannot accept in himself. Three subtypes of the disorder may sometimes be differentiated, depending on the predominant symptoms: hostile, grandiose, and hallucinatory.

295.4 Acute schizophrenic episode

This diagnosis does not apply to acute episodes of schizophrenic disorders described elsewhere. This condition is distinguished by the acute onset of schizophrenic symptoms, often associated with confusion, perplexity, ideas of reference, emotional turmoil, dreamlike dissociation, and excitement depression, or fear. The acute onset distinguishes this condition from simple schizophrenia. In time these patients may take on the characteristics of catatonic, hebephrenic or paranoid schizophrenia, in which case their diagnosis should be changed accordingly. In many cases the patient recovers within weeks, but sometimes his disorganization becomes progressive. More frequently remission is followed by recurrence. (In DSM-I this condition was listed as "Schizophrenia, acute undifferentiated type.")

295.5 Schizophrenia, latent type

This category is for patients having clear symptoms of schizophrenia but no history of a psychotic schizophrenic episode. Disorders sometimes designated as incipient, prepsychotic, pseudoneurotic, pseudopsychopathic, or borderline schizophrenia are categorized here. (This category includes some patients who were diagnosed in DSM-I under "Schizophrenic reaction, chronic undifferentiated type." Others formerly included in that DSM-I category are now classified under *Schizophrenia, other [and unspecified types]* (q.v.).)

295.6 Schizophrenia, residual type

This category is for patients showing signs of schizophrenia but who, following a psychotic schizophrenic episode, are no longer psychotic.

295.7 Schizophrenia, schizo-affective type

This category is for patients showing a mixture of schizophrenic symptoms and pronounced elation or depression. Within this category it may be useful to distinguish excited from depressed types as follows:

295.73* Schizophrenia, schizo-affective type, excited*
295.74* Schizophrenia, schizo-affective type, depressed*

295.8* Schizophrenia, childhood type*

This category is for cases in which schizophrenic symptoms appear before puberty. The condition may be manifested by autistic, atypical, and withdrawn behavior; failure to develop identity separate from the mother's; and general unevenness, gross immaturity and inadequacy in development. These developmental defects may result in mental retardation, which should also be diagnosed. (This category is for use in the United States and should not appear in ICD-8. It is equivalent to "Schizophrenic reaction, childhood type" in DSM-I.)

295.90* Schizophrenia, chronic undifferentiated type*

This category is for patients who show mixed schizophrenic symptoms and who present definite schizophrenic thought, affect and behavior not classified under the other types of schizophrenia. It is distinguished from *Schizoid personality* (q.v.). (This category is equivalent to "Schizophrenic reaction, chronic undifferentiated type" in DSM-I except that it does not include cases now diagnosed as *Schizophrenia, latent type* and *Schizophrenia, other [and unspecified] types*.)

295.99* Schizophrenia, other [and unspecified] types*

This category is for any type of schizophrenia not previously described. (In DSM-I "Schizophrenic reaction, chronic undifferentiated type" included this category and also what is now called *Schizophrenia, latent type* and *Schizophrenia, chronic undifferentiated type*.)

---

*Categories not in the International Classification of Diseases, 8th revision, but used exclusively in the United States.

BIBLIOGRAPHY

Adams, H. B. "Mental illness" or interpersonal behavior. *American Psychologist*, 1964, *19*, 191–197.

Al-Issa, I. Cross-cultural studies of symptomatology in schizophrenia. *Canadian Psychiatric Association Journal*, 1968, *13*, 147–157.

Albee, G. W., Lane, E. A., Corcoran, C. & Werneke, A. Childhood and intercurrent performance of adult schizophrenics. *Journal of Consulting Psychology*, 1963, *27*, 364–366.

Albee, G. W., Lane, E. A., & Reuter, J. M. Childhood intelligence of future schizophrenics and neighborhood peers. *Journal of Psychology*, 1964, *58*, 141–144.

American Psychiatric Association. *Diagnostic and statistical manual of mental disorders.* Washington, D. C. APA, 1952.

American Psychiatric Association. *Diagnostic and statistical manual of mental disorders.* 2nd Ed. (DSM–II). Washington, D. C.: APA, 1968.

Arieti, S. *Interpretation of schizophrenia.* New York: Brunner, 1955.

Arieti, S. Schizophrenic cognition. In P. Hoch & J. Zubin (Eds.), *Psychopathology of schizophrenia.* New York: Grune & Stratton, 1966. Pp. 37–48.

Asch, S. E. Studies of independence and conformity: I. A minority of one against a unanimous majority. *Psychological Monographs*, 1956, *70* (9,Whole No. 416).

Astrup, C. *Schizophrenia: Conditional reflex studies.* Springfield, Ill.: Charles C. Thomas, 1962.

Astrup, C. The prognostic importance of genetic factors in functional psychoses. *British Journal of Psychiatry*, 1966, *112*, 1293–1297.

Astrup, C., Fossum, A., & Holmboe, R. *Prognosis in functional psychoses.* Springfield, Ill.: Charles C. Thomas, 1962.

Atthowe, J. M., Jr., & Krasner, L. Preliminary report on the application of contingent reinforcement procedures (token economy) on a "chronic" psychiatric ward. *Journal of Abnormal Psychology*, 1968, *73*, 37–43.

Ayllon, T., & Azrin, N. *The token economy.* New York: Appleton-Century-Crofts, 1968.

151

Ayllon, T., & Haughton, E. Modification of symptomatic verbal behaviour of mental patients. *Behaviour Research and Therapy,* 1964, *2,* 87–97.

Ayllon, T., Haughton, E., & Hughes, H. B. Interpretation of symptoms: Fact or fiction? *Behaviour Research and Therapy,* 1965, *3,* 1–7.

Ayllon, T., & Michael, J. The psychiatric nurse as a behavioral engineer. *Journal of the Experimental Analysis of Behaviour,* 1959, *2,* 323–334.

Ban, T. *Conditioning and psychiatry.* Chicago: Aldine Publishing, 1964.

Bannister, D. The nature and measurement of schizophrenic thought disorder. *Journal of Mental Science,* 1962, *108,* 825–842.

Bannister, D. The logical requirements of research into schizophrenia. *British Journal of Psychiatry,* 1968, *114,* 181–188.

Bannister, D., & Fransella, F. A grid test of schizophrenic thought disorder. *British Journal of Social and Clinical Psychology,* 1966, *5,* 95–102.

Bannister, D., & Salmon, P. Schizophrenic thought disorder: Specific or diffuse? *British Journal of Medical Psychology,* 1966, *39,* 215–219.

Bateson, G., Jackson, D. D., Haley, J., & Weakland, J. Toward a theory of schizophrenia. *Behavioral Science,* 1956, *1,* 251–264.

Benjamin, J. D. A method for distinguishing and evaluating formal thinking disorders in schizophrenia. In J. S. Kasanin (Ed.), *Language and thought in schizophrenia.* Berkeley: Univ. Calif., 1944. Pp. 65–88.

Berkowitz, H. Effects of prior experimenter-subject relationships on reinforced reaction time of schizophrenics and normals. *Journal of Abnormal and Social Psychology,* 1964, *69,* 522–530.

Blaufarb, H. A demonstration of verbal abstracting ability in chronic schizophrenics under enriched stimulus and instructional conditions. *Journal of Consulting Psychology,* 1962, *26,* 471–475.

Bleuler, E. P. The physiogenic and psychogenic in schizophrenia. *American Journal of Psychiatry,* 1930, *87,* 203–211.

Bleuler, E. P. *Dementia praecox or the group of schizophrenias.* New York: International Universities Press, 1950. (Translated by J. Zinkin).

Blumenthal, R., & Meltzoff, J. Social schemas and perceptual accuracy in schizophrenia. *British Journal of Social and Clinical Psychology,* 1967, *6,* 119–128.

Boardman, W. K., Goldstone, S., Reiner, M. L., & Fathauer, W. F. Anchor effects, spatial judgments, and schizophrenia. *Journal of Abnormal and Social Psychology,* 1962, *65,* 273–276.

Brengelmann, J. C. The effects of exposure time in immediate recall on abnormal and questionnaire criteria of personality. *Journal of Mental Science,* 1958, *104,* 665–680.

Brengelmann, J. C. Expressive movements and abnormal behavior. In H. J. Eysenck (Ed.), *Handbook of abnormal psychology.* New York: Pitman, 1960. Pp. 62–107.

Bridger, W. H. Contributions of conditioning principles to psychiatry. In Symposium No. 9. *Pavlovian conditioning and American psychiatry.* New York: Group for the Advancement of Psychiatry, 1964. Pp. 181–198.

Broadhurst, A. Experimental studies of the mental speed of schizophrenics–II. *Journal of Mental Science,* 1958, *104,* 1130–1135.

Brody, E. B. Socio-cultural influences on vulnerability to schizophrenic behavior. In J. Romano (Ed.), *The origins of schizophrenia.* Amsterdam: Excerpta Medica Foundation, 1967. Pp. 228–238.

Broen, W. E., Jr. *Schizophrenia: Research and theory.* New York: Academic Press, 1968.

Broen, W. E., Jr., & Storms, L. H. The differential effect of induced muscular tension (drive) on discrimination in schizophrenics and normals. *Journal of Abnormal and Social Psychology,* 1964, *68,* 349–353.

Broen, W. E., Jr., & Storms, L. H. A theory of response interference in schizophrenia. In B. A. Maher (Ed.), *Progress in experimental personality research*, Vol. 4. New York: Academic Press, 1967. Pp. 269–312.

Broen, W. E., Jr., Storms, L. H., & Goldberg, D. H. Decreased discrimination as a function of increased drive. *Journal of Abnormal and Social Psychology*, 1963, *67*, 266–273.

Burdock, E. I., Hakerem, G., Hardesty, A. S., & Zubin, J. A. ward behavior rating scale for mental hospital patients. *Journal of Clinical Psychology*, 1960, *16*, 246–247.

Burdock, E. I., & Hardesty, A. S. Behavior patterns of chronic schizophrenics. In P. Hoch & J. Zubin (Eds.), *Psychopathology of schizophrenia*. New York: Grune & Stratton, 1966. Pp. 182–204.

Buss, A. H. *Psychopathology*. New York: Wiley, 1966.

Buss, A. H., & Lang, P. J. Psychological deficit in schizophrenia: affect, reinforcement, and concept attainment. *Journal of Abnormal Psychology*, 1965, *70*, 2–24.

Callaway, E., III. Response speed, the EEG Alpha cycle, and the autonomic cardiovascular cycle. In A. T. Welford, & J. E. Birren (Eds.), *Behavior, aging and the nervous system*. Springfield, Ill.: Charles C. Thomas, 1965.

Cameron, N. Experimental analysis of schizophrenic thinking. In J. S. Kasanin (Ed.), *Language and thought in schizophrenia*. Berkeley: Univ. Calif., 1944. Pp. 50–63.

Campbell, D. T., Hunt, W. A., & Lewis, N. A. The effects of assimilation and contrast in judgments of clinical materials. *American Journal of Psychology*, 1957, *70*, 347–360.

Carroll, J. B., Kjeldergaard, P. M., & Carton, A. S. Number of opposites versus number of primaries as a response measure in free-association tests. *Journal of Verbal Learning and Verbal Behavior*, 1962, *1*, 22–30.

Carson, R. C. Intralist similarity and verbal rote learning performance of schizophrenic and cortically damaged patients. *Journal of Abnormal and Social Psychology*, 1958, *57*, 99–106.

Carson, R. C. Proverb interpretation in acutely schizophrenic patients. *Journal of Nervous and Mental Disease*, 1962, *135*, 556–564.

Cavanaugh, D. K. Improvement in the performance of schizophrenics on concept formation tasks as a function of motivational change. *Journal of Abnormal and Social Psychology*, 1958, *57*, 8–12.

Cawley, R. H. The present status of physical methods of treatment of schizophrenia. In A. Coppen & A. Walk (Eds.), *Recent developments in schizophrenia: A symposium*. London: Headley Bros., Ltd., 1967. Pp. 97–114.

Chambers, J. L. Perceptual judgment and associative learning ability of schizophrenics and nonpsychotics. *Journal of Consulting Psychology*, 1956, *20*, 211–214.

Chapman, L. J. Distractibility in the conceptual performance of schizophrenics. *Journal of Abnormal and Social Psychology*, 1956, *53*, 286–291.

Chapman, L. J. A reinterpretation of some pathological disturbance in conceptual breadth. *Journal of Abnormal and Social Psychology*, 1961, *62*, 514–519.

Chapman, L. J. Illusory correlation in observational report. *Journal of Verbal Learning and Verbal Behavior*, 1967, *6*, 151–155.

Chapman, L. J., & Baxter, J. C. The process-reactive distinction and patients' subculture. *Journal of Nervous and Mental Disease*, 1963, *136*, 352–359.

Chapman, L. J., Chapman, J. P., & Miller, G. A. A theory of verbal behavior in schizophrenia. In B. A. Maher (Ed.), *Progress in Experimental Personality Research, Vol. 1*, New York: Academic Press, 1964. Pp. 49–77.

Chapple, E. D. The standard experimental (stress) interview as used in interaction chronograph investigations. *Human Organization*, 1953, *12*, 23–32.

Chapple, E. D., Chapple, M. F., Wood, L. A., Miklowitz, A., Kline, N. S., & Saunders, J. C. Interaction chronograph method for analysis of differences between schizophrenics and controls. *Archives of General Psychiatry*, 1960, *3*, 160–167.

Cheek, F. E., & Amarel, M. Some techniques for the measurement of changes in verbal communication. In K. Salzinger & S. Salzinger (Eds.). *Research in verbal behavior and some neurophysiological implications.* New York: Academic Press, 1967, Pp. 327–343.

Clark, W. C. The "psyche" in psychophysics: a sensory-decision theory analysis of the effect of instructions on flicker sensitivity and response bias. *Psychological Bulletin,* 1966, *65,* 358–366.

Clark, W. C., Brown, J. C., & Rutschmann, J. Flicker sensitivity and response bias in psychiatric patients and normal subjects. *Journal of Abnormal Psychology,* 1967, *72,* 35–42.

Clausen, J. An evaluation of experimental methods of time judgment. *Journal of Experimental Psychology,* 1950, *40,* 756–761.

Clausen, J. A. Interpersonal factors in the transmission of schizophrenia. In D. Rosenthal & S. S. Kety (Eds.), *The transmission of schizophrenia.* New York: Pergamon, 1968. Pp. 251–263.

Cohen, A. J. Estimating the degree of schizophrenic pathology from recorded interview samples. *Journal of Clinical Psychology,* 1961, *17,* 403–406.

Cohen, B. D., & Camhi, J. Schizophrenic performance in a word-communication task. *Journal of abnormal Psychology,* 1967, *72,* 240–246.

Cooper, R. Objective measures of perception in schizophrenics and normals. *Journal of Consulting Psychology,* 1960, *24,* 209–214.

Craig, W. J. Objective measures of thinking integrated with psychiatric symptoms. *Psychological Reports,* 1965, *16,* 539–546.

Crandall, V. J., & Bellugi, U. Rating personal adjustment through an analysis of social reinforcements. *Journal of Consulting Psychology,* 1956, *20,* 49–52.

Crider, A. B., Grinspoon, L., & Maher, B. A. Autonomic and psychomotor correlates of premorbid adjustment in schizophrenia. *Psychosomatic Medicine,* 1965, *27,* 301–206.

Crider, A. B., Maher, B. A., & Grinspoon, L. The effect of sensory input on the reaction time of schizophrenic patients of good and poor premorbid history. *Psychonomic Science,* 1965, *2,* 47–48.

Cromwell, R. L., & Dokecki, P. R. Schizophrenic language: A disattention interpretation. In S. Rosenberg & J. H. Koplin (Eds.), *Developments in applied psycholinguistics research.* New York: Macmillan, 1968. Pp. 209–260.

Crookes, T. G. Size constancy and literalness in the Rorschach test. *British Journal of Medical Psychology,* 1957, *30,* 99–106.

Davis, D., Cromwell, R. L., & Held, J. M. Size estimation in emotionally disturbed children and schizophrenic adults. *Journal of Abnormal Psychology,* 1967, *72,* 395–401.

Davis, R. H., & Harrington, R. W. The effect of stimulus class on the problem-solving behavior of schizophrenics and normals. *Journal of Abnormal and Social Psychology,* 1957, *54,* 126–128.

Deering, G. Affective stimuli and disturbance of thought processes. *Journal of Consulting Psychology,* 1963, *27,* 338–343.

DeWolfe, A. S. The effect of affective tone on the verbal behavior of process and reactive schizophrenics. *Journal of Abnormal and Social Psychology,* 1962, *64,* 450–455.

Dies, R. R. Electroconvulsive therapy: A social learning theory interpretation. *Journal of Nervous and Mental Disease,* 1968, *146,* 334–342.

Dillon, D. J. Length judgment in psychotic and control populations. *Perceptual and Motor Skills,* 1961, *13,* 335–341. (a)

Dillon, D. J. A test for patient-control differences with a modified version of the Mueller-Lyer illusion. *Perceptual and Motor Skills,* 1961, *13,* 391–397. (b)

Dinoff, M., Horner, R. F., Kurpiewski, B. S., & Timmons, E. O. Conditioning verbal behavior of schizophrenics in a group therapy-like situation. *Journal of Clinical Psychology,* 1960, *16,* 367–370.

Dokecki, P. R., Cromwell, R. L., & Polidoro, L. G. The premorbid adjustment and chronicity dimensions as they relate to commonality and stability of word associations in schizophrenics. *Journal of Nervous and Mental Disease,* 1968, *146,* 310–311.

Dokecki, P. R., Polidoro, L. G., & Cromwell, R. L. Commonality and stability of word association responses in good and poor premorbid schizophrenics. *Journal of Abnormal Psychology,* 1965, *70,* 312–316.

von Domarus, E. The specific laws of logic in schizophrenia. In J. S. Kasanin (Ed.), *Language and thought in schizophrenia.* Berkeley: Univ. Calif., 1944.

Donahoe, J. W., Curtin, M. E., & Lipton, L. Interference effects with schizophrenic subjects in the acquisition and retention of verbal material. *Journal of Abnormal and Social Psychology,* 1961, *62,* 553–558.

Downing, R. W., Ebert, J. N., & Shubrooks, S. J. Effect of phenothiazines on the thinking of acute schizophrenics. *Perceptual and Motor Skills,* 1963, *17,* 511–520. (a)

Downing, R. W., Ebert, J. N., & Shubrooks, S. J. Effects of three types of verbal distractors on thinking in acute schizophrenia. *Perceptual and Motor Skills,* 1963, *17,* 881–882. (b)

Downing, R. W., Shubrooks, S. J., & Ebert, J. N. Intrusion of associative distractors into conceptual performance by acute schizophrenics: Role of associative strength. *Perceptual and Motor Skills,* 1966, *22,* 460–462.

Draguns, J. G. Responses to perceptual and cognitive ambiguity in schizophrenics. Unpublished doctoral dissertation, University of Rochester, 1962.

Draguns, J. G. Responses to cognitive and perceptual ambiguity in chronic and acute schizophrenics. *Journal of Abnormal and Social Psychology,* 1963, *66,* 24–30.

Epstein, S. A study of over-inclusion in a schizophrenic and control group. Unpublished master's thesis, University of Wisconsin, 1951.

Epstein, S. Toward a unified theory of anxiety. In B. A. Maher (Ed.), *Progress in experimental personality research, Vol. 4.* New York: Academic Press, 1967. Pp. 1–89.

Eysenck, H. J. The effects of psychotherapy. In H. J. Eysenck (Ed.), *Handbook of abnormal psychology.* New York: Pitman Medical Publishing, 1960. Pp. 697–725.

Faibish, G. M. Schizophrenic response to words of multiple meaning. *Journal of Personality,* 1961, *29,* 414–427.

Fairbanks, H. Studies in language behavior: II. The quantitative differentiation of samples of spoken language. *Psychological Monographs,* 1944, *56* (2, Whole No. 255).

Feinberg, I., & Garman, E. M. Studies of thought disorder in schizophrenia. *Archives of General Psychiatry,* 1961, *4,* 191–201.

Feldstein, S. The relationship of interpersonal involvement and affectiveness of content to the verbal communication of schizophrenic patients. *Journal of Abnormal and Social Psychology,* 1962, *64,* 39–45.

Feldstein, S., & Jaffe, J. Vocabulary diversity of schizophrenics and normals. *Journal of Speech and Hearing Research,* 1962, *5,* 76–78.

Ferreira, A. J. The semantics and the context of the schizophrenic's language. *Archives of General Psychiatry,* 1960, *3,* 128–138.

Flavell, J. H. Abstract thinking and social behavior in schizophrenia. *Journal of Abnormal and Social Psychology,* 1956, *52,* 208–211.

Fontana, A. F., & Klein, E. B. Self-presentation and the schizophrenic "deficit." *Journal of Consulting and Clinical Psychology,* 1968, *32,* 250–256.

Foulds, G. A., & Dixon, P. The nature of intellectual deficit in schizophrenia: Part I. A comparison of schizophrenics and neurotics. *British Journal of Social and Clinical Psychology,* 1962, *1,* 7–19. (a)

Foulds, G. A., & Dixon, P. The nature of intellectual deficit in schizophrenia: Part III. A longitudinal study of the sub-groups. *British Journal of Social and Clinical Psychology,* 1962, *1,* 199–207. (b)

Foulds, G. A., Dixon, P., McClelland, M., & McClelland, W. J. The nature of intellectual deficit in schizophrenia: Part II. A cross-sectional study of paranoid, catatonic, hebephrenic and simple schizophrenics. *British Journal of Social and Clinical Psychology,* 1962, *1,* 141–149.

Foulds, G. A., Hope, K., McPherson, F. M., & Mayo, P. R. Paranoid delusions, retardation and overinclusive thinking. *Journal of Clinical Psychology,* 1968, *24,* 177–178.

Friedhoff, A. J. Metabolism of dimethoxyphenethylamine and its possible relationship to schizophrenia. In J. Romano (Ed.), *The origins of schizophrenia.* Amsterdam: Excerpta Medica Foundation, 1967. Pp 27–34.

Gaines, J. A., Mednick, S. A., & Higgins, J. Stimulus generalization in acute and chronic schizophrenia. *Acta Psychiatrica Scandinavica,* 1963, *39,* 601–605.

Garmezy, N. Stimulus differentiation by schizophrenic and normal subjects under conditions of reward and punishment. *Journal of Personality,* 1952, *20,* 253–276.

Garmezy, N. Some determiners and characteristics of learning research in schizophrenia. *American Journal of Orthopsychiatry,* 1964, *34,* 643–651.

Garmezy, N. Process and reactive schizophrenia: Some conceptions and issues. In M. M. Katz, J. O. Cole, & W. E. Barton (Eds.), *The role and methodology of classification in psychiatry and psychopathology.* Washington, D. C.: U. S. Govt. Printing Office, PHS Publ. No. 1584, 1965.

Garmezy, N. The prediction of performance in schizophrenia. In P. Hoch & J. Zubin (Eds.), *Psychopathology of schizophrenia.* New York: Grune & Stratton, 1966. Pp. 129–181.

Gerard, R. W. The nosology of schizophrenia: A co-operative study. *Behavioral Science,* 1964, *9,* 311–333.

Gerver, D. Linguistic rules and the perception and recall of speech by schizophrenic patients. *British Journal of Social and Clinical Psychology,* 1967, *6,* 204–211.

Gewirtz, J. L., & Baer, D. M. The effects of brief social deprivation on behavior for a social reinforcer. *Journal of Abnormal and Social Psychology,* 1958, *56,* 49–56.

Gilinsky, A. The effect of attitude upon the perception of size. *American Journal of Psychology,* 1955, *68,* 173–192.

Gladis, M. Retention of verbal paired-associates by schizophrenic subjects. *Psychological Reports,* 1967, *21,* 241–246.

Goffman, E. Mental symptoms and public order. In D. McK. Rioch & E. A. Weinstein (Eds.), *Disorders of communication.* Baltimore: Williams & Wilkins, 1964.

Goldberg, S. C., Klerman, G. L., & Cole, J. D. Changes in schizophrenic psychopathology and ward behaviour as a function of phenothiazine treatment. *British Journal of Psychiatry,* 1965, *111,* 120–133.

Goldberg, S. C., Schooler, N. R., & Mattsson, N. Paranoid and withdrawal symptoms in schizophrenia: Relationship to reaction time. Prepublication Report No. 7, November 1966.

Goldiamond, I., & Hawkins, W. F. Vexierversuch: The log relationship between word-frequency and recognition obtained in the absence of stimulus words. *Journal of Experimental Psychology,* 1958, *56,* 457–463.

Goldstein, K. Methodological approach to the study of schizophrenic thought disorder. In J. S. Kasanin (Ed.), *Language and thought in schizophrenia.* Berkeley: Univ. Calif., 1944. Pp. 17–39.

Goldstein, R. H., & Salzman, L. F. Proverb word counts as a measure of overinclusiveness in delusional schizophrenics. *Journal of Abnormal Psychology,* 1965, *70,* 244–245.

Goldstein, R. H., & Salzman, L. F. Cognitive functioning in acute and remitted psychiatric patients. *Psychological Reports,* 1967, *21,* 24–26.

Goldstone, S. The human clock: a framework for the study of healthy and deviant time perception. In R. Fisher (Ed.), *Interdisciplinary perspectives of time. Annals of the New York*

Academy of Sciences, 1967, *138,* 767–783.

Goldstone, S. The variability of temporal judgment in psychopathology. Paper presented at Biometrics Research Workshop on Objective Indicators of Psychopathology, Sterling Forest, 1968.

Goodman, D. Performance of good and poor premorbid male schizophrenics as a function of paternal versus maternal censure. *Journal of Abnormal and Social Psychology,* 1964, *69,* 550–555.

Goodstein, L. D., Guertin, W. H., & Blackburn, H. L. Effects of social motivational variables on choice reaction time of schizophrenics. *Journal of Abnormal and Social Psychology,* 1961, *62,* 24–27.

Gottschalk, L. A. Theory and application of a verbal method of measuring transient psychologic states. In K. Salzinger & S. Salzinger (Eds.), *Research in verbal behavior and some neurophysiological implications.* New York: Academic Press, 1967. Pp. 299–325.

Gottschalk, L. A., & Gleser, G. C. *The measurement of psychological states through the content analysis of verbal behavior.* Berkeley: University of California Press, 1969.

Gottschalk, L. A., & Gleser, G. C. Distinguishing characteristics of the verbal communications of schizophrenic patients. In D. McK. Rioch & E. A. Weinstein (Eds.), *Disorders of communication.* Baltimore: Williams & Wilkins, 1964. Pp. 400–413.

Gottschalk, L. A., Gleser, G. C., Daniels, R. S., & Block, S. L. The speech patterns of schizophrenic patients: A method of assessing relative degree of personal disorganization and social alienation. *Psychiatric Research Reports 10,* 1958, 141–158.

Gould, L. N. Verbal hallucinations and activity of vocal musculature: An electromyographic study. *American Journal of Psychiatry,* 1948, *105,* 367–372.

Gould, L. N. Auditory hallucinations and subvocal speech: Objective study in a case of schizophrenia. *Journal of Nervous and Mental Disease,* 1949, *109,* 418–427.

Gould, L. N. Verbal hallucinations as automatic speech: The reactivation of dormant speech habit. *American Journal of Psychiatry,* 1950, *107,* 110–119.

Greenspoon, J. The reinforcing effect of two spoken sounds on the frequency of two responses. *American Journal of Psychology,* 1955, *68,* 409–416.

Greenspoon, J., & Gersten, C. D. A new look at psychological testing: Psychological testing from the standpoint of a behaviorist. *American Psychologist,* 1967, *22,* 848–853.

Grisell, J. L., & Rosenbaum, G. Effects of auditory intensity on simple reaction time of schizophrenics. *Perceptual and Motor Skills,* 1964, *18,* 396.

Grossberg, J. M. Behavior therapy: A review. *Psychological Bulletin,* 1964, *62,* 73–88.

Hall, K. R. L. The testing of abstraction, with special reference to impairment in schizophrenia. *British Journal of Medical Psychology,* 1951, *24,* 118–131.

Hamlin, R. M., Haywood, H. C., & Folsom, A. T. Effect of enriched input on schizophrenic abstraction. *Journal of Abnormal Psychology,* 1965, *70,* 390–394.

Hammer, M. Influence of small social networks as factors on mental hospital admission. *Human Organization,* 1963–1964, *22,* 243–251.

Hammer, M. Schizophrenia: Some questions of definition in cultural perspective. In A. R. Kaplan (Ed.), *Genetic factors in schizophrenia.* Springfield, Ill.: C. C. Thomas, 1972.

Hammer, M., & Salzinger, K. Some formal characteristics of schizophrenic speech as a measure of social deviance. *Annals of New York Academy of Science,* 1964, *105,* 861–889.

Hammer, M., & Zubin, J. Evolution, culture, and psychopathology. *Journal of General Psychology,* 1968, *78,* 151–164.

Hare, E. H. The epidemiology of schizophrenia. In A. Coppen & A. Walk (Eds.), *Recent developments in schizophrenia.* London: Headley Bros., 1967. Pp. 9–24.

Harris, J. G. Size estimation of pictures as a function of thematic content for schizophrenic and normal subjects. *Journal of Personality,* 1957, *25,* 651–671.

Hartman, A. M. Apparent size of after-images in delusional and non-delusional schizophrenics.

American Journal of Psychology, 1962, *75,* 587–595.

Harway, N. I., & Salzman, L. F. Size constancy in psychopathology. *Journal of Abnormal and Social Psychology,* 1964, *69,* 606–613.

Heath, E. B., Albee, G. W., & Lane, E. A. Predisorder intelligence of process and reactive schizophrenics and their siblings. Paper read at American Psychological Association, 1965.

Heath, R. G. A biochemical hypothesis on the etiology of schizophrenia. In D. D. Jackson (Ed.), *The etiology of schizophrenia.* New York: Basic Books, 1960, Pp. 146–156.

Heath, R. G., Martens, S., Leach, B., Cohen, M., & Feigley, C. Behavioral changes in non-psychotic volunteers following the administration of Taraxein, the substance obtained from serum of schizophrenic patients. *American Journal of Psychiatry,* 1958, *114,* 917–919.

Hefferline, R. F., & Perera, T. B. Proprioceptive discrimination of a covert operant without its observation by the subject. *Science,* 1963, *139,* 834–835.

Herrnstein, R. J. Superstition: A corollary of the principles of operant conditioning. In W. K. Honig (Ed.), *Operant behavior: Areas of research and application.* New York: Appleton-Century-Crofts, 1966.

Herron, W. G. The process-reactive classification of schizophrenia. *Psychological Bulletin,* 1962, *69,* 329–343.

Herron, W. G., & Kantor, R. E. The anatomy of abnormality. *Journal of Psychology,* 1966, *62,* 167–175.

Heston, L. L., & Denney, D. Interactions between early life experience and biological factors in schizophrenia. In D. Rosenthal & S. S. Kety (Eds.), *The transmission of schizophrenia.* New York: Pergamon Press, 1968. Pp. 363–376.

Higgins, J. The concept of process-reactive schizophrenia: criteria and related research. *Journal of Nervous and Mental Disease,* 1964, *138,* 9–25.

Higgins, J. Commonality of word association responses in schizophrenia as a function of chronicity and adjustment: A response to Dokecki, Cromwell, and Polidoro. *Journal of Nervous and Mental Disease,* 1968, *146,* 312–313.

Higgins, J., Mednick, S. A., & Philip, F. J. Associative disturbance as a function of chronicity in schizophrenia. *Journal of Abnormal Psychology,* 1965, *70,* 451–452.

Higgins, J., Mednick, S. A., Philip, F. J., & Thompson, R. E. Associative responses to evaluative and sexual verbal stimuli by process and reactive schizophrenics. *Journal of Nervous and Mental Disease,* 1966, *142,* 223–227.

Higgins, J., Mednick, S. A., & Thompson, R. E. Acquisition and retention of remote associates in process-reactive schizophrenia. *Journal of Nervous and Mental Disease,* 1966, *142,* 418–423.

Higgins, J., & Peterson, J. C. Concept of process-reactive schizophrenia: A critique. *Psychological Bulletin,* 1966, *66,* 201–206.

Hoch, P. H., & Zubin, J. (Eds.), *Comparative epidemiology of the mental disorders.* New York: Grune & Stratton, 1961.

Hoch, P. H., & Zubin, J. (Eds.), *Psychopathology of schizophrenia.* New York: Grune & Stratton, 1966.

Hoffer, A. The adrenochrome theory of schizophrenia: A review. *Diseases of the Nervous System,* 1964, *25,* 173–178.

Holland, R., Cohen, G., Goldenberg, M., Sha, J., & Leifer, A. I. Adrenaline and noradrenaline in the urine and plasma of schizophrenics. *Federation Proceedings,* 1958, *17,* 378.

Honig, W. K. (Ed.), *Operant behavior: Areas of research and application.* New York: Appleton-Century-Crofts, 1966.

Honigfeld, G. Effect of an hallucinogenic agent on verbal behavior. *Psychological Reports,* 1963, *13,* 383–385.

Honigfeld, G. Non-specific factors in treatment: I. Review of placebo reactions and placebo reactors. *Diseases of the Nervous System*, 1964, 25, 145–156. (a)

Honigfeld, G. Non-specific factors in treatment: II. Review of social psychological factors. *Diseases of the Nervous System*, 1964, 25, 225–239. (b)

Honigfeld, G. Cloze analysis in the evaluation of central determinants of comprehensibility. In K. Salzinger & S. Salzinger (Eds.), *Research in verbal behavior and some neurophysiological implications*. New York: Academic Press, 1967. Pp. 345–352.

Hunt, H. F., & Brady, J. V. Some effects of electro-convulsive shock on a conditioned emotional response ("anxiety"). *Journal of Comparative and Physiological Psychology*, 1951, 44, 88–98.

Huston, P. E., Shakow, D., & Riggs, L. A. Studies of motor function in schizophrenia: II. Reaction time. *Journal of General Psychology*, 1937, 16, 39–82.

Inglis, J. *The scientific study of abnormal behavior*. New York: Aldine, 1966.

Isaacs, W., Thomas, J., & Goldiamond, I. Application of operant conditioning to reinstate verbal behavior in psychotics. *Journal of Speech and Hearing Disorders*, 1960, 25, 8–12.

Jackson, D. D. Schizophrenia the nosological nexus. In J. Romano (Ed.), *The origins of schizophrenia*. Amsterdam: Excerpta Medica Foundation, 1967. Pp. 111–120.

Jannucci, G. I. Size constancy in schizophrenia: A study of subgroup differences. *Dissertation Abstracts*, 1965, 26, 503.

Johannsen, W. J. Motivation in schizophrenic performance: A review. *Psychological Reports*, 1964, 15, 839–870.

Johannsen, W. J., Friedman, S. H., & Liccione, J. V. Visual perception as a function of chronicity in schizophrenia. *British Journal of Psychiatry*, 1964, 110, 561–570.

Johannsen, W. J., & O'Connell, M. J. Institutionalization and perceptual decrement in chronic schizophrenia. *Perceptual and Motor Skills*, 1965, 21, 244–246.

Johannsen, W. J., & Testin, R. F. Assimilation of visual information: A function of chronicity in schizophrenia. *Archives of General Psychiatry*, 1966, 15, 492–498.

Johnson, R. C., Weiss, R. L., & Zelhart, P. F. Similarities and differences between normal and psychotic subjects in responses to verbal stimuli. *Journal of Abnormal and Social Psychology*, 1964, 68, 221–226.

Johnson, W. Studies in language behavior: I. A program of research. *Psychological Monographs*, 1944, 56, (2, Whole No. 255).

Kallmann, F. J. The genetic theory of schizophrenia. An analysis of 691 schizophrenic twin index families. *American Journal of Psychiatry*, 1946, 103, 309–322.

Kanfer, F. H., & Phillips, J. S. A survey of current behavior therapies and a proposal for classification. In C. M. Franks (Ed.), *Behavior therapy: Appraisal and status*. New York: McGraw-Hill, 1969. Pp. 445–475.

Kanfer, F. H., & Saslow, G. Behavioral analysis: An alternative to diagnostic classification *Archives of General Psychiatry*, 1965, 12, 529–538.

Kanfer, F. H., & Saslow, G. Behavioral diagnosis. In C. M. Franks (Ed.), *Behavior therapy: Appraisal and status*. New York: McGraw-Hill, 1969. Pp. 417–444.

Kantor, R. E., & Herron, W. G. *Reactive and process schizophrenia*. Palo Alto, Calif.: Science & Behavior Books, 1966.

Kaplan, M. (Ed.), *Essential works of Pavlov*. New York: Bantam Books, 1966.

Karras, A. The effects of reinforcement and arousal on the psychomotor performance of chronic schizophrenics. *Journal of Abnormal and Social Psychology*, 1962, 65, 104–111.

Karras, A. The effect of stimulus-response complexity on the reaction time of schizophrenics. *Psychonomic Science*, 1967, 7, 75–76.

Kasanin, J. S. (Ed.), *Language and thought in schizophrenia*. Berkeley: Univ. Calif., 1944. (a)

Kasanin, J. S. The disturbance of conceptual thinking in schizophrenia. In J. S. Kasanin (Ed.), *Language and thought in schizophrenia*. Berkeley: Univ. Calif., 1944. Pp. 41–49. (b)

Kausler, D. H., Lair, C. V., & Matsumoto, R. Interference transfer paradigms and the performance of schizophrenics and controls. *Journal of Abnormal and Social Psychology,* 1964, *69,* 584–587.

Keller, F. S., & Schoenfeld, W. N. *Principles of psychology.* New York: Appleton-Century-Crofts, 1950.

Kelly, G. A. *The psychology of personal constructs.* New York: Norton, 1955.

Kelm, H. The figural after-effect in schizophrenic patients. *Journal of Nervous and Mental Disease,* 1962, *135,* 338–345.

Kelm, H. Visual figural after-effect in schizophrenic and nonschizophrenic patients. *Journal of Abnormal Psychology,* 1968, *73,* 273–275.

Kelm, H., & Hall, R. W. Hoffer-Osmond diagnostic test and figural after-effect. *Journal of Nervous and Mental Disease,* 1967, *144,* 305–307.

Kety, S. S. Biochemical theories of schizophrenia. *Science,* 1959, 29, 1–12.

Kety, S. S. Recent biochemical theories of schizophrenia. In D. D. Jackson (Ed.), *The etiology of schizophrenia.* New York: Basic Books, 1960. Pp. 120–145.

Kety, S. S. The relevance of biochemical studies to the etiology of schizophrenia. In J. Romano (Ed.), *The origins of schizophrenia.* Amsterdam: Excerpta Medica Foundation, 1967. Pp. 35–41.

Kety, S. S., Rosenthal, D., Wender, P. H., & Schulsinger, F. The types and prevalence of mental illness in the biological and adoptive families of adopted schizophrenics. In D. Rosenthal & S. S. Kety (Eds.), *The transmission of schizophrenia.* New York: Pergamon Press, 1968. Pp. 345–362.

Kidd, A. H. The effect of stimulus color and content upon schizophrenics. *Journal of Psychology,* 1963, *56,* 29–41.

Kidd, A. H. Monocular distance perception in schizophrenics. *Journal of Abnormal and Social Psychology,* 1964, *68,* 100–103.

King, G. F., Armitage, S. G., & Tilton, J. R. A therapeutic approach to schizophrenics of extreme pathology: An operant-interpersonal method. *Journal of Abnormal and Social Psychology,* 1960, *61,* 276–286.

King, G. F., Merrell, D. W., Lovinger, E., & Denny, M. R. Operant motor behavior in acute schizophrenics. *Journal of Personality,* 1957, *25,* 317–326.

King, H. E. *Psychomotor aspects of mental disease.* Cambridge, Mass.: Harvard University Press, 1954.

King, H. E. Psychomotor techniques. In J. Zubin & E. I. Burdock (Eds.), *Experimental abnormal psychology.* Biometrics Research, New York State Department of Mental Hygiene. Mimeographed, 1960.

King, H. E. Reaction-time as a function of stimulus intensity among normal and psychotic subjects. *Journal of Psychology,* 1962, *54,* 299–307.

King, H. E. Psychomotor correlates of behavior disorder. Paper presented at Biometrics Research Workshop on Objective Indicators of Psychopathology, Sterling Forest Conference, Tuxedo, N. Y., 1968.

Klein, E. B., Cicchetti, D., & Spohn, H. A test of the censure-deficit model and its relation to premorbidity in the performance of schizophrenics. *Journal of Abnormal Psychology,* 1967, *72,* 174–181.

Kolb, L. C., *Noyes' modern clinical psychiatry.* New York: Saunders, 1968.

Kramer, M. Classification of mental disorders for epidemiological and medical care purposes: Current status, problems, and needs. In M. M. Katz, J. O. Cole, & W. E. Barton (Eds.), *The role and methodology of classification in psychiatry and psychopathology.* Washington, D. C.: U. S. Govt. Printing Office, PHS Publ. No. 1584, 1965.

Kreitman, N., & Smythies, J. R. Schizophrenia: genetic and psychosocial factors. In J. R. Smythies, A. Coppen, & N. Kreitman (Eds.), *Biological psychiatry.* New York: Springer-Verlag, 1968. Pp. 1–24.

Kriegel, J., & Sutton, S. Effect of modality shift on reaction time in schizophrenia. Paper read at Conference on *Objective Indicators in Psychopathology,* Sterling Forest, New York. February, 1968.

Kringlen, E. Schizophrenia in male monozygotic twins. *Acta Psychiatrica Scandinavica, Supplementum 178,* 1964, 40, 1–76.

Kringlen, E. Twin study in schizophrenia. *Psychosomatic Medicine,* 1966, *134,* 119–122.

Kringlen, E. Heredity and social factors in schizophrenic twins—an epidemiological clinical study. In J. Romano (Ed.), *The origins of schizophrenia.* Amsterdam: Excerpta Medica Foundation, 1967. Pp. 2–14.

Kristofferson, M. W. Shifting attention between modalities: A comparison of schizophrenics and normals. *Journal of Abnormal Psychology,* 1967, 72, 388–394.

Laffal, J. The contextual associates of sun and God in Schreber's autobiography. *Journal of Abnormal and Social Psychology,* 1960, *61,* 474–479.

Laffal, J. Changes in the language of a schizophrenic patient during psychotherapy. *Journal of Abnormal and Social Psychology,* 1961, *63,* 422–427.

Laffal, J. *Pathological and normal language.* New York: Atherton Press, 1965.

Laffal, J., Lenkoski, L. D., & Ameen, L. "Opposite speech" in a schizophrenic patient. *Journal of Abnormal and Social Psychology,* 1956, *52,* 409–413.

Laing, R. D. The study of family and social contexts in relation to the origin of schizophrenia. In J. Romano (Ed.), *The origins of schizophrenia.* Amsterdam: Excerpta Medica Foundation, 1967. Pp. 139–146.

Landis, C., & Bolles, M. M. *Textbook of abnormal psychology.* New York: Macmillan, 1950.

Lane, E. A., & Albee, G. W. Childhood intellectual development of adult schizophrenics. *Journal of Abnormal and Social Psychology,* 1963, *67,* 186–189.

Lane, E. A., & Albee, G. W. Early childhood intellectual differences between schizophrenic adults and their siblings. *Journal of Abnormal and Social Psychology,* 1964, *68,* 193–195.

Lane, E. A., & Albee, G. W. Childhood intellectual differences between schizophrenic adults and their siblings. *American Journal of Orthopsychiatry,* 1965, *35,* 747–753.

Lane, E. A., & Albee, G. W. Intellectual and perinatal antecedents of adult schizophrenia. Paper read at Conference on Life History Studies in Psychopathology, Teachers College, Columbia University, May 12, 1967.

Lane, E. A., & Albee, G. W. On childhood intellectual decline of adult schizophrenics: A reassessment of an earlier study. *Journal of Abnormal Psychology,* 1968, *73,* 174–177.

Lang, P. J. The effect of aversive stimuli on reaction time in schizophrenia. *Journal of Abnormal and Social Psychology,* 1959, *59,* 263–268.

Lang, P. J., & Buss, A. H. Psychological deficit in schizophrenia II: Interference and activation. *Journal of Abnormal Psychology,* 1965, *70,* 77–106.

Lang, P. J., & Luoto, K. Mediation and associative facilitation in neurotic, psychotic, and normal subjects. *Journal of Abnormal and Social Psychology,* 1962, *64,* 113–120.

Langner, T. S. Environmental stress and mental health. In P. H. Hoch & J. Zubin (Eds.), *Comparative epidemiology of the mental disorders.* New York: Grune & Stratton, 1961. Pp. 32–44.

Lawson, J. S., McGhie, A., & Chapman, J. Perception of speech in schizophrenia. *British Journal of Psychiatry,* 1964, *110,* 375–380.

Lehmann, H. E. Pharmacotherapy of schizophrenia. In P. H. Hoch & J. Zubin (Eds.), *Psychopathology of schizophrenia.* New York: Grune & Stratton, 1966. Pp. 388–411.

Lehmann, H. E. Types and characteristics of objective measures of psychopathology. Paper presented at Biometrics Research Workshop on Objective Indicators of Psychopathology, Sterling Forest Conference Center, Tuxedo, New York, 1968.

Leibowitz, H. W., & Pishkin, V. Perceptual size constancy in chronic schizophrenia. *Journal of Consulting Psychology,* 1961, *25,* 196–199.

Levitt, H. Performance deficit and auditory inefficiencies in schizophrenia. *Journal of Nervous and Mental Diseases*, 1965, *140*, 290–296.

Levy, R., & Maxwell, A. E. The effect of verbal context on the recall of schizophrenics and other psychiatric patients. *British Journal of Psychiatry*, 1968, *114*, 311–316.

Lewinsohn, P. M., & Elwood, D. L. The role of contextual constraint in the learning of language samples in schizophrenia. *Journal of Nervous and Mental Disease*, 1961, *133*, 79–81.

Lewis, D. J., & Maher, B. A. Neural consolidation and electroconvulsive shock. *Psychological Review*, 1965, *72*, 225–239.

Lewis, N. D. C. History of the nosology and the evolution of the concepts of schizophrenia. In P. H. Hoch & J. Zubin (Eds.), *Psychopathology of schizophrenia*. New York: Grune & Stratton, 1966. Pp. 1–18.

Lhamon, W. T., & Goldstone, S. The time sense: estimation of one second durations by schizophrenic patients. *AMA Archives of Neurology and Psychiatry*, 1956, *76*, 625–629.

Lhamon, W. T., Goldstone, S., & Goldfarb, J. L. The psychopathology of time judgment. In P. H. Hoch & J. Zubin (Eds.), *Psychopathology of perception*. New York: Grune & Stratton, 1965. Pp. 164–188.

Lindsley, O. R. Operant conditioning methods applied to research in chronic schizophrenia. *Psychiatric Research Reports 5*. American Psychiatric Association, 1956.

Lindsley, O. R. Characteristics of the behavior of chronic psychotics as revealed by free-operant conditioning methods. *Diseases of the Nervous System*, Monograph Supplement, 1960, *21*, 66–78.

Lindsley, O. R. Operant conditioning methods in diagnosis. In J. Nodine & J. Moyer (Eds.), *Psychosomatic medicine: The first Hahnemann Symposium*. Philadelphia: Lea & Febiger, 1962.

Lindsley, O. R. Direct measurement and functional definition of vocal hallucinatory symptoms. *Journal of Nervous and Mental Disease*, 1963, *136*, 293–297.

Lindsley, O. R., & Conran, P. Operant behavior during EST: A measure of depth of coma. *Diseases of the Nervous System*, 1962, *23*, 407–409.

Lindsley, O. R., & Skinner, B. F. A method for the experimental analysis of the behavior of psychotic patients. *American Psychologist*, 1954, *9*, 419–420. (Abstract)

Lloyd, D. N. Overinclusive thinking and delusions in schizophrenic patients: A critique. *Journal of Abnormal Psychology*, 1967, *72*, 451–453.

Lorr, M., Klett, C. J., & McNair, D. M. *Syndromes of psychosis*. New York: Macmillan, 1963.

Lovinger, E. Perceptual contact with reality in schizophrenia. *Journal of Abnormal and Social Psychology*, 1956, *52*, 87–91.

Ludwig, A. M., Wood, B. S., & Downs, M. P. Auditory studies in schizophrenia. *American Journal of Psychiatry*, 1962, *119*, 122–127.

Luria, A. R. The regulative function of speech in its development and dissolution. In K. Salzinger & S. Salzinger (Eds.), *Research in verbal behavior and some neurophysiological implications*. New York: Academic Press, 1967. Pp. 405–422.

Maher, B. A. *Principles of psychopathology*. New York: McGraw Hill, 1966.

Mahl, G. F. Disturbances and silences in the patient's speech in psychotherapy. *Journal of Abnormal and Social Psychology*, 1956, *53*, 1–15.

Mandelbrot, B. Logique, langage et theory de l'information. University of Paris: Publ. Inst. Statist. 2, 1953. (Thesis).

Mann, M. B. Studies in language behavior: III. The quantitative differentiation of samples of written language. *Psychological Monographs*, 1944, *56*, 41–74.

Matarazzo, J. D., Saslow, G., Matarazzo, R. G., & Phillips, J. S. Differences in interview interaction patterns among five diagnostic groups. Paper read at American Psychological Association, New York City, 1957.

Mattsson, N. B., & Gerard, R. W. Typology of schizophrenia based on multidisciplinary observational vectors. In M. M. Katz, J. O. Cole, & W. E. Barton (Eds.), *The role and methodology of classification in psychiatry and psychopathology.* Washington, D. C.: U. S. Gov't. Printing Office, PHS Publ. No. 1584, 1965.

McGaughran, L. S., & Moran, L. J. "Conceptual level" vs. "conceptual area" analysis of object-sorting behavior of schizophrenic and non-psychiatric groups. *Journal of Abnormal and Social Psychology,* 1956, *52,* 43–50.

McGhie, A. Studies of cognitive disorder in schizophrenia. In A. Coppen & A. Walk (Eds.), *Recent developments in schizophrenia.* London: Headley Bros. Ltd., 1967. Pp. 69–78.

McGhie, A., Chapman, J., & Lawson, J. S. The effect of distraction on schizophrenic performance (I) Perception and immediate memory. *British Journal of Psychiatry,* 1965, *111,* 383–390.

McGinnies, E., & Adornetto, J. Perceptual defense in normal and in schizophrenic observers. *Journal of Abnormal and Social Psychology,* 1952, *47,* 833–837.

McKinnon, T., & Singer, G. Schizophrenia and the scanning cognitive control: a reevaluation. *Journal of Abnormal Psychology,* 1969, *74,* 242–248.

McNemar, Q. Twin resemblances in motor skills and the effect of practice thereon. *Journal of Genetic Psychology,* 1933, *42,* 70–99.

McReynolds, P. Anxiety, perception and schizophrenia. In D. D. Jackson (Ed.), *The etiology of schizophrenia.* New York: Basic Books, 1960, Pp. 248-292.

McReynolds, P. Reactions to novel and familiar stimuli as a function of schizophrenic withdrawal. *Perceptual and Motor Skills,* 1963, *16,* 847-850.

McReynolds, P., Collins, B., & Acker, M. Delusional thinking and cognitive organization in schizophrenia. *Journal of Abnormal and Social Psychology,* 1964, *69,* 210–212.

McReynolds, P., & Guevara, C. Attitudes of schizophrenics and normals toward success and failure. *Journal of Abnormal Psychology,* 1967, *72,* 303-310.

Meadow, A., Greenblatt, M., Levine, J., & Solomon, H. C. The discomfort-relief quotient as a measure of tension and adjustment. *Journal of Abnormal and Social Psychology,* 1952, *47,* 658-661.

Meadow, A., Greenblatt, M., & Soloman, H.C. "Looseness of association" and impairment in abstraction in schizophrenia. *Journal of Nervous and Mental Disease,* 1953, *118,* 27-35.

Mednick, M. T., & Lindsley, O. R. Some clinical correlates of operant behavior. *Journal of Abnormal and Social Psychology,* 1958, *57,* 13-16.

Mednick, S. A. Distortions in the gradient of stimulus generalization related to cortical brain damage and schizophrenia. *Journal of Abnormal and Social Psychology,* 1955, *51,* 536-542.

Mednick, S. A. A learning theory approach to research in schizophrenia. *Psychological Bulletin,* 1958, *55,* 316-327.

Mednick, S. A. The children of schizophrenics: Serious difficulties in current research methodologies which suggest the use of the "high-risk group" method. In J. Romano (Ed.), *The origins of schizophrenia.* Amsterdam: Excerpta Medica Foundation, 1967. Pp. 179-200.

Mednick, S. A., & DeVito, R. Associative competition and verbal learning in schizophrenia. Paper read at the Eastern Psychological Association, Philadelphia, Pa., 1958.

Mednick, S. A., & McNeil, T. F. Current methodology in research on the etiology of schizophrenia: Serious difficulties which suggest the use of the high-risk-group method. *Psychological Bulletin,* 1968, *70,* 681-693.

Mednick, S. A., & Schulsinger, F. Some premorbid characteristics related to breakdown in children with schizophrenic mothers. In D. Rosenthal & S. S. Kety (Eds.), *The transmission of schizophrenia.* New York: Pergamon Press, 1968. Pp. 267-292.

Meehl, P. E. Schizotaxia, schizotypy, schizophrenia. *American Psychologist,* 1962, *17,* 827-838.

Millenson, J. R. *Principles of behavioral analysis.* New York: Macmillan, 1967.

Miller, G. A., & Chapman, L. J. Response bias and schizophrenic beliefs. *Journal of Abnormal Psychology,* 1968, *73,* 252-255.

Miller, G. A., & Selfridge, J. A. Verbal context and the recall of meaningful material. *American Journal of Psychology*, 1950, *63*, 176–185.

Miller, N. E. Learning of visceral and glandular responses. *Science*, 1969, *163*, 434–445.

Mishler, E. G., & Waxler, N. E. Family interaction processes and schizophrenia: A review of current theories. *Merrill-Palmer Quarterly*, 1965, *11*, 269–315.

Mittenecker, E. Eine neue quantitative Methode in der Sprachanalyse und ihre Anwendung bei Schizophrenen. *Monatschrift für Psychiatrie und Neurologie*, 1951, *121*, 364–375.

Moon, A. F., Mefferd, R. B., Jr., Wieland, B. A., Pokorny, A. D., & Falconer, G. A. Perceptual dysfunction as a determinant of schizophrenic word associations. *Journal of Nervous and Mental Disease*, 1968, *146*, 80–84.

Moran, L. J., Mefferd, R. B., Jr., & Kimble, J. P., Jr. Idiodynamic sets in word association. *Psychological Monographs*, 1964, *78*, 1-22.

Morris, J. R., Hannon, J. E., & Dinoff, M. A note on generalization by schizophrenics. *Psychological Reports*, 1963, *13*, 155-157.

Murray, E. J., & Cohen, M. Mental illness, milieu therapy, and social organization in ward groups. *Journal of Abnormal and Social Psychology*, 1959, *58*, 48-54.

Nachmani, G., & Cohen, B. D. Recall and recognition free learning in schizophrenics. *Journal of Abnormal Psychology*, 1969, *74*, 511-516.

Nathan, P. E., Schneller, P., & Lindsley, O. R. Direct measurement of communication during psychiatric admission interviews. *Behavior Research and Therapy*, 1964, *2*, 49-57.

Neale, J. M., & Cromwell, R. L. Size estimation in schizophrenics as a function of stimulus-presentation time. *Journal of Abnormal Psychology*, 1968, *73*, 44-48.

NIMH—Psychopharmacology Research Branch Collaborative Study Group. Short-term improvement in schizophrenia: The contribution of background factors. *American Journal of Psychiatry*, 1968, *124*, 900-909.

O'Kelly, L. I., & Muckler, F. A. *Introduction to psychopathology.* Englewood Cliffs, N. J.: Prentice-Hall, 1955.

Orbach, C. E. Perceptual misinterpretations and distortions of social reality in schizophrenia. Unpublished doctoral dissertation, Columbia University, 1952.

Orme, J. E. Time estimation and the nosology of schizophrenia. *British Journal of Psychiatry*, 1966, *112*, 37-39.

Orme, J. E., Smith, M. R., & Berry, C. Perceptual abnormality in schizophrenia. *British Journal of Social and Clinical Psychology*, 1968, *7*, 13-15.

Orzack, M. H., Kornetsky, C., & Freeman, H. The effects of daily administration of carphenazine on attention in the schizophrenic patient. *Psychopharmacologia*, 1967, *11*, 31–38.

Osmond, H., & Smythies, J. Schizophrenia: a new approach. *Journal of Mental Science*, 1952, *98*, 309-315.

Parks, J. R. A committee report on schizophrenic language. *Behavioral Science*, 1961, *6*, 79-83.

Pasamanick, B., Dinitz, S., & Lefton, M. Psychiatric orientation and its relation to diagnosis and treatment in a mental hospital. *American Journal of Psychiatry*, 1959, *116*, 127-132.

Payne, R. W. Cognitive abnormalities. In H. J. Eysenck (Ed.), *Handbook of abnormal psychology.* New York: Pitman, 1960.

Payne, R. W. The measurement and significance of overinclusive thinking and retardation in schizophrenic patients. In P. H. Hoch & J. Zubin (Eds.), *Psychopathology of schizophrenia.* New York: Grune & Stratton, 1966. Pp. 77–97.

Payne, R. W. Attention, arousal and thought disorder in psychotic illness. Paper read at Biometrics Research Workshop on Objective Indicators of Psychopathology, Sterling Forest, Tuxedo, New York, February 13-15, 1968.

Payne, R. W., Caird, W. K., & Laverty, S. G. Overinclusive thinking and delusions in schizophrenic patients. *Journal of Abnormal and Social Psychology*, 1964, *68*, 562-566.

Payne, R. W., Mattussek, P., & George, E. I. An experimental study of schizophrenic thought disorder. *Journal of Mental Science*, 1959, *105*, 627-652.

Pearl, D. Language processing ability of process and reactive schizophrenics. *Journal of Psychology*, 1963, *55*, 419-425.

Peastrel, A. L. Studies in efficiency: Semantic generalization in schizophrenia. *Journal of Abnormal and Social Psychology*, 1964, *69*, 444-449.

Peters, H. N. Multiple choice learning in the chronic schizophrenic. *Journal of Clinical Psychology*, 1953, *9*, 328-333.

Phillips, L. Case history data and prognosis in schizophrenia. *Journal of Nervous and Mental Disease*, 1953, *117*, 515–525.

Phillips, L. Social competence, the process-reactive distinction, and the nature of mental disorder. In P. H. Hoch and J. Zubin (Eds.), *Psychopathology of schizophrenia*. New York: Grune & Stratton, 1966. Pp. 471-481.

Phillips, L., Broverman, I. K., & Zigler, E. Social competence and psychiatric diagnosis. *Journal of Abnormal Psychology*, 1966, *71*, 209-214.

Pishkin, V. Experimenter variable in concept identification feedback of schizophrenics. *Perceptual and Motor Skills*, 1963, *16*, 921-922.

Pishkin, V. Perceptual judgment of schizophrenics and normals as a function of social cues and symbolic stimuli. *Journal of Clinical Psychology*, 1966, *22*, 3-10.

Pishkin, V., Smith, T. E., & Leibowitz, H. W. The influence of symbolic stimulus value on perceived size in chronic schizophrenia. *Journal of Consulting Psychology*. 1962, *26*, 323-330.

Pollin, W., & Stabenau, J. R. Biological, psychological and historical differences in a series of monozygotic twins discordant for schizophrenia. In D. Rosenthal and S. S. Kety (Eds.), *The transmission of schizophrenia*. New York: Pergamon Press, 1968. Pp. 317-332.

Rabin, A. I. Time estimation of schizophrenics and non-psychotics. *Journal of Clinical Psychology*, 1957, *13*, 88-90.

Rado, S. Dynamics and classification of disordered behavior. *American Journal of Psychiatry*, 1953, *110*, 406–416.

Raeburn, J. M., & Tong, J. E. Experiments on contextual constraint in schizophrenia. *British Journal of Psychiatry*, 1968, *114*, 43-52.

Ramsay, R. W., & Broadhurst, A. The non-randomness of attempts at random responses: Relationships with personality variables and psychiatric disorder. *British Journal of Psychology*, 1968, *59*, 299-304.

Rappaport, M. Competing voice messages: Effects of message load and drugs on the ability of acute schizophrenics to attend. *Archives of General Psychiatry*, 1967, *17*, 97-103.

Rappaport, M. Attention to competing voice message by non-acute schizophrenic patients: Effects of message load, drugs, dosage levels and patient background. *Journal of Nervous and Mental Disease*, 1968, *146*, 404-411.

Rappaport, M., Rogers, N., Reynolds, S., & Weinmann, R. Comparative ability of normal and chronic schizophrenic subjects to attend to competing voice messages: Effects of method of presentation, message load and drug. *Journal of Nervous and Mental Disease*, 1966, *143*, 16-27.

Raskin, A. Effect of background conversation and darkness on reaction time in anxious, hallucinating, and severely ill schizophrenics. *Perceptual and Motor Skills*, 1967, *25*, 353-358.

Rausch, H. L. Perceptual constancy in schizophrenia: I. Size constancy. *Journal of Personality*, 1952, *21*, 176-187.

Rickard, H. C., Dignam, P. J., & Horner, R. F. Verbal manipulation in a psychotherapeutic relationship. *Journal of Clinical Psychology*, 1960, *16*, 364-367.

Ringuette, E. L., & Kennedy, T. An experimental study of the double bind hypothesis. *Journal of Abnormal Psychology*, 1966, *71*, 136–141.

Rodnick, E. H., & Garmezy, N. An experimental approach to the study of motivation in schizophrenia. In M. Jones (Ed.), *Nebraska symposium on motivation.* Lincoln: Univ. Nebraska, 1957, Pp. 109-184.

Rodnick, E. H., & Shakow, D. Set in the schizophrenic as measured by a composite reaction time index. *American Journal of Psychiatry,* 1940, *97,* 214-225.

Roff, M., & Ricks, D. F. *Life history research in psychopathology.* Minneapolis, Minn.: Univ. Minn. Press, 1970.

Romano, J. (Ed.) *The origins of schizophrenia.* Amsterdam: Excerpta Medica Foundation, 1967.

Rosenbaum, G. Feedback mechanisms in schizophrenia. In G. Tourney & J. S. Gottlieb (Eds.), *Lafayette Clinic studies in schizophrenia.* Detroit, Michigan: Wayne State Univ., 1971. Pp. 163–185.

Rosenbaum, G., Flenning, F., & Rosen, H. Effects of weight intensity on discrimination thresholds of normals and schizophrenics. *Journal of Abnormal Psychology,* 1965, *70,* 446-450.

Rosenbaum, G., Mackavey, W. R., & Grisell, J. L. Effects of biological and social motivation on schizophrenic reaction times. *Journal of Abnormal and Social Psychology,* 1957, *54,* 364-368.

Rosenthal, D., & Frank, J. D. Psychotherapy and the placebo effect. *Psychological Bulletin,* 1956, *53,* 294-302.

Rosenthal, D., & Kety, S. S. (Eds.), *The transmission of schizophrenia.* New York: Pergamon Press, 1968.

Rosenthal, D., Lawlor, W. G., Zahn, T. P., & Shakow, D. The relationship of some aspects of mental set to degree of schizophrenic disorganization. *Journal of Personality,* 1960, *28,* 26-38.

Rotter, J. B. *Social learning and clinical psychology.* New York: Prentice-Hall, 1954.

Salzinger, K. Shift in judgment of weights as a function of anchoring stimuli and instructions in early schizophrenics and normals. *Journal of Abnormal and Social Psychology,* 1957, *55,* 43-49.

Salzinger, K. A method of analysis of the process of verbal communication between a group of emotionally disturbed adolescents and their friends and relatives. *Journal of social Psychology,* 1958, *47,* 39-53.

Salzinger, K. The experimental analysis of the interview. In J. Zubin (Ed.), *Experimental abnormal psychology.* New York: University Book Store, 1960.

Salzinger, K. Behavior theory models of abnormal behavior. Paper read at the Biometrics Research Workshop on Objecitve Indicators of Psychopathology, Sterling Forest Conference Center, Tuxedo, New York. February, 1968.

Salzinger, K. *Psychology: The science of behavior.* New York: Springer, 1969.(a)

Salzinger, K. The place of operant conditioning of verbal behavior in psychotherapy. In C. M. Franks (Ed.), *Behavior therapy: Appraisal and status.* New York: McGraw-Hill, 1969. (b)

Salzinger, K. An hypothesis about schizophrenic behavior. *American Journal of Psychotherapy,* 1971, *25,* 601–614. (a)

Salzinger, K. The immediacy hypothesis and schizophrenia. In H. M. Yaker, H. Osmond & F. Cheek (Eds.), *The future of time.* New York: Doubleday Doran, 1971. (b)

Salzinger, K. & Pisoni, S. Reinforcement of affect responses of schizophrenics during the clinical interview. *Journal of Abnormal and Social Psychology,* 1958, *57,* 84–90.

Salzinger, K., & Pisoni, S. Reinforcement of verbal affect responses of normal subjects during the interview. *Journal of Abnormal and Social Psychology,* 1960, *60,* 127–130.

Salzinger, K., & Pisoni, S. Some parameters of the conditioning of verbal affect responses in schizophrenic subjects. *Journal of Abnormal and Social Psychology,* 1961, *63,* 511–516.

Salzinger, K., Pisoni, S., Feldman, R. S., & Bacon, P. M. The effect of drugs on verbal behavior.

Presented at the American Association for the Advancement of Science Symposium, Denver, Col., 1961.

Salzinger, K., & Portnoy, S. Verbal conditioning in interviews: Application to chronic schizophrenics and relationship to prognosis for acute schizophrenics. *Journal of Psychiatric Research,* 1964, *2,* 129.

Salzinger, K., Portnoy, S., & Feldman, R. S. The effect of order of approximation to the statistical structure of English on the emission of verbal responses. *Journal of Experimental Psychology,* 1962, *64,* 52–57.

Salzinger, K., Portnoy, S., & Feldman, R. S. Experimental manipulation of continuous speech in schizophrenic patients. *Journal of Abnormal and Social Psychology,* 1964, *68,* 508–516. (a)

Salzinger, K., Portnoy, S., & Feldman, R. S. Verbal behavior of schizophrenic and normal subjects. *Annals of the New York Academy of Sciences,* 1964, *105,* 845–860. (b)

Salzinger, K., Portnoy, S., & Feldman, R. S. Verbal behavior in schizophrenics and some comments toward a theory of schizophrenia. In P. H. Hoch & J. Zubin (Eds.), *Psychopathology of schizophrenia.* New York: Grune & Stratton, 1966. Pp. 98–128.

Salzinger, K., Portnoy, S. Pisoni, D., & Feldman, R. S. The immediacy hypothesis and response-produced stimuli in schizophrenic speech. *Journal of Abnormal Psychology,* 1970, *76,* 258–264.

Salzinger, K., & Salzinger, S. (Eds.), *Research in verbal behavior and some neurophysiological implications.* New York: Academic Press, 1967.

Salzman, L. F., Goldstein, R. H., Atkins, R., Babigian, H. Conceptual thinking in psychiatric patients. *Archives of General Psychiatry,* 1966, *14,* 55–59.

Saslow, G., & Matarazzo, J. D. A technique for studying changes in interview behavior. In *Research in Psychotherapy.* Washington, D. C.: APA, 1959.

Saucer, R. T., & Deabler, H. L. Perception of apparent motion in organics and schizophrenics. *Journal of Consulting Psychology,* 1956, *20,* 385–389.

Schaffner, A., Lane, E. A., & Albee, G. W. Intellectual differences between suburban preschizophrenic children and their siblings. *Journal of Consulting Psychology,* 1967, *31,* 326–327.

Schooler, C., & Spohn, H. E. The susceptibility of chronic schizophrenics to social influence in the formation of perceptual judgments. *Journal of Abnormal and Social Psychology,* 1960, *61,* 348–354.

Schuman, A. I. The double-bind hypothesis a decade later. *Psychological Bulletin,* 1967, *68,* 409–416.

Schwartz, M., & Shagass, C. Note on the relation between autokinesis and psychiatric diagnosis. *Perceptual and Motor Skills,* 1960, *11,* 253–257.

Schwartz, S. Cognitive deficit among remitted schizophrenics: The role of a life-history variable. *Journal of Abnormal Psychology,* 1967, *72,* 54–58.

Segal, J., & Kety, S. S. *Research in schizophrenia.* NIMH Superintendent of Documents, U. S. Gov't. Printing Office, 1964.

Senf, R., Huston, P. E., & Cohen, B. D. Thinking deficit in schizophrenia and changes with amytal. *Journal of Abnormal and Social Psychology,* 1955, *50,* 383–387.

Seth, G., & Beloff, H. Language impairment in a group of schizophrenics. *British Journal of Medical Psychology,* 1959, *32,* 288–293.

Shakow, D. The nature of deterioration in schizophrenic conditions. *Nervous and Mental Disease Monographs.* No. 70. New York: Coolidge Foundation, 1946.

Shakow, D. Segmental set: A theory of the formal psychological deficit in schizophrenia. *Archives of General Psychiatry,* 1962, *6,* 1–17.

Shakow, D. Psychological deficit in schizophrenia. *Behavioral Science,* 1963, *8,* 275–305.

Shakow, D. The role of classification in the development of the science of psychopathology with particular reference to research. In M. M. Katz, J. O. Cole, & W. E. Barton (Eds.),

The role and methodology of classification in psychiatry and psychopathology. Washington, D. C.: U. S. Gov't. Printing Office, 1965. (PHS Publ. No. 1584.) Pp. 116–143.

Shakow, D. Some psychophysiological aspects of schizophrenia. In J. Romano (Ed.), *The origins of schizophrenia.* Amsterdam: Excerpta Medica Foundation, 1967. Pp. 54–69.

Shakow, D., Rosenzweig, S., & Hollander, L. Auditory apperceptive reactions to the tautophone by schizophrenic and normal subjects. *Journal of Nervous and Mental Disease,* 1966, *143,* 1–15.

Shannon, C. E. A mathematical theory of communication. *Bell System Technical Journal,* 1948, *27,* 379–423, 623–656.

Sherman, J. A. Use of reinforcement and imitation to reinstate verbal behavior in mute psychotics. *Journal of Abnormal Psychology,* 1965, *70,* 155–164.

Shields, J., Gottesman, I. I., & Slater, E. Kallmann's 1946 schizophrenic twin study in the light of new information. *Acta Psychiatrica Scandinavica,* 1967, *43,* 385–396.

Sidle, A., Acker, M., & McReynolds, P. "Stimulus-seeking" behavior in schizophrenics and nonschizophrenics. *Perceptual and Motor Skills,* 1963, *17,* 811–816.

Silverman, J. The problem of attention in research and theory in schizophrenia. *Psychological Review,* 1964, *71,* 352–379. (a)

Silverman, J. Scanning-control mechanism and "cognitive filtering" in paranoid and nonparanoid schizophrenia. *Journal of Consulting Psychology,* 1964, *28,* 385–393. (b)

Silverman, J. Variations in cognitive control and psychophysiological defense in the schizophrenias. *Psychosomatic Medicine,* 1967, *29,* 225–251.

Skinner, B. F. The verbal summator and a method for the study of latent speech. *Journal of Psychology,* 1936, *2,* 71–107.

Skinner, B. F. The processes involved in the repeated guessing of alternatives. *Journal of Experimental Psychology,* 1942, *30,* 495–503.

Skinner, B. F. *Science and human behavior.* New York: Macmillan, 1953.

Smith, K., Pumphrey, M. W., & Hall, J. C. The "last straw": the decisive incident resulting in the request for hospitalization in 100 schizophrenic patients. *American Journal of Psychiatry,* 1963, *120,* 228–233.

Smythies, J. R., Coppen, A., & Kreitman, N. *Biological psychiatry.* New York: Springer-Verlog, 1968.

Snyder, S., Rosenthal, D., & Taylor, I. A. Perceptual closure in schizophrenia. *Journal of Abnormal and Social Psychology,* 1961, *63,* 131–136.

Sommer, R., Dewar R., & Osmond, H. Is there a schizophrenic language? *Archives of General Psychiatry,* 1960, *3,* 665–673.

Sommer, R., Witney, G., & Osmond, H. Teaching common associations to schizophrenics. *Journal of Abnormal and Social Psychology,* 1962, *65,* 58–61.

Spear, F. G. Delayed auditory feedback: Some effects on the speech of psychiatric patients. *British Journal of Psychiatry,* 1963, *109,* 235–242.

Spear, F. G., & Bird, R. L. Delayed auditory feedback: Vocal intensity changes in schizophrenia. *British Journal of Psychiatry,* 1963, *109,* 240–242.

Spence, J. T., & Lair, C. V. Associative interference in the verbal learning performance of schizophrenics and normals. *Journal of Abnormal and Social Psychology,* 1964, *68,* 204–209.

Spence, J. T., & Lair, C. V. Associative interference in the paired-associate learning of remitted and nonremitted schizophrenics. *Journal of Abnormal Psychology,* 1965, *70,* 119–122.

Spence, J. T., Lair, C. V., & Goodstein, L. D. Effects of different feedback conditions on verbal discrimination learning in schizophrenic and nonpsychiatric subjects. *Journal of Verbal Learning and Verval Behavior,* 1963, *2,* 339–345.

Spitzer, R. L., & Endicott, J. Diagno: A computer program for psychiatric diagnosis utilizing the differential diagnostic procedure. *Archives of General Psychiatry,* 1968, *18,* 746–756.

Staats, A. W. Learning theory and "opposite speech". *Journal of Abnormal and Social Psycho-*

logy, 1957, *55,* 268–269.

Starr, B. J., Leibowitz, H. W., & Lundy, R. M. Size constancy in catatonia. *Perceptual and Motor Skills,* 1968, *26,* 747–752.

Stannard, R., Singer, G., & Over, R. The effect of operant conditioning on size judgments of schizophrenics. *British Journal of Psychology,* 1966, *57,* 329–334.

Staudt, V. M., & Zubin, J. A biometric evaluation of the somatotherapies in schizophrenia. *Psychological Bulletin,* 1957, *54,* 113–118.

Stedman, J. M. Mediation in the A-B, A-B[1] transfer paradigm for schizophrenic and control subjects. *Journal of Experimental Research in Personality,* 1967, *2,* 212–219.

Stengel, E. Recent developments in classification. In A. Coppen & A. Walk (Eds.), *Recent developments in schizophrenia.* London: Headley Bros., 1967.

Stephens, J. H., Astrup, C., & Mangrum, J. C. Prognostic factors in recovered and deteriorated schizophrenics. *American Journal of Psychiatry,* 1966, *122,* 1116–1121.

Stilson, D. W., & Kopell, B. S. The recognition of visual signals in the presence of visual noise by psychiatric patients. *Journal of Nervous and Mental Disease,* 1964, *139,* 209–221.

Stilson, D. W., Kopell, B. S., Vandenbergh, R., & Downs, M. P. Perceptual recognition in the presence of noise by psychiatric patients. *Journal of Nervous and Mental Disease,* 1966, *142,* 235–247.

Storms, L. H., Broen, W. E., Jr., & Levin, I. P. Verbal associative stability and commonality as a function of stress in schizophrenics, neurotics, and normals. *Journal of Consulting Psychology,* 1967, *31,* 181–187.

Stotsky, B. A. Motivation and task complexity as factors in the psychomotor responses of schizophrenics. *Journal of Personality,* 1957, *25,* 327–343.

Strecker, E. A., & Ebaugh, F. G. *Practical clinical psychiatry.* Philadelphia: Blakiston Co., 1940.

Sturm, I. E. "Conceptual area" among pathological groups: A failure to replicate. *Journal of Abnormal and Social Psychology,* 1964, *69,* 216–223.

Sturm, I. E., Overinclusion and concreteness among pathological groups. *Journal of Consulting Psychology,* 1965, *29,* 9–18.

Sutton, S., Hakerem, G., Zubin, J., & Portnoy, M. The effect of shift of sensory modality on serial reaction time: a comparison of schizophrenics and normals. *American Journal of Psychology,* 1961, *74,* 224–232.

Sutton, S., Roehrig, W. C., & Kramer, J. Delayed auditory feedback of speech in schizophrenic and normal subjects. *Annals of the New York Academy of Sciences,* 1964, *105,* 832–844.

Sutton, S., & Zubin, J. Effect of sequence on reaction time in schizophrenia. In A. T. Welford & J. E. Birren (Eds.), *Behavior, Aging and the Nervous System.* Springfield, Ill.: Charles C. Thomas, 1965.

Szasz, T. S. The myth of mental illness. *American Psychologist,* 1960, *15,* 113–118.

Taylor, W. L. Cloze procedure: a new tool for measuring readability. *Journalism Quarterly,* 1953, *30,* 415–433.

Truax, C. B. Reinforcement and nonreinforcement in Rogerian psychotherapy. *Journal of Abnormal Psychology,* 1966, *71,* 1–9.

Trussell, M. A. The diagnostic value of the verbal summator. *Journal of Abnormal and Social Psychology,* 1939, *34,* 533–538.

Turner, R. J., & Zabo, L. J. Social competence and schizophrenic outcome: An investigation and critique. *Journal of Health and Social Behavior,* 1968, *9,* 41–51.

Ullmann, L. P., & Krasner, L. (Eds.), *Case studies in behavior modification.* New York: Holt, Rinehart, & Winston, 1965.

Ullmann, L. P., & Krasner, L. *A psychological approach to abnormal behavior.* Englewood Cliffs, New Jersey: Prentice-Hall, 1969.

Ullmann, L. P., Krasner, L., & Edinger, R. L. Verbal conditioning of common associations in long-term schizophrenic patients. *Behavior Research and Therapy*, 1964, *2*, 15–18.

Venables, P. H. Input dysfunction in schizophrenia. In B. A. Maher (Ed.), *Progress in Experimental Personality Research. Vol. 1.* New York: Academic Press, 1964. Pp. 1–47.

Voth, A. C. An experimental study of mental patients through the autokinetic phenomenon. *American Journal of Psychiatry*, 1947, *103*, 793–805.

Wagner, B. R. The training of attending and abstracting responses in chronic schizophrenics. *Journal of Experimental Research in Personality*, 1968, *3*, 77–88.

Wagner, M. K. Partial reinforcement with chronic schizophrenics. *Psychological Reports*, 1964, *14*, 285–286.

Ward, C. H., Beck, A. T., Mendelson, M., Mock, J. E., & Erbaugh, J. K. The psychiatric nomenclature: reasons for diagnostic disagreement. *Archives of General Psychiatry*, 1962, *7*, 198–205.

Warm, J. S., Morris, J. R., & Kew, J. K. Temporal judgment as a function of nosological classification and experimental method. *Journal of Psychology*, 1963, *55*, 287–297.

Weaver, L. A., Jr., & Brooks, G. W. The use of psychomotor tests in predicting the potential of chronic schizophrenics. *Journal of Neuropsychiatry*, 1964, *5*, 170–180.

Webb, W. W., Davis, D., & Cromwell, R. L. Size estimation in schizophrenics as a function of thematic content of stimuli. *Journal of Nervous and Mental Disease*, 1966, *143*, 252–255.

Webster, F. R., Goldstone, S., & Webb, W. W. Time judgment and schizophrenia: Psychophysical method as a relevant contextual factor. *Journal of Psychology*, 1962, *54*, 159–164.

Weckowicz, T. E. Perception of hidden pictures by schizophrenic patients. *Archives of General Psychiatry*, 1960, *2*, 521–527.

Weckowicz, T. E. Shape constancy in schizophrenic patients. *Journal of Abnormal and Social Psychology*, 1964, *68*, 177–183.

Weckowicz, T. E., & Blewett, D. B. Size constancy and abstract thinking in schizophrenic patients. *Journal of Mental Science*, 1959, *105*, 909–934.

Weckowicz, T. E., Sommer, R., & Hall, R. Distance constancy in schizophrenic patients. *Journal of Mental Science*, 1958, *104*, 1174–1182.

Weiss, R. L. On producing random responses. *Psychological Reports*, 1964, *14*, 931–941.

Weiss, R. L. Operant conditioning techniques in psychological assessment. In P. W. McReynolds (Ed.), *Advances in psychological assessment*. Palo Alto: Science and Behavior Books, 1968.

Weiss, R. L., Krasner, L., & Ullmann, L. P. Responsivity of psychiatric patients to verbal conditioning: "success" and "failure" conditions and pattern of reinforced trials. *Psychological Reports*, 1963, *12*, 423–426.

Wender, P. H. Dementia praecox: the development of the concept. *American Journal of Psychiatry*, 1963, *119*, 1143–1151.

Wertheimer, M., & Herring, F. H. Individual differences in figural after-effects: Some problems and potentials. *Journal of Psychology*, 1968, *68*, 211–214.

Whitehorn, J. C., & Zipf, G. K. Schizophrenic language. *Archives of Neurology and Psychiatry*, 1943, *49*, 831–851.

Whiteman, M. The performance of schizophrenics on social concepts. *Journal of Abnormal and Social Psychology*, 1954, *49*, 266–271.

Wiener, M., Jones, A., Nidorf, L., & Karras, A. Verbal reinforcement combinations and examiner-subject interaction in the verbal learning of normal and schizophrenic subjects. *Psychological Reports*, 1965, *16*, 865–876.

Wilensky, H. The performance of schizophrenic and normal individuals following frustration. *Psychological Monographs*, 1952, *66*, 1–20. No. 12.

Wilensky, H., & Solomon, L. Characteristics of untestable chronic schizophrenics. *Journal of Abnormal and Social Psychology*, 1960, *61*, 155–158.

Williams, M. The effect of context on schizophrenic speech. *British Journal of Social and Clinical Psychology*, 1966, *5*, 161–171.

Willner, A. Impairment of knowledge of unusual meanings of familiar words in brain damage and schizophrenia. *Journal of Abnormal Psychology*, 1965, *70*, 405–411.

Winder, C. L. Some psychological studies of schizophrenics. In D. D. Jackson (Ed.), *The etiology of schizophrenia*. New York: Basic Books, 1960. Pp. 191–247.

Wing, J. K. Social treatment, rehabilitation and management. In A. Coppen & A. Walk (Eds.), *Recent developments in schizophrenia*. London: Headley Bros, 1967. Pp. 79–95.

Wittman, P. A scale for measuring prognosis in schizophrenic patients. *Elgin State Hospital Papers*, 1941, *4*, 20–33.

Woods, W. L. Language study in schizophrenia. *Journal of Nervous and Mental Disease*, 1938, *87*, 290–316.

Wooley, D. W. *The biochemical bases of psychoses.* New York: Wiley, 1962.

Wright, D. J., Goldstone, S., & Boardman, W. K. Time judgment and schizophrenia: Step interval as a relevant contextual factor. *Journal of Psychology*, 1962, *54*, 33–38.

Wurster, S. A. Effects of anchoring on weight judgments of normals and schizophrenics. *Journal of Personality and Social Psychology*, 1965, *1*, 274–278.

Wynne, L. C. Methodologic and conceptual issues in the study of schizophrenics and their families. In D. Rosenthal and S. S. Kety (Eds.), *The transmission of schizophrenia*. New York: Pergamon, 1968. Pp. 185–199.

Yacorzynski, G. K. Perceptual principles involved in the disintegration of a configuration formed in predicting the occurrence of patterns selected by choice. *Journal of Experimental Psychology*, 1941, *29*, 401–406.

Yates, A. J. Abnormalities of psychomotor functions. In H. J. Eysenck (Ed.), *Handbook of abnormal psychology*. New York: Pitman, 1960. Pp. 32–61.

Yates, A. J. Psychological deficit. *Annual Review of Psychology*, 1966, *17*, 111–144.

Yavuz, H. S. The production of random letters sequences in schizophrenics. *Journal of Psychology*, 1963, *56*, 171–173.

Zahn, T. P., Rosenthal, D., & Shakow, D. Reaction time in schizophrenic and normal subjects in relation to the sequence of series of regular preparatory intervals. *Journal of Abnormal and Social Psychology*, 1961, *63*, 161–168.

Zahn, T. P., Rosenthal, D., & Shakow, D. Effects of irregular preparatory intervals on reaction-time in schizophrenia. *Journal of Abnormal and Social Psychology*, 1963, *67*, 44–52.

Zigler, E., & Phillips, L. Psychiatric diagnosis: a critique. *Journal of Abnormal and Social Psychology*, 1961, *63*, 607–618. (a)

Zigler, E., & Phillips, L. Psychiatric diagnosis and symptomatology. *Journal of Abnormal and Social Psychology*, 1961, *63*, 69–75. (b)

Zigler, E., & Phillips, L. Social competence and the process-reactive distinction in psychopathology. *Journal of Abnormal and Social Psychology*, 1962, *65*, 215–222.

Zlotowski, M., & Bakan, P. Behavioral variability of process and reactive schizophrenics in a binary guessing task. *Journal of Abnormal and Social Psychology*, 1963, *66*, 185–187.

Zubin, J. Memory functioning in patients treated with electric shock therapy. *Journal of Personality*, 1948, *17*, 33–41.

Zubin, J. (Ed.), *Field studies in the mental disorders.* New York: Grune & Stratton, 1961.

Zubin, J. A biometric approach to diagnosis and prognosis. Chap. 12. In J. Nodine & J. Moyer (Eds.), *Psychosomatic medicine: The first Hahnemann Symposium*. Philadelphia: Lea & Febiger, 1962, Pp. 71–80.

Zubin, J. Perspective on the conference. In M. M. Katz, J. O. Cole, & W. E. Barton (Eds.), *The role and methodology of classification in psychiatry and psychopathology*. Washington, D. C.: U. S. Gov't. Printing Office, PHS Publ. No. 1584, 1965. (a)

Zubin, J. Biometric assessment of mental patients. In M. M. Katz, J. O. Cole, & W. E. Barton

(Eds.), *The role and methodology of classification in psychiatry and psychopathology.* Washington, D. C.: U. S. Gov't. Printing Office, PHS. Publ. No. 1584, 1965. (b)

Zubin, J. A cross-cultural approach to psychopathology and its implications for diagnostic classification. In L. D. Eron (Ed.), *The classification of behavior disorders.* Chicago: Aldine Publishing Company, 1966. Pp. 43–82.

Zubin, J. Classification of the behavior disorders. *Annual Review of Psychology, 1967, 18,* 373–406.

Zubin, J., & Barrera, S. E. Effect of electric-convulsive therapy on memory. *Proceedings of the Society of Experimental Biology and Medicine, 1941, 48,* 596–597.

Zubin, J., & Burdock, E. I. (Eds.), *Experimental abnormal psychology.* Chapter 14. Techniques for the study of conceptual processes. Biometrics Research, N. Y. State Department of Mental Hygiene. Mimeographed, 1960.

Zubin, J., Burdock, E. I., Sutton, S., & Cheek, F. Epidemiological aspects of prognosis in mental illness. In *Epidemiology of mental disorder.* Washington, D. C.: American Association for the Advancement of Science, 1959.

Zubin, J., & Kietzman, M. L. A cross-cultural approach to classification in schizophrenia and other mental disorders. In P. H. Hoch & J. Zubin (Eds.), *Psychopathology of schizophrenia.* New York: Grune & Stratton, 1966. Pp. 482–514.

Zubin, J., Sutton, S., Salzinger, K., Salzinger, S., Burdock, E. I., & Peretz, D. A biometric approach to prognosis in schizophrenia. In P. H. Hoch & J. Zubin (Eds.), *Comparative epidemiology of the mental disorders.* New York: Grune & Stratton, 1961. Pp. 143–203.

Zubin, J., & Windle, C. Psychological prognosis of outcome in the mental disorders. *Journal of Abnormal and Social Psychology, 1954, 49,* 272–284.

AUTHOR INDEX

SUBJECT INDEX

Abstract ability, 22, 40, 46, 47, 49, 51, 52, 53, 56, 57, 63, 64, 66, 70, 83, 84, 88, 130, 131

Affect, 7, 12, 13, 14, 15, 22, 132, 136
  emotion, 15, 22, 25, 56, 57, 117

Anxiety, 17, 18, 37, 40, 48, 58, 60, 61, 76, 117, 118, 127, 131, 132, 133, 134, 144

Arousal, 60, 61, 94, 108, 109, 118, 124, 128, 131, 132, 133, 134, 144

Association, 7, 56, 57, 58, 59, 60, 61, 62, 63, 65, 69, 70, 73, 78, 81, 83, 84, 102, 126, 132

Attention, 81, 84, 93, 94, 95, 117, 131, 136, 137, 138, 139, 140, 141, 144, 145

Auditory stimuli, 4, 77, 82, 94, 95, 96, 100, 103, 105, 106, 109

Behavior theory, 19, 26, 27, 35, 36, 38, 40, 41, 42, 44, 109, 112, 113, 114, 118, 120, 122, 137, 141, 145, 146

Behavior therapy, see Therapy

Case history, 3–4, 19, 20, 114
Cause, see Etiology
Classical conditioning, see Respondent conditioning
Cloze procedure, 74, 75, 79, 80, 85, 142
Communication, see Language
Comprehensibility, see Speech
Concrete, see Abstract ability
Conditioning, 13, 14, 16, 21, 22, 25, 26, 28, 35, 36, 39, 40, 65, 82, 85, 108, 111, 112, 113, 114, 116, 117, 122, 132, 138, 139, 141, 142, 146. See also Operant conditioning; Respondent conditioning
Constancy, see Perception
Construct deficit, 54
Content analysis, 68, 69, 84
Cooperativeness, 27, 28, 30, 43, 62, 106, 116, 117, 118, 133

Culture, 8, 19, 35, 36, 42, 101, 129, 130

Deficit, intellectual, see Intelligence
Delusions, 3, 4, 7, 9, 29, 39, 88, 93, 119, 134
  of grandeur, 17, 117
  of persecution, 117
Dementia praecox, 7, 20. See also Schizophrenia
Deterioration, 4, 7, 18, 20, 48, 51, 83
Diagnosis, 3, 5, 6, 8, 9, 10, 11, 12, 15, 16, 18, 19, 20, 21, 24, 27, 29, 33, 41, 42, 43, 44, 63, 64, 84, 110, 114, 127, 132, 138, 143
Discomfort-relief quotient (DRQ), 68
Distance estimation, 91
Distractibility, 56, 94, 95, 100, 109, 145
Double-bind, 67, 129, 134
Drugs, 6, 8, 17, 21, 22, 23, 24, 26, 34, 40, 53, 72, 76, 77, 80, 102, 127, 138, 145

Emotion, see Affect
Epidemiology, 36
Etiology, 6, 11, 12, 18, 33, 34, 38, 51, 120, 125, 126, 128, 130
  cause, 1, 7, 8, 32, 33, 34, 35, 44, 114, 120, 125
Experimental neurosis, 120
Extinction, 13, 14, 16, 61, 106, 109, 112, 114, 116, 117, 121, 136, 140, 141

Functional disease, 6–7

Generalization, 65, 117, 118, 119, 121, 122, 132, 140, 141
Genetics, 8, 31, 33, 34, 44, 101, 125, 126, 130, 143

Hallucinations, 3, 4, 7, 9, 17, 28, 40, 41, 42, 48, 77, 78, 85, 109, 126, 134
Heredity, see Genetics